Y0-BDN-142

Form–Meaning Connections in Second Language Acquisition

Second Language Acquisition Research
Theoretical and Methodological Issues
Susan M. Gass and Jacquelyn Schachter, Editors

VanPatten • Processing Instruction: Theory, Research, and Commentary

Tarone/Gass/Cohen • Research Methodology in Second Language Acquisition

Schachter/Gass • Second Language Classroom Research: Issues and Opportunities

Birdsong • Second Language Acquisition and the Critical Period Hypotheses

Ohta • Second Language Acquisition Processes in the Classroom: Learning Japanese

Major • Foreign Accent: Ontogeny and Phylogeny of Second Language Phonology

---

Monographs on Research Methodology

Gass/Mackey • Stimulation Recall Methodology in Second Language Research

Yule • Referential Communication Tasks

Markee • Conversation Analysis

Dörnyei • Questionnaires in Second Language Research: Construction, Administration, and Processing

---

Of Related Interest

Gass/Sorace/Selinker • Second Language Learning Data Analysis, Second Edition

Gass/Selinker • Second Language Acquisition: An Introductory Course, Second Edition

Form–Meaning Connections in Second Language Acquisition

Edited by

Bill VanPatten
University of Illinois at Chicago

Jessica Williams
University of Illinois at Chicago

Susanne Rott
University of Illinois at Chicago

Mark Overstreet
University of Illinois at Chicago

LAWRENCE ERLBAUM ASSOCIATES, PUBLISHERS
2004 Mahwah, New Jersey London

Camera ready copy for this book was provided by the author.

Lawrence Erlbaum Associates, Inc., Publishers
10 Industrial Avenue
Mahwah, New Jersey 07430

Library of Congress Cataloging-in-Publication Data

Form-meaning connections in second language acquisitions / edited by Bill VanPatten ... [et al.].
p. cm.

Includes bibliographical references and index.

ISBN 0-8058-4913-0 (cloth : alk. paper)

1. Second language acquisition—Congresses. 2. Grammar, Comparative and general—Congresses. 3. Semantics—Congresses. I. VanPatten, Bill.

P118.2.F67 2004
418—dc22 2003049520
CIP

Books published by Lawrence Erlbaum Associates are printed on acid-free paper, and their bindings are chosen for strength and durability.

Printed in the United States of America
10 9 8 7 6 5 4 3 2 1

Table of Contents

Preface

This volume is a selected and substantially revised set of papers presented[1] at the conference on Form–Meaning Connections in Second Language Acquisition (February 21–24, 2002, Chicago, IL[2]). Some 50 papers were presented and plenary speakers included Catherine Doughty, Nick Ellis, Susan Gass, Jan Hulstijn, Elaine Klein, and Bill VanPatten. The concept of form–meaning connections has been around in one guise or another since contemporary first language and second language research began in the 1960s. That the conference theme attracted researchers and scholars from around the world and stimulated lively discussion during and after sessions, suggests that serious interest in this area has not disappeared since the early days of the morpheme studies. The very positive response of the participants and attendees underscored the importance of this topic and the need for it to be a continuing part of mainstream SLA research. We are grateful that we have the opportunity to provide such a focus with the present volume.

As the reader may well know, conferences are not held without the assistance and support of many people and institutions. First, thanks to Stanley Fish, Dean of the College of Liberal Arts and Sciences at the University of Illinois at Chicago, for his substantial financial contribution and for his stimulating and encouraging opening remarks the first night of the conference. We also thank Christopher Maurer and the Department of Spanish, French, Italian and Portuguese, for additional substantial monetary support and for supporting us throughout the conference and this publication. We also thank the Departments of English, Germanic Studies, Latin American and Latino Studies, and Psychology, and the Instituto Cervantes (Chicago branch) for additional monies and support. Last, and certainly not least, we thank all the graduate student volunteers who helped with the conference details and who worked at the registration and information tables as well as Nancy Velez in the SFIP department. As for the volume, we would like to thank Cathleen Petree who had the volume reviewed and then signed it on, Bonita D'Amil who moved the volume on to the next stage, and Sara Scudder and the team at Lawrence Erlbaum Associates, Inc., for their work.

We are also indebted to our friends and families who occasionally had to put up with us while we pulled our hair out during that last few days before and, of course, during the conference. Your continued patience as we worked on this volume reminds us of why you are in our lives.

[1] The exceptions are the first chapter by VanPatten, Williams, and Rott and the final commentary by Larsen-Freeman, who graciously agreed to spend some of her already overstretched time to read the other contributors' chapters and share her reactions. Bardovi-Harlig's and Shirai's chapters were on the program but were not presented at the conference because of scheduling conflicts.

[2] The conference was originally scheduled for September 19, 2001. The attacks on the World Trade Center and Pentagon and the tragedy of United 703 that occurred just one week before rightfully caused considerable distress to many participants flying in from other cities and countries. We felt obliged to postpone accordingly.

CHAPTER 1
Form–Meaning Connections in Second Language Acquisition

Bill VanPatten, Jessica Williams, and Susanne Rott
University of Illinois at Chicago

Form–meaning connections (FMCs) have long occupied the interest of second language acquisition (SLA) researchers. From the early research on acquisition orders to current day minimalist discussion of the interface between syntax and morphology, FMCs have been an integral component of SLA. Learners must grapple with verb inflections, nominal inflections, particles, determiners, and other FMCs as they work their way toward the creation of a linguistic system that bears resemblance to the L2. Just what is involved in the creation of FMCs? Are the processes different from those involving syntax, for example? To what extent does their creation involve multiple processes? What are the relative contributions of learner internal factors and aspects of the input itself?

This volume offers perspectives on FMCs from a variety of disciplines. This introductory chapter attempts to link these strands of research in a unified discussion by turning attention to questions of processing. Empirical and theoretical literature on FMCs has looked at a wide range of behavioral and cognitive subprocesses, beginning with the initial link between a lexical or grammatical form and its meaning(s) to the use of the form by the L2 learner. This introduction examines learner and input factors as they affect different stages of the processing of input. The discussion addresses the following specific aspects of language learning: the establishment, subsequent processing, and use of FMCs. Many questions posed here underlie the more practical issue of the effect of instruction: To what extent must attention be paid to L1-L2 contrasts in teaching? Do universal processing mechanisms overshadow any pedagogical efforts that might be made? Do different aspects of language require different pedagogical strategies? How can factors in the L2 environment be manipulated more effectively. A deeper understanding of how FMCs are made and maintained may help answer some of these questions. The discussion begins with some fundamental considerations, namely, the nature of FMCs themselves.

WHAT IS A FORM–MEANING CONNECTION?

What Is Form?

We take form to mean a surface feature of language or a surface manifestation of an underlying representation. Surface features can include the following:

- lexemes: *eat* (Eng.), *com-* (Span.), *mang-* (Fr.),
- verbal inflections: *-ed* (Eng.), *-ó/-é* (Span.), *-it/-u* (Fr.)
- nominal inflections: *he/him* (Eng.), *él/le/lo* (Span.), *il/lui/le* (Fr.)

- nominal derivational inflections: *dis-advantage, thought-less*
- adjectival inflections: *abierto/abierta* (Span.), *overt/overte* (Fr.)[1]
- functors including complementizers, classifiers, determiners, and particles such as *wa* and *ga* in Japanese

To be sure, not all languages share the same surface features and not all languages make use of the features to the same degree. Agglutinative languages, such as Quechua, make much more use of inflections on nouns and verbs to convey meanings that Indo-European languages, for example, would convey by prepositions, adverbs, or some other free-standing lexical item or morpheme (Langacker, 1972; Spencer & Zwicky, 1998).

All of the forms listed correspond to target language features and categories. The chapters in this volume use the term form as suggested by the previous list; that is, form is viewed as lexicon, inflections, particles, and the like.[2] These are not the only units of language acquisition, however. Formulaic expressions and routines larger than individual words (e.g., Bardovi-Harlig, 2000; Ellis, 1996; Krashen, 1981; Myles, Hooper & Mitchell, 1998; Myles, Mitchell & Hooper, 1999; Peters, 1985; Skehan, 1998; Weinert, 1995; Wong Fillmore, 1976) can be considered forms in the sense that learners can extract them from the input and assign them a meaning or function.

What Is Meaning?

Meaning is understood in a variety of ways. In the field of linguistics, lexical semantics has tended to dominate the field, with extensive research on the lexical–semantic–syntactic interface underscoring the importance of verbs in projecting sentential syntax. For example, the verb *dry* contains information related to its meaning: <agent, patient> and [[X ACT] CAUSE [Y BECOME DRY]]. This information reveals that both an agent and patient are involved in making the activity of dry to come about and that the activity involves a change of state that is caused by something (Levin & Hovav, 1998).

Looking at meaning as it applies to surface features of language, it can minimally refer to the following:

- concrete semantic referential meaning: in English, [*kaet*] means a four-legged feline
- displaced or abstract semantic referential meaning: *-aba-* in Spanish means nonpunctual so that when a speaker is narrating some past event, that person is indicating an event or state in progress

[1] These forms are somewhat unusual in that they do not encode meaning. For this reason, they are not discussed further in this chapter.
[2] The one exception is Klein, who in Chapter 8 argues for an examination of the role of L2 parsing in SLA, which means looking at entire sentences in addition to some individual surface features.

- sociolinguistic meaning: when *vous* is used instead of *tu* in French the speaker indicates something about politeness, deference, and/or social distance
- pragmatic meaning: when someone says "Why don't you take a break?" the intent of this utterance is understood, that is, it is a suggestion and not a real *Wh*-question that demands a "because..." answer

In the present volume, it is clear that the various authors intend the real-world referential definition of meaning with semantic content. In this discussion, meaning is also restricted to this narrower sense. Thus, this volume is concerned with concrete, displaced, or abstract referential value such as number, temporal reference, agency, aspect, and lexical reference.

What Is a Form–Meaning Connection?

It may seem obvious that a form–meaning connection is a situation in which a form encodes some kind of referential meaning. However, the situation is a bit more complicated. Three distinct possibilities present themselves:

1. one form encodes one meaning
2. one form encodes multiple meanings
   a. in different contexts
   b. in a single context
3. multiple forms encode the same meaning

Forms with a one-to-one correspondence with meaning do exist, although this is not the only type of form–meaning relationship. In Japanese, *ga* means only one thing: "subject or agent" in a nonpassive sentence. In Turkish, *lar* means "more than one." In Spanish *–mos* exclusively means first person plural. Forms that have multiple meanings are more complex. In Spanish, the pronoun *se* can refer to real-world reflexivity as in *Juan se ve* 'John sees himself', and it can refer to unspecified subjects as in *Aquí se vive bien* 'One lives well here.' It can also refer to datives (i.e., stand in for dative pronouns) when direct object pronouns follow in sequence as in *Juan se lo dio a María* 'John gave it to Mary'. With lexical forms, homonyms are examples of one form having multiple meanings. The word [*plen*] (spelled either 'plain' or 'plane') can refer to at least the following: simple; not pretty; a flat expanse of terrain; a type of craft for air transportation; a tool used to shave off small amounts of wood; the act of shaving off small amounts of wood; the act of tires skimming on wet pavement. Thus, the same form may encode different meanings depending on context. It is also possible for a form that encodes multiple meanings at once. For example, the German article *dem* encodes many components of meaning: definiteness, dative case, singular, and either masculine or neuter gender. No part of the form can be uniquely linked to a specific component of meaning.

Finally, some forms share meaning. This is not unusual in the case of lexical items and bound morphemes. For example, pastness can be encoded by both a temporal lexical item ('yesterday', 'before') as well as bound and unbound morphemes ('was', '-ed'). Plurality can be encoded by quantifying modifiers ('many', 'two') as well as by bound and unbound morphemes ('teeth', '-s'). Different bound morphemes may map onto the same meaning: In Spanish, *-aba-* and *-ía-* both encode pastness and nonpunctual aspect. They only differ in that they must be used with particular classes of verbs whose distinction is not semantic. *-aba-* can only be used with verbs with *a* for a theme vowel (e.g., *hablar*), whereas *-ía-* can only be used with verbs with theme vowels *e/i* (e.g., *decir, beber*). Another example of forms sharing meaning are the derivational inflections *dis-*, *non-* and *un-* in English (e.g., dishonest, nonnative, uneven). These morphemes all mean "opposite of" or "not" and their distribution is based on nonsemantic features of their words they attach to (e.g., in general, *non-* attaches to nouns; *dis-* attaches to nouns, adjectives, and verbs; and *un-* attaches to adjectives). Bound morphemes can also overlap in meaning. As noted, in Spanish *-aba* encodes pastness, first/third person singular, and nonpunctual aspect; in contrast, *-ió* encodes the meanings of pastness, third person singular, and punctual aspect. Thus, these two verb inflections overlap in their encoding of pastness, but they do not encode exactly the same meanings.

The discussion has identified FMCs as connections between an *L2* form and its *L2* meaning. However, L2 forms can also be connected to meanings that are not L2-like. For example, Jarvis and Odlin (2002) reported that Swedish learners of English mapped L2 prepositions onto L1-based spatial concepts. Similarly, referential meaning can be connected to a form that is not L2-like (or only partially so). A learner of French may incorrectly assign *ne* to the meaning of negation, based on the distributional bias (Andersen, 1990) of this form in negative declaratives (e.g., *Le chien ne mange pas* 'The dog is not eating') in the L2. In fact, it serves a purely grammatical function in certain kinds of expressions (e.g., *Je n'ai que deux class* 'I only have two classes'). Unanalyzed chunks, such as *comment t'appelles, lookit,* or *dunno*, are further examples of L2 derived interlanguage (IL) forms that learners may map on to specific referential meanings (Myles, et al., 1999; Wong-Fillmore, 1976).

WHY LOOK AT FORM–MEANING CONNECTIONS?

The establishment of FMCs is a fundamental aspect of both first and second language acquisition. All but a few L2 learners pursue meaning first, in an effort to communicate and to understand the world around them. Research in a variety of contexts attests to this impulse (e.g., W. Klein & Perdue, 1997; Krashen, 1982; Perdue, 2002; VanPatten, 1996). This often, though not always, means that lexical acquisition takes precedence over the acquisition of grammatical features of the language. Indeed, it has been argued that processes involved in the acquisition of the semantic and formal components of words are distinct (N. Ellis, 1994).

However, establishing FMCs goes beyond lexical learning. The acquisition of important subsystems in interlanguage grammars involves almost exclusively the relationship between forms, their meanings, and how the connections between the two are established. The most researched of these is the tense-aspect system. In the present volume, this robust area of research is represented by Bardovi-Harlig's study on the acquisition of the future system and Shirai's overview and discussion of the development of tense-aspect in general. These complex systems within a larger grammatical system evolve over time much as other parts of the learner's grammar do. How and why they evolve is critical to understanding interlanguage development as a whole.

Despite the clear importance of FMCs, they have not often been a central focus in SLA research. In the burgeoning research from a Chomskyan perspective since the mid-1980s, syntax has continued to be the center of the bulk of research from a theoretical perspective (for an overview, see Hawkins, 2001). However, this strand of research may be more closely connected to FMCs than it first appears, and there is good reason for those exploring second language syntax to concern themselves with FMCs. Current Minimalist perspectives clearly link syntax and morphology (i.e., inflections and allomorphs, which are aspects of FMCs) either in terms of what is called "feature checking" or in terms of the interface between morphology and syntax for understanding the development of syntax itself (e.g., Beck, 1998; Radford, 1997; White, 2003).

It seems that continued examination of the what, why, and how of establishing FMCs during second language acquisition is a profitable endeavor. Its payoff may be seen in theory (e.g., the role that FMCs may play in the development of syntax) and in application (e.g., the effects of instruction). We now consider the processes involved in the acquisition of FMCs.

ACQUISITION AND FORM–MEANING CONNECTIONS

Following the ideas of others (e.g., Carroll, 2001; Harrington, 2003;VanPatten, 1996, 2003), we adopt the idea that acquisition must consist of multiple, distinct but related processes that together make up what is commonly referred to as the process of acquisition. Given that the concern here is FMCs, three processes associated with their acquisition are discussed. These processes can be considered stages in that an FMC must go through each process in order to be fully acquired. We will refer to these processes/stages as (1) making the initial connection, (2) subsequent processing of the connection, and (3) accessing the connection for use.

Making the Initial Connection

An FMC is initially made when a learner somehow cognitively registers a form, a meaning, and the fact that the form encodes that meaning in some way. The learner either accesses a semantic, conceptual, or functional meaning from existing knowledge to process a new form, or the learner notes from the surrounding linguistic or social context that there is a new meaning or concept to be acquired and that a particular form expresses that meaning. An example of the first is familiar: The L2 learner attaches the concept of 'airplane' with the new form, *avión*, based on prior (L1) experience (e.g., Jiang, 2002). An example of the second might result from an initial encounter with honorifics by an L2 Japanese learner (e.g., Cook, 2001). The learner would have to create a new meaning and connect it to a form encountered in the input (see also Bogaards, 2001; R. Ellis, 1995). This process differs from Schmidt's idea of noticing in two ways. First, Schmidt's noticing is restricted to some kind of registration of a form in working memory but does not necessarily entail a simultaneous connection to a meaning or function (see, e.g., Schmidt 1990, 1995, 2001, also Carroll, 2003; Williams, chap. 10 in this vol.). Second, no claims are made about level of awareness involved. Although it is likely that learners may be aware of encountering a novel lexical form ("I wonder what that word means?"), we cannot say that they have the same level of awareness or any at all for various kinds of grammatical form. It is not necessary for the present discussion whether a FMC is made with or without awareness. What is necessary is an exploration of why some FMCs are made but not others.

Given the range of aspects of a given form or meaning that learners must acquire, it is likely that many FMCs are not made all at once. For example, although the lexical form *Vogel* might be clearly linked to the referent 'bird' on the first encounter and available for immediate retrieval, other scenarios are also likely. Initial FMCs may be placed on any point on various continua: partial to complete, weak to robust, nontargetlike to targetlike.

Completeness of FMCs. It is possible for a learner to only connect part of a new form to its meaning, or a new form to part of its meaning. If learners encounter the word *Vogel* aurally, they may remember only a vague pronunciation or know that "it starts with an [f] sound and has two syllables." If learners encounter it in written form, they may remember just the first few letters. Another possibility of an incomplete FMC may occur with more complex forms, which, unlike *Vogel*, are conceptually more complex or linked to multiple meanings. Returning to the example of the German definite article, *dem*, learners may make FMCs between the form and only one of the meanings encoded into that form. They may simply connect the form with its most salient meaning, arguably, definiteness, and ignore the case, gender, and number components of its meaning (Andersen, 1983). Similar arguments have been made for the acquisition of tense-aspect morphology, with learners first establishing FMCs for prototypical components of meaning, such as "action-in-progress" for the progressive aspect (Shirai & Andersen, 1995). It is likely that FMCs continue to be elaborated with increased exposure as learners add complex layers of meaning and usage to the connections they have made. This is certainly true of lexical forms; after learners have made a basic connection between a word and its meaning, they will encounter additional, perhaps somewhat different, meanings for the form, distributional restrictions, and collocational regularities (Bahns & Eldaw, 1993; Schmitt, 1998).

Robustness of FMCs. Completeness is not the only measure of an FMC. A learner may make a complete FMC, but it may initially be weak, that is, the connection may quickly fade if not strengthened by subsequent input. N. Ellis

(2002, chap. 3 in this vol.) argues persuasively for the importance of frequency in language processing and acquisition, a perspective consistent with the notion of the increasing robustness of FMCs that are confirmed by subsequent input. A learner's first encounter with *Vogel* may leave a trace of the entire word in memory, lightly "penciled in" (see VanPatten, chap. 2 in this vol.) such that the learner's next encounter with this form in the input will result in a stronger connection (see next section). This initial lack of either completeness or robustness of a memory trace can be caused by any kind interference while processing the new form that causes attentional resources to be overwhelmed (Baddeley, 1990). This does not necessarily mean, however, that the default situation is that learners tend to make complete and robust connections from the outset and that interference in processing disturbs the connections. It is more likely that learners—especially in the early and intermediate stages, if not longer—tend to make incomplete initial mappings and less than robust connections.

Target-like Nature of FMCs. There is no guarantee that an FMC will be target-like or even reflect target language categories. It is possible that the learner would link *Vogel* to 'chicken', or that *comía* would be linked to conditional rather than the target-like imperfect meaning, or that *comió* will be overgeneralized to other past contexts. There is extensive evidence of initial FMCs between perfective marking and telic meaning (Bardovi-Harlig, 2000; Collins, 2002; Lee, 2001; Shirai, chap. 5 in this vol.) in spite of the fact that the distribution of form and meaning in the L2 may not always reflect this connection. Finally, it is also possible that meaning will be linked to unanalyzed L2 forms, in other words, incorporated into the developing IL as chunks, separate from its components. This has been shown to occur with the English *dunno* (Bybee, 2002).

Subsequent Processing

Once an initial FMC has been made, what happens next? We argue that there are always psycholinguistic consequences of the initial FMC, however weak or incomplete they may be. According to N. Ellis (chap. 3 in this vol.), "any event, any experience produces a distributed pattern of activity in many parts of the cognitive system." Repeated exposure to the forms in these incipient FMCs offer several possibilities regarding robustness, completeness, and proximity to target: Initially incomplete FMCs, in which only one or some of the possible connections have been made, may be filled in for a more complete mapping. An initially weak FMC may be strengthened. It is also possible that if the processing of subsequent input results in conflicts with an existing FMC (possibly a nontarget-like one), then the learner's language system will be forced to make adjustments both to that FMC or possibly to others as well.

Filling in. If the initial FMC is incomplete, then subsequent encounters may fill in additional elements of either the form or its meaning. For the lexical item *Vogel*, if the initial connection resulted in the partial entry, "starts with an [f] sound and has two syllables," further exposure may allow the learner to establish a more complete phonological representation. Meaning and concepts may be filled in a similarly incremental fashion. Following multiple encounters, semantic boundaries of a word may be expanded (Schmitt, 1998) and conceptual characteristics refined. L2 learners may discover in a specific context that words have specific pragmatic functions, belong to a certain register, or collocate with other words redefined (Bahns & Eldaw, 1993). Regarding grammatical forms, it was noted earlier that many forms, such as the German definite article *dem*, are more complex than concrete nouns. The initial FMC may link the form to definiteness; a subsequent FMC may be made between the same form and dative case, another with singular, and so on.

Strengthening

If the initial encounter with a form in the input results in a weak connection with its meaning, subsequent encounters in the input may add to the robustness of this FMC, increasing the likelihood of long-term retention, although not guaranteeing availability for use. Conversely, lack of subsequent input may have the opposite effect: The FMC may fade and eventually disappear from memory. This is the case with such forms as verbs in the subjunctive mood in Romance languages, which are often taught early on. At the time of instruction, learners may be exposed to appropriate input that contains subjunctive forms and the connections may be initiated. But according to frequency counts in Spanish, for example, the subjunctive makes up about 3% of the verb forms that learners encounter in communicative input (Bull, 1947). Thus, the FMC may fade away and in some cases, show no signs of return. What is more, it has been shown that frequency of one form that is “in competition” with another for meaning may cause the less frequent form to fade. This scenario is illustrated by the well-known U-shaped acquisition of irregular past tenses, which are temporarily “pushed out” by the overwhelmingly more frequent past tense forms. This leads to the next process.

Restructuring. So far, the process of making an FMC has been presented as a relatively simple one: A new FMC is made, it is strengthened, becomes more complex (if the FMC itself is complex), or, if there is no subsequent encounter with the form, eventually fades away. However, as already noted, the input often contains forms that are potentially in competition with one another, a situation that may require restructuring of the FMC and more broadly, of the learner's developing IL.

Bardovi-Harlig (2000) and Shirai (chap. 5 in this vol.) describe systems in which there are several formal options for encoding past events. According to Andersen's (1984) One-to-One Principle, learners will initially prefer to match one form to one meaning. In a language such as Spanish, which has a complex system for marking pastness, establishing target-like FMCs may take extensive exposure to and processing of input (see VanPatten, chap 2 in this vol.). A learner who initially associates the ending *-ía* with pastness rather than pastness plus nonpunctuality, may create incorrect forms such as **tuvía* 'was having', in which an irregular preterit tense ending (which may be in the processing of being penciled in) is conflated with the "new" past tense ending. In short, the learner takes two different pieces of two different verbs that have been coded for pastness and fuses them. However, continued exposure to *tuve* and *tenía* would presumably force learners to modify their original nontarget-like FMC. This process of restructuring can help trim nontarget forms from the IL. A second type of restructuring will affect the initial FMC, but other FMCs in the lexical component of the IL as well. Continuing with the example of Spanish tense, one past tense is used to mark punctual, completed events, another, to mark nonpunctual events and activities. Thus, if the learner's system only contains forms such as *llamó* 'called' to mark any event or action in the past, recognition that the form *llamaba* 'was calling' also refers to the past may prompt a new FMC. Unlike in the first example of **tuvía*, in this second example there is no nontarget-like form, rather, this is an L2 form used incorrectly. In this case, it is not just the FMC that needs to be restructured, but also how it relates to other FMCs in the IL. Accommodation of this new FMC may force reorganization of part of the IL, in this case, the tense-aspect system.

Restructuring may also have impact beyond the lexical component of the developing IL. In current syntactic theory, there are both lexical and functional categories and languages seem to vary according to functional features (e.g., Radford, 1997). The surface representations of many of these functional features are precisely the types of grammatical forms under discussion here: inflections, particles, determiners, complementizers, and so on. The properties associated with these features are said to drive much of syntactic movement. If an L1 and an L2 differ in terms of movement rules, then the learner must somehow begin penciling in the inflectional features (along with their properties) so that the grammar can evolve toward the correct L2 system of rules. Learning a particular form–meaning connection, for example, could be the catalyst or trigger for such evolution. VanPatten (chap. 2 in this vol.) discusses how learners of English must come to know that English disallows verb movement. He suggests that the FMC contained in *do* may be the catalyst for this knowledge. Such cases are actually describing the restructuring of the syntax based on the incorporation of a new FMC in the lexicon. (The debate on the relationship between FMCs and syntactic development is addressed later.)

In a different case, Hawkins (2001) described the scenario in which learners of English L2 may not yet have projected an IP (the inflectional phrase of a syntactic tree). In an argument too complex to review here, he suggested that when learners "get" copular *be*, they will project IP and the syntax will begin to restructure itself, which in turn allows for the incorporation of other grammatical morphology. Thus, the incorporation of just one new FMC can cause a major restructuring of the syntactic component of a grammar.

Access for Use

Access for use applies to both comprehension and production processes. Once an FMC has been integrated into the IL, it is potentially accessible for comprehension and production. Each time the form is accessed for use, the FMC is strengthened, regardless of whether it is target-like. When a form is accessed for comprehension, the process also involves another exposure to the form in context, further strengthening or elaborating the FMC. The important point here is that although access cannot *initiate* FMCs—after all, one cannot access what does not yet exist—it can strengthen those that are already made. Regarding access for production, de Bot (1996) noted, "Output as such does not play a role in the acquisition of completely new declarative knowledge, because learners can only acquire this type of knowledge by using external input" (p. 549). He went on to argue, however, that repeatedly accessing this connection is more effective for learning than simply perceiving it in the input. Thus, access too has an important role in the FMC process.

Earlier in this chapter it was noted that the process in which FMCs are made and processed is not a uniform one. Why are some FMCs made and not others? Why do some connections grow strong and others fade? Such questions have clear pedagogical implications. Whereas a more global view of language acquisition results in very general questions about instruction (e.g., Does output accelerate learning? Is focus on form effective? Does input enhancement work?), the previous outline of FMCs suggests that these questions cannot be answered about second language learning in general, as if it were a uniform process. In addressing the effectiveness of instruction, Williams (in press) notes "Learner interaction with language data changes at different stages of development, and instruction may impact the acquisition process differently at these various points. Instruction should therefore be targeted thoughtfully, based on where learners are in this process. In fact, however, very little work has explicitly addressed the need to differentiate the effect of (instruction) at specific points of IL development." Clearly, research on instructed SLA will need to develop more focused questions that consider what kind of instruction to affect what kind of process for the acquisition of which/what kind of form.

It is likely that the many factors involved in SLA will impact the different stages and processes described in different ways. The next section, reviews current research and the contributions to this volume for evidence of potential mediating factors and their effects.

FACTORS AFFECTING ACQUISITION OF FMCS

We divide the factors that affect the acquisition of FMCs into two broad categories: *learner factors* and *input factors*. Learner factors include knowledge sources shared by learners or groups of learners (e.g., the L1, universals, and universal grammar) and specifics of the individual (e.g., proficiency in the L2). Input factors include aspects of forms and their meanings (e.g., frequency, nature of the L2 form). The discussion concentrates primarily on the initial creation of FMCs, not because this process is most important, but because this has been where research has concentrated. Where possible, the discussion distinguishes among the processes associated with FMCs that have been outlined and the impact that learner and input factors may have on them.

Learner Factors

L1/Other L Knowledge. The most general question about L1 knowledge concerns how L1 features affect the learning of the L2. For example, does L1 limit or enhance how L2 input is perceived and processed? Do all L1 features affect L2 learning in the same way? Do L1 features affect the processing of L2 lexical and grammatical aspects differently? These questions have been part of an active research agenda in second language acquisition for half a century (e.g., Andersen, 1983; Cadierno & Lund, chap. 7 in this vol.; Gass & Selinker, 1992; Jarvis, 2000a, 2000b; Jarvis & Odlin, 2000; Jiang, 2002; Kellerman, 1995; Odlin, 1989, 2002; Pavlenko & Jarvis, 2002; Ringbom, 1987; VanPatten, chap. 2 in this vol.).

Regarding FMCs, their completeness, robustness, and approximation to the target may be mediated by the L1. Researchers who assume that language processing mechanisms operate automatically outside of the conscious control of the learner (Carroll, 2001; VanPatten, chap 2 in this vol.) propose that beginning learners automatically apply L1 parsing procedures when processing the L2. L1 parsing procedures may lead to an indistinct memory trace or even block the processing of particular L2 forms if the constituents in the L1 and the L2 do not follow the same linear order (see Rounds & Kanagy, 1998; VanPatten, chap. 2 in this vol., for examples). It is not only parsing procedures that are affected by the L1. Cadierno and Lund (chap. 2 in this vol.) demonstrate how the encoding of semantic components of events in the L1 can influence their encoding in the L2. If an L2 does not have the same system for encoding two separate semantic components in a single verb (e.g., movement and manner in Danish), connections may only be made between L2 forms and meanings that exist in the L1. In other words, only a partial FMC will be established, one that resembles the L1 more than the L2.

Similarly, for lexical development, L1 concept characteristics may interfere with L2 acquisition because L2 learners conceptualize L2 words through the L1 until they achieve a high level of proficiency (N. Ellis & Beaton, 1993; Jiang, 2002; Kroll & Tokowicz, 2001). That is, an L2 word is initially mapped to an L1 concept, which may not have the same conceptual features. Words that relate to concepts that are firmly grounded in physical reality are more likely to share conceptual features from L1 to L2, but more abstract words do not necessarily share the same boundaries and may vary in attributes across languages (e.g., words such as democracy, guilt, or penance). The influence of the L1 in lexical development may take many forms and is not always predictable. When L2 forms are very different from their L1 equivalents, learners may fail to make FMCs, as Laufer and Eliasson (1993) found for

Hebrew learners of English phrasal verbs. Cognates generally facilitate targetlike FMCs (Ard & Homburg, 1983; Holmes & Ramos, 1993; Lotto & de Groot, 1998; Vidal, 2003), but false cognates, such as English *actual*/German *aktuel*, can result in the connection of nontarget-like meanings to a target form. In addition, although normally L1-L2 similarities do promote FMCs, if the form in question is considered unusual by learners, they may resist making such a connection despite this similarity, as Hulstijn and Marchena (1989) found for Dutch learners' acquisition of English phrasal verbs.

Universals. A fundamental concern in second language acquisition is not so much what is different across language learning contexts, but what is universal. Are there some aspects of second language learning that do not vary, or vary little, across contexts and learners? This question has been investigated by those who believe such universals are inborn and, in the view of some, unique to language, as well as by those who believe linguistic universals emerge and are evidence for the similarity of language learning to other cognitive processes (e.g., N. Ellis, 1998; Gregg, 1996; MacWhinney, 1997; O'Grady, 1999; Schwartz, 1999; White, 2003). In one view, the universals are linguistic and consist of principles that constrain the nature of all human grammars, including second language grammars. In the other view, the universals are related to perception and processing of information from the environment and are sensitive to the nature of information (in the present case, the input). These in turn interact with (or more likely are constrained by) the neural architecture of the brain.

Universal processing mechanisms can variously support, fail to support, or actively hinder the initial establishment of FMCs. VanPatten (1996, 2003) posited processing mechanisms that explain how learners get linguistic data from input and why certain connections, but not others, are made. He explained that L2 learners first establish FMCs for more meaning-bearing forms—in particular, content words—because they are most crucial for message comprehension. Beginning learners do not have the working memory capacity to focus attentional resources to all parts of a message. The information encoded in grammatical forms may be redundant and therefore may not draw their attention. This is the case, for example, when sentences start out with an adverb of time indicating past tense, as in *Yesterday it snowed.* The *-ed* ending as an indicator for past tense is not likely to attract learner attention and instead may be skipped because it does not contribute additional meaning to the sentence. Such forms are only processed if learners do not need attentional resources to process the informational content of the message. E. Klein (chap. 8 in this vol.) summarizes research that goes beyond VanPatten's claims, to examine performance factors in sentence processing. This research suggests that a number of input features may affect processing but that the processing itself involves universal tendencies among learners.

Some universals may be related to the forms themselves. Formal salience may also affect the initial establishment and subsequent processing of FMCs. Most research on the topic seems to share the assumption that FMCs are more likely to be made for salient forms than nonsalient forms (Bardovi-Harlig,

1987; Goldshneider & DeKeyser, 2001). Forms may be salient because of their inherent characteristics (see nature of input form below), their frequency, or their position. Regarding position, an attested processing universal is that initial and final positions in an utterance are more salient compared to middle positions (Barcroft & VanPatten, 1997; Clahsen, 1984; W. Klein, 1986; Rosa & O'Neill, 1998; Slobin, 1985). Forms in middle positions, therefore, may not receive sufficient attentional resources to initiate FMCs.

Another universal processing mechanism that can result in initially nontarget-like FMCs is the One-to-One Principle (Andersen, 1984, 1990), which states that one form is, at least initially, mapped onto a single meaning.[3] As a result, an initial connection between a given form and an additional meaning may be delayed or suppressed altogether. A concept may be represented in the L1 with one form but in the L2 by two forms. The example of the German article *dem* is again relevant here. If the form is initially mapped onto the single meaning definiteness, then adherence to the One-to-One Principle may suppress or delay the additional connections inherent to the target language form. Lexical examples also abound. The verb *to know* is used to express knowing facts and knowing a person in English; in German and French, however, knowing facts is always expressed with the verb *wissen/savoir* and knowing a person with the verb *kennen/connaître.* English learners of German or French may select one L2 form and initially map it onto both L2 meanings.

As for formative universals, it is not clear to what extent Universal Grammar (UG) plays a role in the development of FMCs, especially morphological inflections. White (2003), for example, summarized the debate on this role. On the one hand, there are proponents of the idea that the acquisition of certain FMCs acts as a trigger for the development of specific syntactic features or better yet the strength of such features (e.g., Eubank, 1996; Vainikka & Young-Scholten, 1996). Under this scenario, strong agreement (as a feature of INFL) in Romance languages is not "in place" until the overt surface features of such agreement are in place (e.g., acquisition of all person-number verb endings). Accordingly, morphological acquisition drives the acquisition of certain aspects of the syntax. In opposition to this "morphology-before-syntax" position, White also described the "syntax-before-morphology" position. Here, abstract morphosyntactic features can be represented before acquisition of the corresponding overt (surface) features of language are acquired (e.g., Lardiere, 2000). It is possible, although not necessary, that under this scenario, the acquisition of the abstract syntactic feature drives the acquisition of the FMCs that correspond to it.

It is also possible that, in spite of the "morphology-before-syntax" and "syntax-before-morphology" debate, FMCs are acquired independently of any UG related issues. That is, because FMCs "reside" in the lexicon, they are learned like any other lexical item and are probably subject to the factors that

[3] This principle clearly has its origins in the Uniqueness Principle, proposed for child language acquisition (Wexler & Culicover, 1980).

affect lexical acquisition. This is the position that Hyams (1994) took for child first language acquisition and is also adopted by Herschensohn (2000). Thus, the absence or presence of certain FMCs in a learner's output may be due to problems in the mapping process between syntax and lexicon during speech production (e.g., Lardiere, 2000).

L2 proficiency. This factor can be understood most generally as beginning versus advanced learners, or more narrowly, as regards development of specific structures. It has already been noted that learners in the early stages of acquisition tend to focus on forms and parts of forms that are crucial for communication and thus are less likely to process grammatical FMCs than lexical forms. Lexical learning itself may also vary with proficiency level (Meara, 1997; Vidal, 2003). More advanced learners are better able to make use of linguistic context to discover FMCs. For example, L2 readers with advanced proficiency can make initial FMCs for new items in the input by using the current knowledge of other L2 forms in the surrounding context, knowledge that beginning learners are unlikely to have. Auditory short-term memory may also be affected by proficiency, limiting the amount of input low proficiency learners can process (Call, 1985).

Beyond such general statements, it is clear that learners tackle the language learning process a step at a time, although the nature of these steps has not always been clear. To what extent is second language acquisition constrained by developmental prerequisites? Much of the research in this area of the field has rested on the early work of Pienemann (1984, 1985) (e.g., Mackey, 1999; Spada & Lightbown, 1999) and focused on the issue of developmental readiness within specific linguistic subsystems, such as questions and relative clauses.[4] However, the issue extends beyond these subsystems, with evidence that learners must achieve specific learning milestones, or complete developmental stages, before new FMCs can be made (e.g., Bardovi-Harlig, 1995, 2000; Kasper & Schmidt, 1996; Towell, Hawkins & Bazergui, 1996). Bardovi-Harlig (1995) reported that learners, despite targeted instruction, were unable to connect form and meaning in the acquisition of English past perfect until they had demonstrated stable use of the past and communicative need for the form. More generally, Bardovi-Harlig (2000) demonstrated that learners pass through several stages in the acquisition of the tense-aspect system, beginning with the use of interlocutor scaffolding and other context, moving to the use of adverbials, and only then beginning to acquire the morphological marking of that system. Learners are therefore unlikely to connect temporal/aspectual meaning to grammatical forms that mark them in the early stages of acquisition. Such staged development has also been demonstrated in acquisition of other

[4] Pienemann's earlier work was tied into learning constraints, explaining how developmental readiness came to be a factor in the acquisition of FMCs. Since the late 1980s, however, Pienemann (1998) abandoned learning strategies in favor of an explanation of stages of acquisition based on the acquisition of output procedures within a Leveltian model of speech processing and within the framework of Lexical Functional Grammar.

surface forms, such as those in the pronominal system, in which FMCs are made sequentially, based on person, case, and number (Broeder, 1995; Felix & Hahn, 1985) and of articles (Huebner, 1983; Liu & Gleason, 2002). Thus, both general proficiency level and specific developmental stage are likely to have an impact on whether FMCs are made, strengthened, and to what degree they are complete. Indeed, proficiency may override some of the input features described in the following section, such as frequency and perceptual salience (Gass & Mackey, 2002). It is also not clear if it is possible to store input data for which the developing system is not ready. It has been suggested that exposure to input containing later stage structures may have a positive effect (Lightbown, 1998; Spada & Lightbown, 1999), facilitating future FMCs. This issue, although difficult to investigate empirically, has important pedagogical implications.

Input Features

FMCs are made when learners interact with incoming input. Learner factors are an important element of this interaction, but the nature of the input is also a key factor. There are, of course, many other elements in the linguistic environment, such as what happens to the input during exposure: Is there negotiation, repetition, feedback, and so forth? (e.g., Gass, chap. 4 this vol.). This chapter, however, limits the discussion to inherent properties of the input and how these may affect the formation of FMCs.

Frequency. The effect of input frequency on SLA has been discussed extensively in recent empirical research (e.g., N. Ellis, 2002, chap. 3 in this vol.). Although it seems evident that its impact is important, it is not yet clear if frequency affects all aspects of language in the same way: lexical versus grammatical, more versus less meaning bearing forms. There have been strong claims for the effect of frequency on lexical learning (N. Ellis, 2002; Horst, Cobb, & Meara, 1998; Hulstijn, Holander, & Greidanus, 1996; Rott, 1999, Vidal, 2003), and also on morphology and multiword units (N. Ellis, 1996, 2001; Myles et al., 1998). Regarding FMCs, for example, the issue may be whether frequency is likely to have an impact on the initial establishment, strengthening, or integration of these connections. Although it seems intuitively logical that the more often L2 learners encounter a form, the greater the potential for an initial FMC to be established, this is not always the case. The power of frequency law may fail if the learner is not ready (Gass & Mackey, 2002), if the form is not salient, needs to be processed in a different way, or requires explicit learning because of its complexity (N. Ellis, chap. 3 in this vol.). The prototypical examples are English articles and third person singular *-s*. Both are abundant in the input, but both present learners difficulty.

Even initial FMCs for lexical items may be unaffected by increased frequency (de Groot & Keijzer, 2000). Yet, lexical research on the effect of frequency has shown this factor to be important. It may take up to 8 to 12 encounters with a word before learners demonstrate significant receptive or productive word knowledge (Horst et al., 1998; Nation, 2001), but that some increased knowledge can be measured with as few as three exposures (Hulstijn et al., 1996). It is possible that these discrepancies can be explained by the differential impact of frequency on different phases of FMCs, for example, that its impact on the initial mapping of lexical items is less significant than on subsequent processing of FMCs.

For the initial mapping and subsequent processing of grammatical FMCs, again frequency may interact with the availability of processing resources and the importance of the form for content comprehension. It is possible that the computational mechanisms proposed for lexical acquisition do not operate as efficiently for items such as inflectional morphology. Hulstijn (1995) suggested that higher frequency forms are more likely candidates for lexical learning, that is, learning relies on accumulation of exemplars rather than rules. In fact, research on the effect of increased frequency on grammatical development, in the form of input floods, has shown somewhat mixed results (e.g., Bardovi-Harlig & Reynolds, 1995; Jourdenais, Ota, Stauffer, Boyson, & Doughty, 1995; Lee, 2002; Leeman, Artegoitia, Friedman, & Doughty, 1995; Trahey & White, 1993; White, 1998; Williams & Evans, 1998). This may be in part due to the fact that in contrast to lexical forms, whose frequencies learners may compute, grammatical forms often represent underlying formal abstractions, which learners can neither notice nor compute. It is also important to note two things about the flood studies. Often, the floods were mixed with other treatments. Second, they have often been composed of items that are new to learners, and thus are better considered in terms of their impact on the initial connection than on subsequent processing.

Nature of the L2 form. Frequency is an important input feature, but there are other elements inherent to the forms themselves that may affect FMCs. First, as has been noted several times, it is likely that different aspects of language are processed differentially (N. Ellis, 1994; Schwartz, 1993, VanPatten, 1994). FMCs are perhaps more easily made for lexical items than grammatical forms (Gass, chap. 4 in this vol.; VanPatten, 1990). Two general characteristics of input have been suggested as important elements in the creation and processing of FMCs: form complexity and form salience.

It is generally thought that complex structures are more difficult to acquire than simpler structures (DeKeyser, 1998; Hulstijn, 1995; Hulstijn & deGraaf, 1994). An FMC's complexity may rest on (a) a form's relationship to meaning(s) (one-to-one vs. one-to-many) (Bensoussan & Laufer, 1984, DeKeyser, 1995; Goldschnieder & DeKeyser, 2001; Toth, 2000), (b) its transparency (DeKeyser, 1995; N. Ellis & Beaton, 1993; Laufer, 1997), (c) its regularity (adherence to expected rules) (DeKeyser, 1998; N. Ellis & Beaton, 1993; Goldschnieder & DeKeyser, 2001; Hulstijn, 1995; Hulstijn & De Graaff, 1994) (d) the degree to which it might be confused with other similar forms (Laufer, 1991; Ryan & Meara, 1991), and (e) its ease of pronunciation or spelling (N. Ellis & Beaton, 1993; Laufer, 1997). Although all of these factors have been shown to influence FMCs, it is not clear which are most important or how these factors interact (Vidal, 2003). Further research is also needed to determine the impact these factors may have on various phases of form–meaning mapping (see Shirai, chap. 5 in this vol., for one example).

Salience is also a complex factor that is sometimes difficult to define without circularity[5]: Salient forms are those that are most noticeable; learners tend to notice forms that are salient. It may be related to frequency or it may be seen as a primarily acoustic property. Forms may also gain salience in the context of a given message, independent of its inherent characteristics if it is crucial for message comprehension. Its importance is attested in production as well as acquisition processes (e.g., Pienemann, 1998). Goldschnieder and DeKeyser (2001) attempted a clearer definition for the acoustic salience of inflectional morphemes. Their definition has three components: number of phones, syllabicity, and sonority. The assumption they make is that the greater number of phones in the functor and the more sonorous the functor, the greater its salience, and the more likely it is to draw learner attention. For example, functors with vowels in their surface form are more salient that those without. Goldschnieder and DeKeyser's investigation was limited to inflectional morphemes, but the same principles may be applied more broadly. Forms that consistently draw learner attention are more likely to lead to complete and robust FMCs.

It is important to determine the interactive effect of these factors on FMCs. For example, the FMC for the future marker *be going to* is more complex than *will* because of the number of phonological units to be sequenced (N. Ellis, 1996). Yet, its length may also make it more salient and therefore more likely to draw learner attention. Similarly, Bardovi-Harlig (1987) argued that although preposition stranding may be seen as structurally more complex than pied piping, its relative frequency in the input and its novelty make it more salient than the more typologically common and straightforward pied piping. Some factors, such as salience, may be controlled for pedagogical purposes; others, such as complexity, probably cannot. Yet, even factors such as L1 influence, which would appear to be beyond teacher control, may be addressed and even manipulated to facilitate the establishment of FMCs (VanPatten, 2003). A greater understanding of how these factors impact learners processes will be an important step in advancing the research agenda in instructed language learning (Doughty, chap. 9 in this vol.; Skehan, 2002). For too long, both instructors and researchers have approached instructed language learning by focusing on teaching the product, that is, teaching a particular form or structure. It may be that instruction is more beneficial if it either capitalizes on or manipulates processes that lead to the acquisition of an FMC.

[5] Carroll (2001) argued that salience is not a property of the input at all, but rather that it is a result of the interaction of perceptual systems with certain kinds of stimuli.

CHAPTERS IN THIS VOLUME

This proposed outline of factors and subprocesses underscores the complexity of establishing FMCs and points to the multiplicity of approaches to understanding their acquisition, a multiplicity that ultimately must be integrated into a larger view or model of how FMCs are processed, internalized, and used. The chapters in this volume demonstrate this multiplicity. The first section contains contributions that provide overviews of important factors and processes involved in making FMCs. In Chapter 2, VanPatten reviews the issues surrounding the roles of input and output in making FMCs, arguing against what he calls "the input vs. output debate." He makes the distinction between competence and skill development, maintaining that input plays the primary role in making FMCs and that output is not necessary although it can be beneficial in combination with input. Ellis, in turn, looks at the nature of the form–meaning mapping process from cognitive perspective in Chapter 3 by discussing functional approaches, associations, and the construction of the brain. He claims that a majority of language development is an implicit frequency driven process. In his discussion, he also explains under which conditions frequency fails to drive learning.

Gass addresses the role that context has played in various approaches to second language acquisition in Chapter 4, focusing on the role of attention as a link between internal linguistic/psycholinguistic processes and the context in which learning takes place. She reviews the results of two studies that demonstrate that learners whose attention is focused on a target structure learn more than subjects whose attention is not so directed. Given that one of the focusing devices in her study was an interaction task, Gass concludes that interaction serves as an attention-focusing device that promotes the establishment of FMCs. Her results also support the notion that not all input is inherently equal; syntactic, morphological and syntactic forms may be not all be processed in the same way.

Shirai, in his review of the empirical support for the Aspect Hypothesis in Chapter 5, presents evidence that FMCs are affected by a number of factors including frequency in the input, learning environment, L1 influence, and learner characteristics. These factors interact in complex ways to determine what connections learners make and when they make them. He discusses the development of the interlanguage tense-aspect system and shows how a change in one area can cause changes in another, manifesting the kind of restructuring described earlier in this introduction. The acquisition of the tense-aspect system is also the subject of Bardovi-Harlig's chapter. Her chapter opens the second section of the volume, which offers empirical studies of the development of specific FMCs and their impact on the developing system. In Chapter 6, Bardovi-Harlig traces the restructuring of one function within the developing grammars of L2 learners. Her study examines two form–meaning pairs: *will* and *going to* as markers of futurity. At the beginning, learners make the simplest of form–meaning mappings possible, for example, *will* is used only for temporal reference (e.g., as a form to distinguish future from past and present contexts). Modality and aspectual meanings are mapped subsequently, as *going to* is added and the system is forced to deal with two forms in competition.

L1 influence is undoubtedly one of the most important factors in guiding FMCs. Cadierno and Lund take a new look at L1 influence in Chapter 7, arguing that a typological approach can constitute the basis for theoretically grounded and testable hypotheses on the FMCs made by learners from different L1 backgrounds. Using motion events, they show that even though learners may have made all the FMCs that are part of a sentence (i.e., the learners have all the words and all the forms in the IL), the influence of the L1 on the syntactic component of the L2 may cause them to misinterpret sentences. Indeed, they may not perceive how motion events are constructed in the L2. The syntax thus will continue to contain L1-like structures as long as learners comprehend sentences using that same L1-like structure.

In Chapter 8, Klein explores the impact of new FMCs on the learner's developing grammar. Her review of a number of studies attempts to explain the development of L2 knowledge that lies beyond the abstract principles and parameter-settings of UG; that is, how language-specific input is processed and incorporated into the L2 grammar, and the particular factors that affect the syntactic restructuring process. Specifically, she investigates how performance factors affect processing and whether errors in syntax that look like gaps in competence could be due to performance factors.

The final section focuses on pedagogical implications of FMC research. In Chapter 9, Doughty provides an overview of the effects-of-instruction empirical research. She assesses and critiques the overall findings of this research, which suggest that second language instruction does make a difference and points to the types of instruction that are most effective. She offers suggestions for improvements in design of instructed second language acquisition studies, particularly concerning the conceptualization of L2 instructional treatments and matching them to outcome measures.

The final two chapters report on empirical studies with pedagogical implications. Williams' study of acquisition of determiners in Chapter 10 focuses on the possibility that initial FMCs can be learned implicitly. The results of two experiments suggest that learners fail to make appropriate connections when their attention is not explicitly directed to the relationship between a form and its meaning. His results also suggest that the L1 may play a factor in how learners make these connections. Although he does not make direct pedagogical recommendations based on the results, they suggest that some kind of intervention may be needed for successful acquisition of these FMCs.

In Chapter 11, Barcroft presents research on FMCs in lexical acquisition. His study examines the effects of semantic versus structural elaboration on memory for new words in a second language. The results reveal that semantic elaboration did not positively affect performance, suggesting that this is not an effective intervention for fostering acquisition of new words. Learners who were merely exposed to words learned them just as well as those who were engaged in tasks purported to enhance vocabulary acquisition.

Furthermore, a substantial percentage of learners avoided performing both the semantic and structural elaboration tasks even when instructed to do so, defaulting instead to strategies of their own preference. Juxtaposed to Williams' study, these results suggest that different aspects of L2 learning may respond to intervention differentially.

Larsen-Freeman's Chapter 12 reviews the scope of FMC research and poses several important challenges that such research must face in the future, particularly the place of mental competence in models of SLA and the role of comprehension and production in acquisition processes.

CONCLUSION

Such a collection can only be taken as suggestive of areas in need of investigation. Nonetheless, along with this introductory chapter, they strongly show that research on the acquisition of FMCs must

- ultimately be tied to the input learners are exposed to,
- consider properties of the form in question,
- relate processes and processing to the nature of the form,
- consider the role of the L1 in both processing and restructuring,
- link instructional intervention to learning processes

In spite of the long-standing research on syntax and sentence structure in SLA, the acquisition of FMCs continues to be a central area of vigorous research as investigators chip away at the intricacy of SLA. It should now be clear to everyone that there will never be "a" theory of SLA. Instead, most likely there will be multiple theories and models that account for different aspects of SLA. In the case of FMCs, the present volume demonstrates the various strands of research that bear upon an eventual theory or set of theories that will underlie how the acquisition of FMCs is conceptualized—and this theory or set of theories will be different from one that underlies the acquisition of syntax, the acquisition of phonology, the acquisition of socio-pragmatic competence and perhaps the acquisition of skills, especially productive skills.

REFERENCES

Andersen, R. (1983). Transfer to somewhere. In S. Gass & L. Selinker (Eds.), *Language transfer in language learning* (pp. 177–201). Rowley, MA: Newbury House.

Andersen, R. (1984). The one-to-one principle of interlanguage construction. *Language Learning, 34*, 77–95.

Andersen, R. (1990). Models, process, principles, and strategies: Second language acquisition inside and outside the classroom. In B. VanPatten & J. Lee (Eds.), *Second language acquisition-foreign language acquisition* (pp. 45–71). Clevedon, England: Multilingual Matters.

Ard, J., & Homburg, T. (1983). Verification of transfer. In S. Gass & L. Selinker (Eds.), *Language transfer in language learning* (pp. 157–176). Rowley, MA: Newbury House.

Baddely, A. (1990). *Human memory: Theory and practice.* Needham Heights, MA: Allyn & Bacon.

Bahns, J., & Eldaw, M. (1993). Should we teach EFL students collocations? *System, 21*, 101–114.

Bardovi-Harlig, K. (1987). Markedness and salience in second-language acquisition. *Language Learning, 37*, 385–407.

Bardovi-Harlig, K. (1995). The interaction of pedagogy and natural sequences in the acquisition of tense and aspect. In F. Eckman, D. Highland, P. Lee, J. Mileham, & R. Weber (Eds.), *Second language acquisition theory and pedagogy* (pp. 151–168). Mahwah, NJ: Lawrence Erlbaum Associates.

Bardovi-Harlig, K. (2000). Tense and aspect in second language acquisition: Form, meaning and use. *Language Learning, 50* (Supplement 1).

Bardovi-Harlig, K., & Reynolds, D. (1995). The role of lexical aspect in the acquisition of tense and aspect. *TESOL Quarterly, 29*, 107–131.

Barcroft, J., & VanPatten, B. (1997). Acoustic salience: Testing location, stress and the boundedness of grammatical form in second language acquisition input perception. In W. R. Glass & A. T. Pérez-Leroux (Eds.), *Contemporary perspectives on the acquisition of Spanish: Production, processing, and comprehension* (pp. 109–121). Somerville, MA: Cascadilla Press.

Beck, M. L. (1998). Morphology and its interfaces in second-language knowledge: Introduction. In M.L. Beck (Ed.), *Morphology and its interfaces in second language knowledge* (pp. 1–39). Philadelphia: Benjamins.

Bensoussan, M., & Laufer, B. (1984). Lexical guessing in context in EFL reading comprehension. *Journal of Research in Reading, 7*, 15–32.

Bogaards, P. (2001). Lexical units and the learning of foreign language vocabulary. *Studies in Second Language Acquisition, 23*, 321–343.

Broeder, P. (1995). Acquisition of pronominal reference: A longitudinal perspective. *Second Language Research, 11*, 178–191.

Bull, W. (1947). Modern Spanish verb frequencies. *Hispania, 30*, 451–466.

Bybee, J. (2002). Phonological evidence for exemplar storage of multiword sequences. *Studies in Second Language Acquisition, 24*, 215–221.

Call, M. (1985). Auditory short-term memory, listening comprehension and the input hypothesis. *TESOL Quarterly, 19*, 767-81.

Carroll, S. (2001). *Input and evidence.* Amsterdam: Benjamins.

Carroll, S. (2003). Commentary: Some general and specific comments on input processing and processing instruction. In B. VanPatten (Ed.), *Processing instruction: Theory, research, and commentary.* Mahwah, NJ: Lawrence Erlbaum Associates.

Clahsen, H. (1984). The acquisition of German word order: A test case for cognitive approaches to L2 development. In R. Andersen (Ed.), *Second languages: A cross-linguistic perspective.* Rowley, MA: Newbury House.

Collins, L. (2002). The roles of L1 influence and lexical aspect in the acquisition of temporal morphology. *Language Learning, 52*, 43–94.

Cook, H. (2001). Why can't learners of JFL distinguish polite from impolite speech styles? In K. Rose & G. Kasper (Eds.), *Pragmatics in language teaching* (pp. 80–102). Cambridge, England: Cambridge University Press.

De Bot, K. (1996). The psycholinguistics of the output hypothesis. *Language Learning, 46*, 529–555.

De Groot, A., & Keijzer, R. (2000). What is hard to learn is easy to forget: The role of word concreteness, cognate status and word frequency in foreign-language learning and forgetting. *Language Learning, 50*, 1–56.

DeKeyser, R. (1995). Learning second language grammar rules: An experiment with a miniature linguistic system. *Studies in Second Language Acquisition, 17*, 379–410.

DeKeyser, R. (1998). Beyond focus on form: Cognitive perspectives on learning and practicing second language grammar. In C. Doughty & J. Williams (Eds.), *Focus on form in classroom second language acquisition* (pp. 42–63). Cambridge, England: Cambridge University Press.

Ellis, N. (1994). Consciousness in second language learning: Psychological perspectives on the role of conscious processes in vocabulary acquisition. In J. Hulstijn & R. Schmidt (Eds.), *Consciousness in second language learning (AILA Review 11)* (pp. 37–56).

Ellis, N. (1996). Sequencing in SLA: Phonological memory, chunking, and points of order. *Studies in Second Language Acquisition, 18*, 91–126.

Ellis, N. (1998). Emergentism, connectionism and language learning. *Language Learning, 48*, 631–644.

Ellis, N. (2001). Memory for language In P. Robinson (Ed.), *Cognition and second language instruction* (pp. 33–68). Cambridge, England: Cambridge University Press.

Ellis, N. (Ed.). (2002). Frequency effects in language processing. *Studies in Second Language Acquisition, 24* (2).

Ellis, N., & Beaton, A. (1993). Psycholinguistic determinants of foreign language vocabulary learning. *Language Learning, 43*, 559–617.

Ellis, R. (1995). Modified oral input and the acquisition of word meanings. *Applied Linguistics, 16*, 409–441.

Eubank, L. (1996). Negation in early German-English interlanguage: More valueless features in the L2 initial state. *Second Language Research, 12*, 73–106.

Felix, S., & Hahn, A. (1985). Natural processes in classroom second language learning. *Applied Linguistics, 6*, 223–238.

Gass, S., & Mackey, A. (2002). Frequency effects and second language acquisition: A complex picture? *Studies in Second Language Acquisition, 24*, 249–260.

Gass. S., & Selinker, L. (Eds.). (1992). *Language transfer in language learning* (Rev. ed.). Amsterdam: Benjamins.

Goldschneider, J., & DeKeyser, R. (2001). Exploring the "natural order of L2 morpheme acquisition" in English: A meta-analysis of multiple determinants. *Language Learning, 51*, 1–50.

Gregg, K. (1996). The logical and developmental problems of second language acquisition. In T. Bhatia & W. Ritchie, (Eds.), *Handbook of second language acquisition* (pp. 49–81). New York: Academic Press.

Harrington, M. (2003). Input processing as a theory of processing input. In B. VanPatten (Ed.), *Processing instruction: theory, research, and commentary*. Mahwah, NJ: Lawrence Erlbaum Associates.

Hawkins, R. (2001). *Second language syntax*. Oxford: Blackwell.

Herschensohn, J. (2000). *The second time around: Minimalism and L2 acquisition*. Philadelphia: Benjamins.

Holmes, J., & Ramos, R. (1993). False friends and reckless guessers: Observing cognate recognition strategies. In T. Huckin, M. Haynes, & J. Coady, (Eds.), *Second language reading and vocabulary learning* (pp. 86–108). Norwood, NJ: Ablex.

Horst, M., Cobb, T., & Meara, P. (1998). Beyond *A Clockwork Orange*: Acquiring second language vocabulary through reading. *Reading in a Foreign Language, 11*, 207–223.

Huebner, T. (1983). *A longitudinal analysis of the acquisition of English*. Ann Arbor, MI: Karoma.

Hulstijn, J. (1995). Not all grammar rules are equal: Giving grammar instruction its proper place in foreign language teaching. In R. Schmidt (Ed.), *Attention and awareness in foreign language learning* (pp. 359–386). Honolulu: University of Hawaii Press.

Hulstijn, J., & De Graaff, R. (1994). Under what conditions does explicit knowledge of a second language facilitate the acquisition of implicit knowledge? In J. Hulstijn & R. Schmidt (Eds.), *Consciousness in second language learning (AILA Review 11)* (pp. 97–112).

Hulstijn, J., Holander, M., & Griedanus, T. (1996). Incidental vocabulary learning by advanced foreign language students: The influence of marginal glosses, dictionary use, and reoccurrence of unknown words. *Modern Language Journal, 80*, 327–339.

Hulstijn, J., & Marchena, E. (1989). Avoidance: Grammatical or semantic causes? *Studies in Second Language Acquisition, 11*, 241–255.

Hyams, N. (1996). The underspecification of functional categories in early grammar. In H. Clahsen (Ed.), *Generative perspectives on language acquisition: Empirical findings, theoretical considerations, crosslinguistic comparisons* (pp. 91–127). Philadelphia: Benjamins.

Jarvis, S. (2000a). Methodological rigor in the study of transfer: Identifying L1 influence in the interlanguage lexicon. *Language Learning, 50*, 245–309.

Jarvis, S. (2000b). Semantic and conceptual transfer. *Bilingualism, Language and Cognition, 3*, 19–21.

Jarvis, S., & Odlin, T. (2000). Morphological type, spatial reference and language transfer. *Studies in Second Language Acquisition, 22*, 535–556.

Jiang, N. (2002). Form–meaning mapping in vocabulary acquisition in a second language. *Studies in Second Language Acquisition, 18*, 149–169.

Jourdenais, R., Ota, M., Stauffer, S., Boyson, B., & Doughty, C. (1995). Does textual enhancement promote noticing? A think-aloud protocol analysis. In R. Schmidt (Ed.), *Attention and awareness in foreign language learning* (pp. 183–216). Honolulu: University of Hawaii Press.

Kasper, G., & Schmidt, R. (1996). Developmental issues in interlanguage pragmatics. *Studies in Second Language Acquisition, 22*, 535–556.

Kellerman, E. (1995). Cross-linguistic influence: Transfer to nowhere? In W. Grabe (Ed.), *Annual Review of Applied Linguistics, 15*, 125–150.

Klein, W. (1986). *Second language acquisition*. Cambridge, England: Cambridge University Press.

Klein, W., & Perdue, C. (1997). The basic variety. *Second Language Research, 13*, 301–347.

Krashen, S. (1981). *Second language acquisition and second language learning*. Oxford, England: Pergammon.

Krashen, S. (1982). *Prinicples and practice in second language acquisition*. New York: Pergammon.

Kroll, J.F., & Tokowicz, N. (2001). The development of conceptual representation for words in a second language. In J. L. Nicol (Ed.), *One mind two languages: Bilingual language processing* (pp. 49–71). Cambridge, England: Blackwell.

Langacker, R. W. (1972). *Fundamentals of linguistic analysis*. New York: Harcourt, Brace & Jovanovich.

Lardiere, D. (2000). Mapping features to forms in second language acquisition. In J. Archibald (Ed.), *Second language acquisition and linguistic theory* (pp. 102–129). Oxford, England: Blackwell.

Laufer, B. (1991). The development of L2 lexis in the expression of the advanced language learner. *Modern Language Journal, 75*, 440–448.

Laufer, B. (1997). What's in a word that makes it hard or easy: Some extralinguistic factors that affect the learning of words. In N. Schmitt & M. McCarthy (Eds.), *Vocabulary description acquisition and pedagogy* (pp. 140–155). Cambridge, England: Cambridge University Press.

Laufer, B., & Eliasson, S. (1993). What causes avoidance in L2 learning, L1-L2 difference, L1-L2 similarity or L2 complexity? *Studies in Second Language Acquisition, 15*, 33–48.

Lee, E.-J. (2001). Interlanguage development by two Korean speakers of English with a focus on temporality. *Language Learning, 51*, 591–633.

Lee, J. (2002). The incidental acquisition of Spanish: Future tense morphology through reading in a second language. *Studies in Second Language Acquisition, 24*, 55–80.

Leeman, J., Arteagoitia, I., Friedman, B., & Doughty, C. (1995). Integrating attention to form with meaning: Focus on form in content-based Spanish instruction. In R. Schmidt (Ed.), *Attention and awareness in foreign language learning* (pp. 217–258). Honolulu: University of Hawaii Press.

Levin, B., & Hovav, M. R. (1998). Morphology and lexical semantics. In A. Spencer & A. M. Zwicky (Eds.), *The handbook of morphology* (pp. 248–271). Oxford, England: Blackwell.

Lightbown, P. (1998). The importance of timing in focus on form. In C. Doughty & J. Williams (Eds.), *Focus on form in classroom second language acquisition* (pp. 177–196). Cambridge, England: Cambridge University Press.

Liu, D., & Gleason, J. (2002). Acquisition of the article THE by nonnative speakers of English: An analysis of four nongeneric uses. *Studies in Second Language Acquisition, 24*, 1–26.

Lotto, L., & de Groot, A. (1998). The effects of learning method and word type on acquiring vocabulary in an unfamiliar language. *Language Learning, 48*, 31–69.

Mackey, A. (1999). Input, interaction and second language development: An empirical study of question formation in ESL. *Studies in Second Language Acquisition, 21*, 557–587.

MacWhinney, B. (1997). Second language acquisition and the competition model. In A. deGroot & J. Kroll (Eds.), *Tutorials in bilingualism* (pp. 113–142). Mahwah, NJ: Lawrence Erlbaum Associates.

Meara, P. (1997). Towards a new approach to modeling vocabulary acquisition. In N. Schmitt & M. McCarthy (Eds.), *Vocabulary description acquisition and pedagogy* (pp. 109–121). Cambridge, England: Cambridge University Press.

Myles, F., Hooper, J., & Mitchell, R. (1998). Rote or rule? Exploring the role of formulaic language in the foreign language classroom. *Language Learning, 48*, 323–364.

Myles, F., Mitchell, R. & Hooper, J. (1999). Interrogative chunks in French L2: A basis for creative construction? *Studies in Second Language Acquisition, 21*, 49–80.

Nation, I. S. P. (2001). *Learning vocabulary in another language*. Cambridge, England: Cambridge University Press.

O'Grady, W. (1999). Toward a new nativism. *Studies in Second Language Acquisition, 21*, 621–633.

Odlin, T. (1989). *Language transfer*. Cambridge, England: Cambridge University Press.

Odlin, T. (2002). Language transfer and cross-linguistic studies: Relativism, universalism, and the native language. In R. Kaplan (Ed.), *The Oxford handbook of applied linguistics*. Oxford: Oxford University Press.

Pavlenko, A., & Jarvis, S. (2002). Bidirectional transfer. *Applied Linguistics, 23*, 190–214.

Perdue, C. (2002). The development of L2 functional use. In V. Cook, (Ed.), *Portraits of the L2 user* (pp. 121–144) Clevedon, England: Multilingual Matters.

Peters, A. M. (1985). Language segmentation: Operating principles for the perception and analysis of language. In D. I. Slobin (Ed.), *The cross-linguistic study of language acquisition, Vol. 2: Theoretical issues* (pp. 1029–1067). Hillsdale, NJ: Lawrence Erlbaum Associates.

Pienemann, M. (1984). Psychological constraints on the teachability of languages. *Studies in Second Language Acquisition, 6*, 186–214.

Pienemann, M. (1985). Learnability and syllabus construction. In K. Hyltenstam & M. Pienemann (Eds.), *Modeling and assessing second language acquisition* (pp. 23–75). Clevedon, England: Multilingual Matters.

Pienemann, M. (1998). *Sentence processing and second language development*. Philadelphia: Benjamins.

Radford, A. (1997). *Syntax: A minimalist introduction*. Cambridge, England: Cambridge University Press.

Ringbom, H. (1987). *The role of first language in foreign language learning*. Clevedon, England: Multilingual Matters.

Rosa, E., & O'Neill, M. (1998). Effects of stress and location on acoustic salience at the initial stages of Spanish L2 input processing. *Spanish Applied Linguistics, 2*, 24–52.

Rott, S. (1999). The effect of exposure frequency on intermediate language learners' incidental vocabulary acquisition and retention through reading. *Studies in Second Language Acquisition, 21*, 589–619.

Rounds, P., & Kanagy, R. (1998). Acquiring linguistic cues to identify AGENT: Evidence for children learning Japanese as a second language. *Studies in Second Language Acquisition, 20*, 509–542.

Ryan, A., & Meara, P. (1991). The case of invisible vowels. *Reading in a Foreign Language, 7*, 531–540.

Schmidt, R. (1990). The role of consciousness in second language learning. *Applied Linguistics, 11*, 17–46.

Schmidt, R. (1995). Consciousness and foreign language learning: A tutorial on the role of attention and awareness in learning. In R. Schmidt (Ed.), *Attention and awareness in foreign language learning* (pp. 1–65). Honolulu: University of Hawaii Press,

Schmidt, R. (2001). Attention. In P. Robinson (Ed.), *Cognition and second language instruction* (pp. 3–32). Cambridge, England: Cambridge University Press.

Schmitt, N. (1998). Tracking the incremental acquisition of second language vocabulary: A longitudinal study. *Language Learning, 48*, 281–317.

Schwartz, B. (1993). On explicit and negative data effecting and affecting competence and linguistic behavior. *Studies in Second Language Acquisition, 15*, 147–163.

Schwartz, B. (1999). Let's make up your mind, "Special nativist" perspectives on language acquisition, modularity of mind and nonnative language acquisition. *Studies in Second Language Acquisition, 21*, 635–654.

Shirai, Y., & Andersen, R. (1995). The acquisition of tense-aspect morphology. *Language, 71*, 743–762.

Skehan, P. (1998). *A cognitive approach to language learning*. Oxford, England: Oxford University Press.

Skehan, P. (2002). Theorising and updating aptitude. In P. Robinson (Ed.), *Individual differences and instructed language learning* (pp. 69–93). Amsterdam: Benjamins.

Slobin, D. (Ed.). (1985). *The cross-linguistic study of language acquisition*. Hillsdale, NJ: Lawrence Erlbaum Associates.

Spada, N., & Lightbown, P. (1999). Instruction, first language influence and developmental readiness in second language acquisition. *Modern Language Journal, 83*, 1–22.

Spencer, A., & Zwicky, A. M. (1998). Introduction. In A. Spencer & A. M. Zwicky (Eds.), *The handbook of morphology* (pp. 1–43). Oxford, England: Blackwell.

Toth, P. (2000). The interaction of instruction and learner internal factors in the acquisition of L2 morphosyntax. *Studies in Second Language Acquisition, 22*, 169–208.

Towell, R., Hawkins, R., & Bazergui, N. (1996). The development of fluency in advanced learners of French. *Applied Linguistics, 17*, 84–119.

Trahey, M., & White, L. (1993). Positive evidence and preemption in the second language classroom. *Studies in Second Language Acquisition, 15*, 181–204.

Vainikka, A., & Young-Scholten, M. (1996). Gradual development of L2 phrase structure. *Second Language Research, 12*, 7–39.

VanPatten, B. (2003). Input processing in SLA. In B. VanPatten (Ed.), *Processing instruction: theory, research, and commentary*. Mahwah, NJ: Lawrence Erlbaum Associates.

VanPatten, B. (1996). *Input processing and grammar instruction*. Norwood, NJ: Ablex.

VanPatten, B. (1994). Evaluating the role of consciousness in second language acquisition: Terms, linguistic features and research methodology. *AILA Review 11*, 27–36.

VanPatten, B. (1990). Attending to form and content in the input: An experiment in consciousness. *Studies in Second Language Acquisition, 12*, 287–301.

Vidal, K. (2003). Academic listening: A source of vocabulary acquisition. *Applied Linguistics, 24*, 56–89.

Weinert, R. (1995). The role of formulaic language in second language acquisition. *Applied Linguistics, 16*, 180–205.

Wexler, K., & Cullicover, P. (1980). *Formal principles of language acquisition*. Cambridge, MA: MIT Press.

White, J. (1998). Getting the learners' attention: A typographical input enhancement study. In C. Doughty & J. Williams (Eds.), *Focus on form in second language classroom acquisition* (pp. 91–128). Cambridge, MA: Cambridge University Press.

White, L. (2003). *Second language acquisition and universal grammar*. Cambridge, England: Cambridge University Press.

Williams, J. (in press). Form-focused instruction. In E. Hinkel (Ed.) *Handbook of second language learning and teaching*. Mahwah, NJ: Lawrence Erlbaum Associates.

Williams, J., & Evans, J. (1998). What kind of focus on which forms? In C. Doughty & J. Williams (Eds.), *Focus on form in classroom second language acquisition* (139–155). Cambridge, England: Cambridge University Press.

Wong Fillmore, L. (1976). *The second time around: Cognitive and social strategies in second language acquisition*. Unpublished Ph.D. dissertation, Stanford University.

I
Factors and Processes

CHAPTER 2
Input and Output in Establishing Form–Meaning Connections

Bill VanPatten
University of Illinois at Chicago

With the rise in research on the role of output in SLA, one occasionally sees the phrase "input versus output" or "the input versus output debate," or even "the roles of comprehension and production," in titles of papers[1]. It may seem obvious to most that output plays some kind of role in SLA. What is not clear to all researchers is the extent of that role, its necessity, or what processes it affects or interacts with. To be sure, few discount a role for input and acquisition is generally characterized in just about any theory as being input dependent in some way (see, e.g., the discussion in Gass, 1997). Indeed, the various chapters in this volume assume the input-dependent nature of acquisition. The question then becomes to what extent acquisition can be characterized as output dependent. Because the field of SLA research has begun to explore roles for both input and output, I find it puzzling to see phrases such as "input vs. output" describing the various positions taken by some scholars.

In this chapter, I review the roles of input and output in establishing form–meaning connections. I review them by asking the following questions: What is acquisition? Why do we believe that acquisition is input dependent? Can we speak of acquisition as also being output dependent? In the end I conclude that any strong version that requires a role for output for successful SLA is currently untenable.

WHAT IS ACQUISITION?

I take acquisition to mean the development of some underlying competence on which skills in language use depend. In this sense, I am following a generative tradition (e.g., Hawkins, 2001; Pinker, 1994; Radford, 1997) in distinguishing between a knowledge source and any mechanisms that make use of that knowledge source for comprehension and production (e.g., Levelt, 1989; Pienemann, 1998). This competence is also known as an underlying mental representation, the developing system, the interlanguage, and other terms used in SLA literature. This competence consists of different components that interact at various levels of comprehension and speech production and consists of a lexicon, a phonological component, a syntactic component, a semantic component, and a sociopragmatic component. (For discussions of various components within linguistic theory as applied to SLA, see the various papers in

[1] I am grateful to my colleagues, Susanne Rott, Jessica Williams, Wynne Wong, and James F. Lee for comments on an earlier version of this chapter. But don't hold any shortcomings you find against them.

Archibald, 2000) However, I will focus on form–meaning connections, which I take to reside in the lexicon or are derived from lexical entries (e.g., Bybee, 1991; Jensen & Strong-Jensen, 1984; but see some discussion in Aronoff & Anshen, 1998).

It should be noted that by using terms such as competence or underlying mental representation one should not construe that what is acquired is necessarily a native or native-like competence or mental representation. If one accepts Universal Grammar (UG) as a constraint mechanism on the acquisition of syntax, a learner need not achieve nativelike competence for UG to operate. UG operates all along the way (e.g., Hawkins, 2001; Lardiere, 2000; Schwartz, 1998; Schwartz & Sprouse, 2000; White, 2003). If one does not accept UG as a constraint mechanism, a learner still does not have to achieve native-like performance on any measures for the underlying cognitive mechanisms of acquisition to operate (e.g., Ellis, 2002a, 2002b; MacWhinney, 1997). So, what are these mechanisms and just what is involved in acquisition? Acquisition consists of at least three sets of processes, each of which may contain its own subprocesses and mechanisms. I refer to these sets of processes as input processing, accommodation, and restructuring (VanPatten, 2003, and elsewhere). These terms are not used by everyone, but they are convenient to group the domains in which the various knowledge sources and processes act as we will see.

Input Processing

Input processing consists of two subprocesses. The first is the formation of initial form–meaning connections. The second is parsing. Initial form–meaning connections occur the very first time the learner makes the connection between a form and a meaning (as well as possible function) it may represent. This connection may be whole or partial, correct or incorrect; the point being that some kind of connection is initiated. An example of a whole connection is if the learner processes *–s* on the end of present tense verbs in Spanish connecting it to second person singular. An example of partial form–meaning connection would be if a learner initially processes the relationship between the Spanish verb inflection *–aba* and the past, but not have also attached some kind of progressive or nonperfective aspect to it. In such cases, one might also talk about subsequent form–meaning connections, that is, those that fill out those connections that were initially incomplete. In the case of *–aba*, the initial connection may be to past tense, which is correct but incomplete, and subsequent connections would connect it to its aspectual meaning(s). Input processing is also what determines the categories of words, that is, whether something is a noun, verb, adjective, and so on. Thus, when a learner encounters a new word such as *erase*, the learner not only attaches meaning to it as part of processing but also assigns it a lexical category (or functional category in the case of determiners, complementizers, and others). Input processing results in some kind of linguistic data that are held in working memory, defined as that processing and storage space where online, real-time language computations are made during comprehension (Gathercole & Baddeley, 1993; Just & Carpenter, 1992). Input processing does not refer to the internalization of those data.

Within input processing, *parsing* refers to how learners assign syntactic categories to words they comprehend and to what kind of syntactic representation learners build during comprehension (e.g., Clifton, Frazier, & Rayner, 1994; Harrington, 2001; Pritchett, 1992). When comprehending an utterance, a major function of the learner's parser is to project syntactic phrases associated with lexical items. The results may be accurate or they may be erroneous. Consider two examples. In Spanish, it is well known that learners of English rely on a first-noun strategy to process sentences (see VanPatten, 1996, 2003). L2 sentences that follow canonical order are no problem because SVO and even VO are interpretable by the English L1 parser. But canonical sentences in Spanish represent only about 60% of the sentences one might hear. The other sentences can be either SOV or OVS or even OV. Thus, learners often misinterpret OVS sentences as SVO sentences. That is, the parser takes the first noun or pronoun and projects it into a syntactic phrase that is positioned where subjects are normally positioned within a sentence (i.e., within the IP but above the VP). Thus, the parser, expecting an SVO string, imposes a structure on the sentence that is incorrect and as long as meaning interpretation is not compromised, the result is erroneous form–meaning connection and incorrect data for acquisition. (See VanPatten, 2000, as well as Carroll, 2001, for further discussion.)[2].

Making form–meaning connections and parsing are not necessarily mutually exclusive. It could be (and probably is) the case that either one can influence the other. In parsing with the first-noun strategy, for example, learners commit early on to a sentence structure. Thus, when they hear *Juan no conoce a María bien* ('John does not know Mary well'), they first hear *Juan* and retrieve its lexical information (e.g., noun, proper name, male) and project an NP that in turn is projected into a sentence as the subject. As they hear *no* there is nothing to disconfirm their structural assignment of *Juan* and the parser expects a verb to be next. As they hear *conoce* they retrieve its lexical information, that is, a verb with a particular meaning that requires two arguments and they project the VP and the parser expects to encounter an object NP next. There is still nothing to

[2] Parsing consists also of making use of abstract properties of the grammar during comprehension and the preferences that languages have. For example, some languages show differences in parsing preferences when there is ambiguity (Cuetos, Mitchell, & Corley, 1996; Fernández, 1999). In the sentence *Andrew had dinner with the niece of the teacher who belongs to the communist party*, when asked "Who belongs to the communist party?", there is a tendency among English speakers to say "the teacher." This is called low attachment. In Spanish, the equivalent sentence is *Andrés cenó con la sobrina del maestro que está en el partido comunista* and when asked who is in the communist party Spanish speakers tend to reply that the niece is, showing a preference for high attachment. (See Fernandez, 1999, for these and other examples.) However, note that in these examples we are not talking about correct form–meaning mappings but about interpretation preferences when two interpretations are both possible. In such research, interest is not in form–meaning connections but how a parser uses what it has to effect comprehension. Thus, this research falls outside of the scope of input processing per se.

tell them *Juan* is not the subject and, as they hear *María*, they tag this noun as object after retrieving its lexical information. The same process occurs with *bien* as an adverb and the sentence is successfully computed, with all aspects of parsing being satisfied.

Note, however, that we have said nothing about the function word *a*, which is used in Spanish to mark objects that could be construed as possible subjects, that is, when lexical semantics allows for it. In this case, *María* is case marked with *a* because the verb *conoce* does not rule her out as a possible subject; either she or John is capable of knowing. This contrasts with *la materia* ('the subject matter'), which cannot be a subject for a verb like *conocer* and hence no case marking is needed: *Juan no conoce la materia bien.* In the case of L2 parsing, because the learner commits to sentence structure early on and expectations are fulfilled along the way, the case marker *a* may not be processed initially. The information it conveys is redundant and the parser, having no way to project it into the sentence, simply ignores it and it is dumped from working memory. This is a case where a form may get noticed (i.e., it gets registered somehow in working memory) but not processed (not connected with its meaning or function). In this scenario, parsing impedes the possible connection of form and meaning.

Another example comes from English. It is well known that learners have problems with the acquisition of *do.* As I have suggested elsewhere (VanPatten, 1996), it is possible that learners initially process *do* as a simple question marker, which is a possible surface feature in languages. Japanese has *wa* and French may utilize *est-ce que,* both of which allow the languages to maintain canonical ordering of elements. In English yes/no questions with *do*, canonical order with lexical verbs is maintained, for example, *Do you like chocolate?*, where *you like chocolate* is canonical declarative SVO word order. If learners process *do* as a particle, then they commit to a sentence structure early on in parsing that is not the actual structure of the sentence and subtle abstract properties of *do* as part of Infl (or whatever functional category it belongs to) do not make their way into the grammatical system. The result is erroneous acquisition, which may evidence itself in learner speech, such as *Do you can say this?* (see also, Hawkins, 2001). In this particular scenario, how learners initially connected a form to its meaning (and function) influenced the parsing of the sentence. It would not be until learners somehow note that *do* can carry person-number information as well as tense that the grammar reanalyzes the sentence structure and the parser is forced to commit to a different syntactic structure (i.e., when encountering *do,* it projects an inflectional phrase). In other words, only when learners make the form–meaning connections involving the finite inflections on *do* can parsing be altered.

To summarize so far, input processing consists of two subprocesses: the process of making form–meaning connections and parsing. Both have to do with how learners initially match meaning with form at both its local and sentential levels. Input processing is not equivalent to acquisition and is only one set of processes involved in the creation of an underlying mental representation. The result of input processing is linguistic data held in working memory that is made available for further processing. (See VanPatten, 2004, for a more detailed discussion.) What is this further processing?

Accommodation and Restructuring

Separate from input processing are accommodation and restructuring. *Accommodation* is a term borrowed from the field of schema theory in which learners are said to accommodate (i.e., internalize, incorporate) new schema into their conceptual systems (see, e.g., Rumelhart, 1980). In the present discussion, accommodation refers to either the partial penciling in or complete incorporation of a surface feature (form–meaning connection) of language into the developing system. For example, a past tense marker begins to infiltrate the developing system because an initial and then subsequent connections between a form and its meaning have been made during input processing. However, that a form is processed in input processing does not necessarily mean that it can be accommodated. For a number of reasons (see, e.g., Ellis, 2002b, and Chap. 3 in this vol., and Hawkins, 2001), a form and its meaning may be linked during the act of comprehension, but the developing system may not be ready for it or the connection may simply fade in working memory.

Restructuring is another term borrowed from cognitive psychology (McLaughlin, 1990) and refers to what may happen to the developing system after a form has been accommodated. Restructuring has consequences either in the syntax or other subtle semantico-morphosyntactic aspects of the language (e.g., aspectual systems—see, e.g., Bardovi-Harlig, Chap 6; Shirai, Chap. 5 in this vol.) and is said to involve qualitative rather than quantitative changes in either competence or linguistic behavior (Gass & Selinker, 2001). Within a principles and parameters framework the initial triggering of a parameter, which I take to be an aspect of restructuring, is believed to happen because some formal aspect of an input string has been processed (e.g., Hawkins, 2001; White, 1989, 2003) or because parsing has somehow failed (e.g., Carroll, 2001; Fodor, 1999). An example can be seen in speakers of English going into Spanish as an L2 who are moving from a non-verb-movement language to a verb-movement language. One possible trigger for the restructuring of the underlying system might be the combined form–meaning connection of a lexical verb plus parsing of questions, some declarative sentences, and some embedded clauses. For example, Spanish easily and readily inverts subject and finite lexical verb and in certain contexts inversion is obligatory, as in *¿Qué comió Juan?/*¿Qué Juan comió?* ('What did John eat?'), *¿Ya comió Juan?/*¿Ya Juan comió, Ya comió Juan/Juan ya comió* ('Did John already eat?/John already ate.') and *Maria dice que ya comió Juan* ('Mary says that John already ate.'). The parser notes that the verb is not in the expected position and that the noun following it cannot be an object or patient but has to be the subject or agent. This information, which is readily available in the input, may be the catalyst for restructuring; in this case, parameter setting or resetting for verb movement. The word order VS(O) delivered to the developing system would be evidence that the verb has moved out of its position within the VP.

In going from Spanish to English, the problem is different. English almost always maintains canonical word order with subjects, lexical verbs, and objects. The sequence John-eat-breakfast will almost always appear in that order: *John eats breakfast/Does John eat breakfast?/*Eats John breakfast?, Has John eaten breakfast?, When did John eat breakfast?*, and so on. The question in this scenario becomes "What is the trigger or possible trigger for *not* maintaining verb movement when the possible sentences in English are all possible sentences in Spanish (with the exception of the sentence containing the auxiliary *have*)?" If learners process *do* as a question marker (as suggested earlier), then no appropriate linguistic data are delivered about the underlying nature of inflectional phrases and restructuring may not occur. The form has been accommodated but in the wrong way and has consequences for the syntax. Learners will not reprocess *do* until they have to, that is, when they have to rely on it to retrieve information about tense. (Person-number may be readily recoverable from the subject noun or pronoun). It is not clear under what circumstances this would happen during input processing, so it is possible that the grammar could exist for sometime with a misanalyzed form and no restructuring around a parameter. This example is hypothetical, but when one examines the research on the acquisition of questions and negation in English L2, it is clear that the analysis of *do* as a dummy auxiliary takes some time (see Lightbown & Spada, 1999; Mackey, 1999, for a review)[3]. Such an analysis, however, is consistent with arguments about how Infl[4] is established in the grammars of L2 learners of English as they acquire negation. It is the acquisition of copular *be* that may force a learner's grammar to reanalyze and thus establish Infl (a functional phrase), which in turn impacts on the projection of Neg into the syntax. For discussion, see Hawkins (2001, p. 96-103).

As in the case of input processing, accommodation and restructuring alone are not equivalent to acquisition; they are two of the processes involved. In short, while we often tend to take acquisition to mean one thing, what is actually involved is more complex than generally acknowledged and involves multiple processes, multiple knowledge domains, and multiple interactions of both. The sketch I am making here is necessarily brief, but it certainly hints at the multicomponential nature of acquisition (see also Carroll, 2001, and Klein, Chap. 8 in this vol., for example). To summarize this section, acquisition is viewed as consisting of different processes. Some are responsible for an initial form–meaning connection (input processing) and some are responsible for the establishment of the connection in the learner's developing linguistic system (accommodation). The establishment of a connection may cause a part of the

[3] See also the discussion in Lightfoot (1991) about the move from Old English to Modern English, which involved resetting the verb movement parameter to "no movement." The resetting of English to [- verb movement] involved the appearance of *do,* suggesting that this dummy verb is a surface feature of nonmovement (at least in English).

[4] I am using Infl rather than IP for inflectional phrase to avoid confusion possible by reading IP as "input processing."

system to move in particular directions (restructuring) depending on the nature of the connection made.

WHY DO WE BELIEVE THAT ACQUISITION IS INPUT DEPENDENT?

My argument in this section is that at some level input is the primary initial ingredient for the development of competence, however one construes that competence. This may seem a trivial or silly point to argue given that the role of input is almost universally accepted in SLA. But given the recent emphasis on the role of output in acquisition, my belief is that we should not take for granted that the centrality of input is clear to everyone.

To begin this section, let's examine the assumed role of input in two radically different theories: UG and connectionism. Within a UG framework, an innate knowledge system whose job is to constrain the shape of possible human grammars is said to "guide" language acquisition (Schwartz, 1998; White, 2003). The questions that drive the UG approach to acquisition is "What do learner grammars allow and disallow?" and "How can learners come to know what they know about language with the data they are exposed to?" Within the principles and parameters framework, UG-based researchers can examine to what extent L2 learners adhere to UG-based constraints and to what extent they are capable of (re)setting parameters. (See Gregg, 2001, for some critical commentary on this, as well as Carroll, 2001; Lardiere, 2000.)

In a connectionist framework, there is no innate knowledge structure or special component of the mind that guides language acquisition. If there is a language-specific system, it emerges over time; it is not there from the outset (Ellis, 1998; Elman, et al., 1996). Within this framework, learners construct a neural network of information nodes with links between them. These links are either strengthened or weakened via activation and nonactivation. For example, once a link is established between a particular form and its meaning, that link is increasingly strengthened each time the connection between form and meaning are made. Thus, frequency in the input has an impact on the strength of connections and the mind/brain is predisposed to look for regularities in the input and to create links between associations (Ellis, 2002b, Chap. 3 in this vol.).

Admittedly, the previous descriptions of a UG-based account of acquisition and a connectionist account are limited and incomplete. Nonetheless, they can be used to illustrate that even two theories as divergent as UG and connectionism rely on or imply a fundamental role for input in the creation of a linguistic system. For UG, some of the data needed for grammar construction are to be found in the processed input (the rest, of course, in the principles of UG itself). For connectionism, data for the creation of nodes and associations between them are to be found in the input. Both theories posit a role for input, but they posit completely different mind–brain mechanisms that make use of that input.[5]

Even perspectives on acquisition that do not adhere to a particular theory place input in a central role in acquisition. Schmidt (1995) asked the question, "Can language be learned without some kind of conscious awareness of what one is learning?" Although this question can be researched in a variety of ways, it is important to note that Schmidt refers to awareness during input processing. And his list of "tips" for language learners includes statements such as "Pay attention to input" and "Pay particular attention to whatever aspects of the input that you are concerned to learn" (Schmidt, 1995, p. 45). Although he did not take a stance on theoretical models such as UG or connectionism, Schmidt was clear in his position on the role of input in the development of a linguistic system by L2 learners.

Why is it that current perspectives on SLA posit such a fundamental role for input? As I see it, this largely occurs for the following reason: Even though all theories may not have well-articulated mechanisms that act on input data (in Gregg's terms, what is often missing is a transition theory; see Gregg, 1989, 2001), there is always the matter that learners come to know more than they could possibly know and do things with language that cannot be traced to output practice or, say, explicit learning. The only way for this knowledge to develop is for the internal mechanisms to act on input data (or rather, processed input data; see VanPatten, 1996). Within a UG framework, this point has been made a number of times with different examples. (See Lardiere, 2000; Schwartz, 1993, 1998; Towell & Hawkins, 1994; White, 1989, 2003.) According to this perspective, the principles of UG are responsible for the shape of the interlanguage grammar. If learners acquire the constraints on *Wh-* movement when their first language does not have such movement (e.g., Chinese L1 to English L2) as in, for example, **Which mayor did Mary read the book that praised?* (Martohardjono, 1993), these constraints are a result of UG not allowing certain kinds of *Wh-* extraction. But what is important to note is that UG cannot do what it does without input. Unless there is input to provide raw data for acquisition, there is nothing for UG to act on, there is no grammar to constrain, there are no parameters to reset. It is worth repeating that the learner need not reach native-like competence in order to show the interactions of UG with input data, a point Schwartz (1998) clearly and elegantly made and is echoed in the work of Lardiere (2000), among others.

Within a connectionist framework, evidence for learners "going beyond the input data" is found in the so-called U-shape behavior by which learners initially do something correctly, then seem to do it incorrectly, and then do it correctly later on. Examples in the literature include Lightbown's (1983) study

[5] It is sometimes said that within UG the role of input is downplayed. That if learners come to know more than what they are exposed to, it is because of the principles contained in UG, not because of something in the input. However, my discussion in this section is meant to suggest that in the totality of acquisition within a UG framework, input is necessary. According to White (2003), "Acquisition proceeds on the basis of input interacting with principles and parameters of UG…" (p. 131).

of the learning of *–ing* (e.g, He is taking a cake → He take a cake → He is taking a cake) and learners' acquisition of the simple past tense forms (see, e.g., Elman et al., 1996). Here learners move from first using accurately a number of irregular past tense forms (e.g., *came, went*). This is followed by the emergence of regular past tense forms, which in turn is followed by the regularization of irregulars (e.g., *wented, camed*). Later, the irregular forms reemerge and forms such as *wented* are purged from the grammar. The argument made by connectionists is that as regular forms are incorporated into the network of nodes where "language is stored," the sheer frequency of regulars in the input overwhelms the system and causes changes in the strengths of links among past tense forms (see, e.g., Ellis, 2002a, p. 166, for some discussion of token and frequency data affecting acquisition). This restructuring of the past tense system can only happen based on the frequency that learning mechanisms compute on the input data they receive.[6] So, in this scenario, even though we are dealing with a morphological issue rather than a syntactic issue, learners still do something with the language that represents more than what they were exposed to. (See also Kellerman, 1985, for discussion of U-shaped L2 behavior.)

When discussing the role of input, an often-overlooked aspect of SLA is vocabulary acquisition. It is a given among researchers of vocabulary acquisition that the bulk L2 words known by a learner come from interaction with input,[7] especially reading (see, e.g., the collection in Coady & Huckin, 1997, and the discussion in Hulstijn, 2001, pp. 266–275). However, the bulk of research on incidental vocabulary acquisition tends to focus on acquisition of word meaning and automaticity of use. I would like to examine here, instead, the interface between syntax, semantics, and words—the domain in which the input-dependent nature of acquisition is clearly evident. As an example, verbs contain syntactic information in that their use in a sentence implies syntactic projections (i.e., there is a semantic-syntactic interface). There also may be slight differences in meaning depending on context or the syntactic environment of a word. For example, the verb *poner* in Spanish is generally translated as 'to put' and as a bare verb requires a complement (e.g., *Puso la torta en el horno* 'He put the pie in the oven'/**Puso en el horno.* 'He put in the oven'). However, when used with the pronoun *se*, the verb can either be transitive and reflexive (*Se puso un sombrero* 'He put a hat on [himself]') or it can be intransitive and require different English translations depending on what follows (*Se puso rojo* 'He turned red', *Se puso a correr* 'He began to run'). In the latter case, there are slight nuances in meaning between *Empezó a correr* ('He began to run') and *Se puso a correr* where the latter implies some kind of flight or deliberateness and the former does not. Learners tend not to make errors such as *Se puso a tener celos* ('He began to be jealous'), which although grammatical is semantically

[6] I am not arguing here that a connectionist account of U-shaped phenomena is correct. For arguments against it, see Pinker (1994).

[7] These arguments are based on what is considered to be a minimal amount of words necessary for a learner to function with oral and written language on nonspecialist topics. See Hulstijn (2001) for discussion of this "threshold," which he claims to be about 10,000 words.

anomalous and instead learners correctly produce *Empezó a tener celos*. Such subtle distinctions are not taught and are learned through the interaction of input with internal learning mechanisms and/or UG. (See Juffs, 2000, for a discussion of such matters, as well as the research on L2 learner acquisition of dative alternation, e.g., Mazurkewich & White, 1984, and acquisition of unaccusative constructions, Sorace, 1999, as discussed in White, 2003.)

Perhaps the best argument for the fundamental role of input in the creation of an implicit linguistic system is made by Larsen-Freeman and Long (1991) in their discussion of comprehensible input (Krashen, 1982 and elsewhere): There are no cases of successful learners who have not been exposed to lots of input; at the same time, a common factor among unsuccessful learners is restricted or inaccessible (my term) input. Most advanced learners of a language have not been restricted to classroom practice, Berlitz tapes/cds, or exercise books. Instead, they read in the L2, watch movies and TV, have friends in their own country who speak the L2 as an L1, have lived abroad, married into the culture, or have sought interactions with the language in other ways. (It is true they would be engaged in making output as well, a point addressed in the next section.)

Summary

The point of the preceding section was to demonstrate in no uncertain terms that SLA is input dependent. I have discussed matters related to form–meaning connections, extended the discussion to syntax as it relates to form–meaning connections, and also touched on vocabulary acquisition. Much of the previous argumentation is not new, but exists in one form or another in the literature and some readers may have shrugged their shoulders at various points saying, "So? We all know this." My answer would be "Yes, many, maybe even most, researchers know all this. But some must not. Hence their claim that there is an 'input vs. output' debate." That an increase in attention has been given to the role of output in SLA should not be construed as somehow undermining the fundamental role that input plays. I would now like to examine the role of output.

CAN WE SPEAK OF SLA AS BEING OUTPUT DEPENDENT?

In contemporary SLA research, the role of output in the construction of an L2 grammar is perhaps best attributed to Swain's (1985) seminal paper. In reviewing the ability of L2 learners whose context of learning is a French immersion program in Canada, Swain observed that their production is distinctly non-native like. On oral and written production tests involving various grammatical structures, discourse features, and some sociolinguistic aspects of language use, immersion students scored significantly lower than native speakers even after 7 years of immersion. After reviewing various possibilities, including Long's (1983) and Varonis and Gass' (1985) positions on the role of negotiated interactions (which she said are inadequate to account for what she and her colleagues had been observing in the immersion data), Swain concluded that what is missing is output. She explained, "[Smith] has argued that one learns to read by reading, and to write by writing. Similarly, it can be argued that one learns to speak by speaking" (p. 248).

I would like to examine this statement in the context of SLA research in general. The reader will recall that I defined SLA as the development of some underlying competence on which eventual (if not developmental) skills in language use depend. Swain's claim could be taken one of two ways. The first is that output somehow impacts the underlying competence. That is, by making output, the learner makes changes in the underlying grammar. The second is that output is necessary for accuracy and fluency, which are aspects of L2 use that lay outside of the internalized grammar.

That output leads to changes in the underlying competence or grammar is what Swain (1985) had in mind when she indicated that "producing the target language may be the trigger that forces the learner to pay attention to the means of expression needed in order to successfully convey his or her own intended meaning" (p. 249). Swain characterized this process as a move from purely semantic to more syntactic analysis of language. I take this to mean that output pushes learners to be better processors of input, albeit it in a more purposeful way. (See, e.g., the follow up discussion in Swain, 1998, on the possible role of output in promoting noticing.) Gass (1997) took the same position:

> If what is crucial about interaction is the fact that input becomes salient in some way (i.e., enhanced), then it matters little how salience comes about—whether through a teachers' self-modification, one's own request for clarification, or observation of another's request for clarification. The crucial point is that input becomes available for attentional resources and attention is focused on a particular form or meaning. When learners are in an interactive mode, they can focus on what is necessary for them. (p. 129; see also Chap. 4 in this vol.)

What Gass argued, it seems, is that interaction alters the task demands placed on a learner during input processing. The change in task demands frees up attentional resources allowing learners to process something they might miss otherwise. It must be made clear that this position does not suggest that by producing the form in question during the interaction the learner is acquiring that form; the position is that by interacting the learner gets crucial data from another interlocutor. The following example is illustrative and was overheard in a locker room after a tennis match. "Bob" is a native speaker of English and "Tom" is a non-native speaker with Chinese as a first language:

BOB: So where's Dave?

TOM: He vacation.
BOB: He's on vacation?
TOM: Yeah. On vacation.
BOB: Lucky guy.

In this particular interaction, Bob's clarification/confirmation request allowed Tom to notice the use of *on* with *vacation*. That Tom incorporated it subsequently into a confirmation does not mean that he has acquired it; it does show that he has focused his attention on it, something that Gass claimed may be part of the process of acquisition (Chap. 4 in this vol.). (See also Schmidt 1990, 1995.).

What I think is worth pointing out is that examples of interaction leading to some impact on the morphosyntactic system of a learner's internalized grammar are few and far between (e.g., Mackey, 1999; Williams, 1999; also, see the discussion on this topic in Mitchell & Meyers, 1998). Gass (1997) was clear on this point when she said, "Few [studies], however, have established a link between actual negotiation and subsequent learning, operationally defined as change in linguistic knowledge" (p. 126).[8] Those that do tend to show learners becoming aware of very clear and somewhat simple form–meaning connections as in the case with Tom and Bob, above. There is no evidence from interactional studies that I am aware of that demonstrates any impact from interaction on subtle and/or abstract properties of the grammar, such as the tense-aspect system, constraints on movement and binding, and similar properties. My hypothesis is that such studies cannot and will never show such an effect because of the nature of the processes engaged during interaction. As in the Tom and Bob scenario, studies on interaction suggest that learners are quite focused on performing the task and tend to be "alert" to meaning-making during interaction, especially when it comes to vocabulary, as Markee (2000) demonstrated in the well-known "Coral Episode" in which a learner becomes fixated on the meaning of coral and struggles with the word throughout the classroom interaction. Because learners are engaging explicit processes (probably overt hypothesis testing), they can only focus on those aspects of language that allow such overt and explicit processing, namely, vocabulary and easy transparent form–meaning connections (such as most prepositions, third-person *–s*, and others). This does not mean that the acquisition of these features requires explicit processes or that some aspects of acquisition require explicit processes and others implicit. I am merely suggesting that vocabulary and easy transparent form–meaning connections are

[8] In Mackey (1999) interaction was seen to have an effect, but this was constrained by learnability issues as framed by Pienemann (1998). In short, interaction or output can only have an effect if learners are about to acquire a structure anyway in the normal sequence of development. Within the Pienemann approach, learners acquire output procedures; he purposefully avoided the issue of how underlying competence comes about. Thus, his framework would not make any claims about output causing a change in underlying competence.

the only kind that could engage explicit processes and this is why they tend to be the forms "affected" in the research on interaction.

Following more closely Swain's notion of "pushed output," experimental studies that seek to manipulate output as a variable (as opposed to those that look at interactions in or out of the classroom) might suggest that learners can pay attention to all sorts of things. An exemplary study along these lines is Izumi (2002). In this study, learners of English were exposed to input only or input+output cycles in learning relative clause constructions. Some groups received cycles of unenhanced input with no tasks requiring production. Others received cycles of enhanced input, in which the relative clause marking was highlighted (all input was written in this study as was all output). Other groups received either of these two treatments, plus intervening cycles of tasks that required the production of relative clauses. They were subsequently tested on interpretation tasks, grammaticality judgment tasks, sentence combination tasks, and sentence completion tasks. The results are somewhat difficult to interpret because all gains and test scores are reported as combined scores from all four tests. Nonetheless, the following is clear: The input+output groups made greater gains compared with the input-only groups. Despite this support for a role for output, the following is also clear from the results: All groups made gains and the tests on which the lowest gains could be observed were the grammaticality judgment task and the sentence completion task. Izumi reported that a multivariate analysis of variance (MANOVA) revealed a significant effect for output only on the sentence combination and the interpretation tests.

What are we to make of such a study? The only reasonable conclusion is that output promotes acquisition but does not appear to be necessary. In fact, Izumi (2002) concludes: "on exposure to relevant input immediately after their production experience, the heightened sense of problematicity would lead [learners] to pay closer attention to what was indentified to be a problematic area in their IL. In short, pushed output can induce the learners to process the input effectively for their greater IL development" (p. 566). Recall that all groups made gains, but that the input+output groups made more gains. With time and additional exposure, the input-only groups may have caught up with the others. This is a testable hypothesis and if supported would mean that input alone may be sufficient for this particular form–meaning connection and that pushed output's role is similar to any focus-on-form technique: to speed up acquisition.

Returning to Swain's original reason for positing the "output hypothesis," it may do well to examine the argument in which it (and related ones, such as focus on form) are made. That argument is the "insufficiency of input alone" for the development of learner's grammars. In various ways, the argument is that learners who receive input alone don't do so well, meaning they may fall far short of native-like abilities (See, e.g., the introductory discussion of the motivation for a focus on form in Doughty & Williams, 1998). Thus, something other than input must be necessary for acquisition. In the current discussion, that something is output. But it would do well to keep in mind that non-nativeness is the norm for second language acquisition. If this is the norm, and it is the norm under a variety of conditions (e.g., instructed/non-instructed, rich input/poor input), then perhaps a different conclusion is warranted, namely, nothing else is necessary because non-nativeness is always the result anyway. Hence, the sketchy empirical or observational evidence for any strong role for output in the development of the learner's competence (see also the questions raised by Sato, 1986). Now, by saying that nothing else is necessary does not mean that it is true. I am simply pointing out an alternative conclusion that is generally overlooked in SLA research.[9]

Summary

What I have argued in this section on the role of output is that despite the claim that pushed output may lead to changes in the grammar, we have little if any experimental or observational/case data that clearly show that acquisition (defined as development of an internal grammar) is somehow output dependent. Research tends to show some effect for vocabulary acquisition (or use) and some effect for simple and transparent form–meaning connections (exactly the kind that Krashen claimed years ago were the ones that could be affected by conscious processes of learning). In Izumi's well-designed study, the case for a facilitative role for pushed output in the classroom is clear. But the role of output in how and when learners make initial form–meaning connections in general and its role in strengthening these connections is far from evident. We cannot make the claim that somehow acquisition—in the specific case of making form–meaning connections—is output dependent. This conclusion is the same that Larsen-Freeman and Long (1991) arrived at in their discussion of the role of conversation in developing syntax: "cases of language learning without any production at all (e.g., Fourcin, 1975) show that conversation, although probably facilitative in some cases, is not necessary for success" (p. 132).

CONCLUSION

In this chapter, I have argued two main points. First, the input-dependent nature of the acquisition of an underlying grammar—and in terms of the present volume, initially making and subsequently strengthening form–meaning connections—is essentially correct. From the lexicon to the syntax, acquisition will not be successful without access to input. Second, we cannot claim along the same lines that acquisition of an underlying grammar is somehow output dependent. The current evidence does not warrant such a position.

Placing these arguments in the context of my own research, I have argued elsewhere that within a focus on form (or, more correctly, an overt

[9] Doughty and Williams (1998) did not overlook this possibility. They pointed out, "A somewhat weaker claim [about the role for focus on form] is that even if such a focus may not be absolutely necessary, it may be part of a more efficient language learning experience in that it can speed up natural acquisition processes" (p. 2). Again, we are confronted with the idea that something other than input may facilitate acquisition but ultimately not be necessary.

intervention in instructed SLA), structured input alone is sufficient to cause change in learner competence (VanPatten, 2002; VanPatten & Oikennon, 1996). This conclusion is supported by recent research that examines the effect of providing learners with structured input alone (e.g., Benati, 2004; Farley, 2004; Sanz & Morgan-Short, 2004; Wong, 2004)[10]. Although this evidence does not rule out the possibility that factors other than input could play significant roles in acquisition, they do suggest that some kind of input alone can be sufficient.

This chapter should not be construed as concluding that output plays no role at all in language use. In the case of skill building (i.e., developing fluency and accuracy), output is most likely necessary. Unfortunately, skill development is seriously understudied in SLA (see DeKeyser, 1997, and Schmidt, 1992) and any comments about it here would be speculative. Pienemann's work on Processability Theory in which output processing procedures are seen to be a separate acquisition process from the development of any kind of competence would be a good point of departure in this domain (Pienemann, 1998). The hypothesis would be that learners may be able to develop an underlying competence without output but only output would push them to develop the procedures described by Pienemann—and only output would push learners toward increasing degrees of fluency. The point to be underscored here is that we are currently unable to support any specific role for output in the creation of an underlying competence that contains form–meaning connections. At best, we can say that input is necessary for acquisition, but input+output may be better—we just do not know how or under what circumstances.

REFERENCES

Archibald, J. (Ed.). (2000). *Second language acquisition and linguistic theory*. Oxford, England: Blackwell.

Aronoff, M., & Anshen, F. (1998). Morphology and the lexicon: Lexicalization and productivity. In A. Spencer & A. M. Zwicky (Eds.), *The handbook of morphology* (pp. 235–247). Oxford, England: Blackwell.

Benati, A. (2004). The effects of structured input activities and explicit information on the acquisition of the Italian future tense. In B. VanPatten (Ed.), *Processing instruction: Theory, research, and commentary* (pp. 207–225). Mahwah NJ: Lawrence Erlbaum & Associates.

Bybee, J. (1991). Natural morphology: The organization of paradigms and language acquisition. In. T. Huebner & C. Ferfuson (Eds.), *Crosscurrents in second language acquisition and linguistic theories* (pp. 67–91). Philadelphia: Benjamins.

Carroll, S. (2001). *Input and evidence: The raw material of second language acquisition*. Philadelphia: Benjamins

[10] This research should be contrasted with research on text enhancement (e.g., White, 1998; Wong, 2003) in which targeted items are merely highlighted in the input. The results of this line of research are rather disappointing and are used by some to argue that input alone is not sufficient. A different conclusion is that input alone is sufficient, but some learners benefit by qualitatively different types of input.

Clifton, C., Frazier, L., & Rayner, K. (1994). Introduction. In C. Clifton, L. Frazier, & K. Rayner (Eds.), *Perspectives on sentence processing* (pp. 1–12). Hillsdale, NJ: Lawrence Erlbaum & Associates.

Coady, J., & Huckin, T. (Eds.). (1997). *Second language vocabulary acquisition*. Cambridge, England: Cambridge University Press.

Cuetos, F., Mitchell, D. C., & Corley, M. M. B. (1996). Parsing in different languages. In M. Carreiras, J. E. García-Albea, & N. Sebastián-Gallés (Eds.), *Language processing in Spanish* (pp. 145–187). Mahwah, NJ: Lawrence Erlbaum & Associates.

DeKeyser, R. (1997). Beyond explicit rule learning: Automatizing second language syntax. *Studies in Second Language Acquisition, 19*, 195–221.

Doughty, C., & Williams, J. (1998). Issues and terminology. In C. Doughty & J. Williams (Eds.), *Focus on form in classroom second language acquisition* (pp. 1–11). Cambridge, England: Cambridge University Press.

Ellis, N. C. (1998). Emergentism, connectionism, and language learning. *Language Learning, 48*, 631–664.

Ellis, N. C. (2002a). Frequency effects in language processing: A review with implications for theories of implicit and explicit language acquisition. *Studies in Second Language Acquisition, 24*, 143–188.

Ellis, N. C. (2002b). Reflections on frequency effects in second language acquisition. *Studies in Second Language Acquisition, 24*, 297–339.

Elman, J., Bates, E., Johnson, M. H., Karmiloff-Smith, A., Parisi, D., & Plunkett, K. (1996). *Rethinking innateness: a connectionist perspective on development*. Cambridge, MA: MIT Press.

Farley, A. P. (2004). Processing instruction and the Spanish subjunctive: Is explicit information needed? In B. VanPatten (Ed.), *Processing instruction: theory, research, and commentary* (pp. 227–239) . Mahwah, NJ: Lawrence Erlbaum & Associates.

Fernández, E. (1999). Processing strategies in second language acquisition: Some preliminary results. In E. Klein & G. Martohardjono (Eds.), *The development of second language grammars: A generative approach* (pp. 217–239). Philadelphia: Benjamins.

Fodor, J. D. (1999). Learnability theory: Triggers for parsing with. In E. Klein & G. Martohardjono (Eds.), *The development of second language grammars: a generative approach* (pp. 363–406). Philadelphia: Benjamins.

Fourcin, A. (1975). Language development in the absence of expressive speech. In E. Lenneberg & E. Lenneber (Eds.), *Foundations of language development* (pp. 263–268). New York: Academic Press.

Gass, S. M. (1997). *Input, interaction, and the second language learner*. Mahwah, NJ: Lawrence Erlbaum & Associates.

Gass, S. M. & Selinker, L. (2001). *Second language acquisition: An introductory course*. Mahwah, NJ: Lawrence Erlbaum & Associates.

Gathercole, S. E., & Baddeley, A. D. (1993). *Working memory and language*. Hillsdale, NJ: Lawrence Erlbaum & Associates.

Gregg, K. D. (1989). Second language acquisition theory: The case for a generative perspective. In S. M. Gass & J. Schachter (Eds.), *Linguistic perspectives on second language acquisition* (pp. 15–40). Cambridge, England: Cambridge University Press.

Gregg, K. D. (2001). Learnability and second language acquisition theory. In P. Robinson (Ed.), *Cognition and second language instruction* (pp. 152–180). Cambridge, England: Cambridge University Press.

Harrington, M. K. (2001). Sentence processing. In P. Robinson (Ed.), *Cognition and second language instruction* (pp. 91–124). Cambridge, England: Cambridge University Press.

Hawkins, R. (2001). *Second language syntax*. Oxford, England: Blackwell.

Hulstijn, J. (2001). Intentional and incidental second language vocabulary learning: A reappraisal of elaboration, rehearsal and automaticy. In P. Robinson (Ed.), *Cognition and second language instruction* (pp. 258–286). Cambridge, England: Cambridge University Press.

Izumi, S. (2002). Output, input enhancement, and the noticing hypothesis: an experimental study on ESL relativization. *Studies in Second Language Acquisition, 24*, 541–577.

Jensen, J. T., & Strong-Jensen, M. (1984). Morphology in the lexicon! *Linguistic Inquiry, 15*, 474–498.

Juffs, A. (2000). An overview of the second language acquisition of links between verb semantics and morpho-syntax. In J. Archibald (Ed.) *Second language acquisition and linguistic theory* (pp. 187–227). Oxford, England: Blackwell.

Just, M. A., & Carpenter, P. A. (1992). A capacity theory of comprehension: Individual differences in working memory. *Psychological Review, 99*, 122–149.

Kellerman, E. (1985). In S. M. Gass & C. Madden (Eds.), *Input in second language acquisition* (pp. 345–353). Rowley, MA: Newbury House.

Krashen, S. D. (1982). *Principles and practice in second language acquisition*. Oxford, England: Pergamon.

Lardiere, D. (2000). Mapping features to forms in second language acquisition. In J. Archibald (Ed.), *Second language acquisition and linguistic theory* (pp. 102–129). Oxford: Blackwell.

Larsen-Freeman, D., & Long, M. H. (1991). *Introduction to second language acquisition research*. London: Longman.

Levelt, W. J. M. (1989). *Speaking: from intention to articulation*. Cambridge, MA: MIT Press.

Lightbown, P. M. (1983). Exploring relationships between developmental and instructional sequences in L2 acquisition. In H. Seliger & M. Long (Eds.), *Classroom-oriented research in second language acquisition* (pp. 217–243). Rowley, MA: Newbury House.

Lightbown, P. M., & Spada, N. (1999). *How languages are learned* (rev. ed.). Oxford, England: Oxford University Press.

Lightfoot, D. (1991). *How to set parameters. Arguments from language change*. Cambridge, MA: MIT Press.

Long, M. H. (1983). Linguistic and conversational adjustments to nonnative speakers. *Studies in Second Language Acquisition, 5*, 177–193.

Mackey, A. (1999). Input, interaction and second language development: An empirical study of question formation in ESL. *Studies in Second Language Acquisition, 19*, 557–597.

MacWhinney, B. (1997). SLA and the Competition Model. In A. M. B. de Groot & J. F. Kroll (Eds.), *Tutorials in bilingualism* (pp. 113–142). Mahwah, NJ: Lawrence Erlbaum & Associates.

Markee, N. (2000). *Conversation analysis*. Mahwah, NJ: Lawrence Erlbaum & Associates.

Martohardjono, G. (1993). *Wh- movement in the acquisition of a second language*. Unpublished doctoral dissertation, Cornell University.

Mazurkewich, I. & White, L. (1984). The acquisition of the dative alternation: unlearning overgeneralizations. *Cognition, 16*, 261–283.

McLaughlin, B. (1990). Restructuring. *Applied Linguistics, 11*, 113–128.

Mitchell, R. & Meyers, F. (1998). *Second language learning theories*. London: Arnold.
Pienemann, M. (1998). *Language processing and second language development: Processability theory*. Philadelphia: Benjamins.
Pinker, S. D. (1994). *The language instinct*. New York: HarperCollins.
Pritchett, B. L. (1992). *Grammatical competence and parsing performance*. Chicago: University of Chicago Press.
Radford, A. (1997). *Syntax: a minimalist introduction*. Cambridge, England: Cambridge University Press.
Rumelhart (1980). Schemata: The building blocks of cognition. In R. Spiro, B. Bruce & W. Brewer (Eds.), *Theoretical issues in reading comprehension* (pp. 33–35). Hillsdale, NJ: Lawrence Erlbaum & Associates.
Sanz, C., & Morgan-Short, K. (2003). Positive evidence vs. explicit rule presentation and explicit negative feedback: A computer-assisted study. *Language Learning, 53*.
Sato, C. (1986). Conversation and interlanguage development: Rethinking the connection. In R. R. Day (Ed.), *Talking to learn: Conversation in second language acquisition* (pp. 23–45). Rowley, MA: Newbury House.
Schmidt, R. W. (1990) The role of consciousness in second language learning. *Applied Linguistics, 11*, 129–158.
Schmidt, R. W. (1992). Psychological mechanisms underlying second language fluency. *Studies in Second Language Acquisition, 14*, 357–385.
Schmidt, R. W. (1995). Consciousness and foreign language learning: A tutorial on the role of attention and awareness in learning. In R. W. Schmidt (Ed.), *Attention and awareness in foreign language learning* (pp. 1–63). Honolulu: University of Hawaii Press.
Schwartz, B. D. (1993). On explicit and negative data effecting and affecting competence and linguistic behavior. *Studies in Second Language Acquisition, 15*, 147–163.
Schwartz, B. D. (1998). The second language instinct. *Lingua, 106*, 133–160.
Schwartz, B. D. & Sprouse, R. (2000). When syntactic theories evolve. In J. Archibald (Ed.), *Second language acquisition and linguistic theory* (pp. 156–186). Oxford, England: Blackwell.
Sorace, A. (1999). Initial states, end states and residual optionality in L2 acquisition. In A. Greenbill, H. Littlefield, & C. Tano (Eds.), *Proceedings of the 23rd annual Boston University conference on language development* (pp. 666–674). Somerville, MA: Cascadilla Press.
Swain, M. (1985). Communicative competence: some roles of comprehensible input and comprehensible output in its development. In S. M. Gass & C. Madden (Eds.), *Input in second language acquisition* (pp. 235–253). Rowley, MA: Newbury House.
Swain, M. (1998). Focus on form through conscious reflection. In C. Doughty & J. Williams (Eds.), *Focus on form in classroom second language acquisition* (pp. 64–81). Cambridge, England: Cambridge University Press.
Towell, R. & Hawkins, D. (1994). *Approaches to second language acquisition*. Clevedon, England: Multilingual Matters.
VanPatten, B. (1996). *Input processing and grammar instruction: Theory and research*. Norwood, NJ: Ablex.
VanPatten, B. (2000). Processing instruction as form–meaning connections: Issues in theory and research. In J. F. Lee & A. Valdman (Eds.), *Form and meaning: multiple perspectives* (pp. 43-68). Boston: Heinle & Heinle.
VanPatten, B. (2002). Processing instruction: an update. *Language Learning, 52*, 755–803.
VanPatten, B. (2003). *From input to output: A teacher's guide to second language acquisition*. New York: McGraw-Hill.

VanPatten, B. (2004). Input processing in SLA. In B. VanPatten (Ed.), *Processing instruction: theory, research, and commentary* (pp. 5–31) Mahwah, NJ: Lawrence Erlbaum & Associates.

VanPatten, B. & Oikkenon, S. (1996). Explanation versus structured input in processing instruction. *Studies in Second Language Acquisition, 18*, 495–510.

Varonis, E. M. & Gass, S. M. (1985). Nonnative/nonnative conversations: A model for negotiation of meaning. *Applied Linguistics, 6*, 71–90.

White, J. (1998). Getting the learner's attention: a typographical input enhancement study. In C. Doughty & J. Williams (Eds.), *Focus on form in classroom second language acquisition* (pp. 85–113). Cambridge, England: Cambridge University Press

White, L. (1989). *Universal grammar and second language acquisition*. Phihladelphia: Benjamins.

White, L. (2003). *Second language acquisition and universal grammar*. Cambridge, England: Cambridge University Press.

Williams, J. (1999). Learner-generated attention to form. *Language Learning, 49*, 583–625.

Wong, W. (2003). Textual enhancement and simplified input: Effects on L2 comprehension and acquisition of non-meaningful grammatical form. *Applied Language Learning, 13*, 109–132.

Wong, W. (2004). Processing instruction in French: the roles of explicit information and structured input. In B. VanPatten (Ed.), *Processing instruction: Theory, research, and commentary* (pp. 187–205). Mahwah, NJ: Lawrence Erlbaum & Associates.

CHAPTER 3
The Processes of Second Language Acquisition

Nick C. Ellis
University of Wales, Bangor

What are the mental representations that underpin second language acquisition (SLA)? What is the nature of the mapping processes involved in learning them? To what extent are these representations learned unconsciously, a result of implicit learning while engaging in communication in a second language? And to what extent are explicit learning or explicit instruction necessary in order to attain native-like competence, fluency, and idiomaticity?[1]

The first section outlines a usage-based account holding that SLA is the learning of constructions that relate form and meaning. The second section concerns how these form–meaning relations are probabilistic. Some constructions and interpretations are much more frequent than others. Fluent speakers of a language implicitly know this and their processing systems are tuned to expect them accordingly. Every element of surface language form is multiply ambiguous in its interpretation, just as every meaning can be expressed in a variety of ways. Fluent language learners are tuned to these mapping strengths: They know implicitly the most likely interpretation of a linguistic cue as well as the relative likelihoods of the range of alternatives and how these change in differing contexts. Their language processing is sensitive to input frequency at all levels of grain: phonology and phonotactics, reading, spelling, lexis, morphosyntax, formulaic language, language comprehension, grammaticality, sentence production, and syntax. Thus, SLA must involve acquisition of the strengths of these associations. The third section shows how this involves implicit learning from experience of input. But there are many aspects of SLA where the learner seems impervious to certain aspects of the language, where input fails to become intake. The fourth section considers various ways in which SLA commonly fails to reflect the input: failing to notice cues because they are not salient, failing to notice that a feature needs to be processed in a different way from that relevant to L1, failing to acquire a mapping because it involves complex associations that cannot be acquired implicitly, or failing to build a construction as a result of not being developmentally ready in terms of having the appropriate representational building blocks. Such failings reflect limits of implicit learning, working memory, or representational precursors. In these cases, it is necessary for learners first to notice certain input cues. The fifth section returns to the question of the nature of the interface: Is there no-, weak-, or strong-interface between explicit and implicit knowledge of language? It considers the role of noticing and attention in the initial acquisition of constructions, along with other ways in

[1] These themes were developed in the 2002 special issue of Studies in Second Language Acquisition, 24(2), "Frequency Effects in Language Processing: A Review with Commentaries."

which explicit learning is involved in SLA. The final section reviews research concerning the cognitive neuroscience of complementary memory systems and of noticing, and demonstrates that although these are separate representational systems, nevertheless, explicit knowledge can affect implicit learning in a variety of ways.

SLA IS THE LEARNING OF CONSTRUCTIONS RELATING FORM AND MEANING

The task of the language learner is to make sense of language. Understanding is built, or falls, depending on the adequacy of the learner's construction set for meanings. Language construction sets are as infinitely combinatorial and creative as are Lego and Meccano, and as limiting also. Without the right piece, the support buckles and the structure crashes. Without preparatory organization and practice, activity focuses on searching for the right block rather than the process of building itself. Less tangible than plastic or metal, the language learner's kit consists of constructions that map forms and meanings—the recurrent patterns of linguistic elements that serve some well-defined linguistic function. They may be complex structures, like Lego arches, trucks, or houses (e.g., at the sentence level, imperatives, ditransitives, and yes–no questions). Some frequent, smaller structures, like generic Lego arches, walls, and wheeled axles, are abstract patterns—the noun phrase, the prepositional phrase, and so forth. Others come preformed, like Lego windows, doors, and beams (where kit frequency inversely relates to beam size)—formulas like "how are you?", "I think I'll...", "a great deal of...", and "survival of the fittest." More common still, like the workaday blocks that appear in every set, ambiguous when still loose in the box, are the grammatical morphemes, the closed class words, the articles, versatile, essential, but often lacking structural salience—just another brick in the wall.

A construction is part of the linguistic system, accepted as a convention in the speech community, and entrenched as grammatical knowledge in the learner's mind. Constructions may be complex, as in [Det Noun], or simple, as in [Noun]; they may represent complex structure above the word level, as in [Adj Noun], or below the word level, as in [NounStem-PL]; and they may be schematic, as in [Det Noun], or specific, as in [the United Kingdom]. Hence, "morphology," "syntax," and "lexicon" are uniformly represented in construction grammar, unlike both traditional grammar and generative grammar, and chunks of language much larger than the analytic units of morphemes or words are the usual units of storage and processing. Constructions are symbolic: In addition to specifying the defining properties of morphological, syntactic, and lexical form, a construction also specifies the semantic, pragmatic, and discourse functions associated with it. Constructions form a structured inventory of a speaker's knowledge of language, in which schematic constructions can be abstracted over the less schematic ones that are inferred inductively by the learner in acquisition. A construction may provide a partial specification of the structure of an utterance, and, inversely, utterance structure is usually specified by a number of distinct constructions. Constructions are independently represented units in a speaker's mind. Any construction with unique, idiosyncratic formal or functional properties must be represented independently. However, absence of any unique property of a construction does not entail that it is not represented independently and simply derived from other, more general or schematic constructions. Frequency of occurrence may lead to independent representation of even so-called regular constructional patterns. In the context of this usage-based perspective (Bybee & Hopper, 2001; Croft, 2001; Fillmore & Kay 1993; Goldberg, 1995; Langacker, 1987; Tomasello, 1998), the acquisition of grammar is the piecemeal learning of many thousands of constructions and the frequency-biased abstraction of regularities within them.

Many constructions are based on particular lexical items, ranging from the simple *Wow!* to more complex formulae *Beauty is in the eye of the beholder*. But other constructions are more abstract. Goldberg (1995) focused on complex argument structure constructions, such as the ditransitive *Caroline faxed Bill the letter* and the caused motion *Bill pushed the book over the counter*, and showed that these abstract and complex constructions themselves carry meaning, independently of the particular words in the sentence. For example, even though *sneeze* is typically intransitive, *Pat sneezed the napkin off the table* is readily interpretable as a "caused motion" construction. These abstract argument structure constructions, extracted inductively from the evidence of particular exemplars that fit the schematic pattern, thus create an important top-down component to linguistic processing. They allow, for example, a reasonable analogical understanding of the novel sentence *Eloquence is in the ear of the hearkener*. Constructions show prototype effects. For example, ditransitive constructions can be comprehended based on the prototype Agent-successfully-causes-recipient-to-receive-patient, *Bill gave [handed, passed, threw, took] her a book,* and various more peripheral meanings such as future-transfer, *Bill bequeathed [allocated, granted, reserved] her a book*, and enabling-transfer, *Bill allowed* or *permitted her one book*.

If language is represented as a community of constructions, induced from exemplars and evidencing classic prototype effects, then the understanding of language acquisition can be informed by classic psychological research on category formation, schema learning, and classification. Construction-based theories of child language acquisition (Tomasello, 1998, 2000; Tomasello & Bates, 2001) emphasize the piecemeal learning of concrete exemplars and widespread lexical-specificity in L1 grammar development. A high proportion of children's early multiword speech is produced from a developing collection of slot-and-frame patterns based around chunks of one or two words or phrases (e.g., *I can't* + verb; *where's* + noun + *gone?*). Children are very productive with these patterns and both the number of patterns and their structure develop over time. They are, however, lexically specific: A child who consistently uses two patterns, *I can't* + *X* and *I don't* + *X*, will typically show little or no overlap in the verbs used in the X slots of these two constructions (Lieven, Pine, & Dresner Barnes, 1992; Pine & Lieven, 1993, 1997; Pine, Lieven, & Rowland, 1998; Tomasello, 1992, 2000). Such observations suggest that at this age (a) the patterns are not related through an underlying grammar (i.e., the child does not "know" that *can't* and *don't* are both auxiliaries or that the words that appear in the patterns all belong to a category of Verb); (b) there is no evidence for abstract grammatical patterns in the 2- to 3-year-old child's speech; and (c) in contrast, the children are picking up frequent patterns from what they hear around them and only slowly making more abstract generalizations as the database of related utterances grows. Although verbs predominate in seeding low-scope patterns and eventually more abstract generalizations, Pine et al. (1998) showed that such islands are not exclusive to verbs and that Tomasello's (1992) "Verb Island Hypothesis" should be extended to include limited patterns based on other lexical types such as bound morphemes, auxiliary verbs, and case-marking pronouns.

In sum, theories of the acquisition of first language grammatical constructions maintain that there is a developmental sequence from formula, through low-scope pattern, to construction. Second and foreign language acquisition is different from L1 acquisition in numerous respects. First, it differs in conceptual development: In child language acquisition, knowledge of the world and knowledge of language are developing simultaneously, whereas adult SLA builds upon preexisting conceptual knowledge. Moreover, adult learners have sophisticated formal operational means of thinking and can treat language as an object of explicit learning, that is, of conscious problem solving and deduction, to a much greater degree than can children (Ellis, 1994). Second, it differs in language input: The typical L1 pattern of acquisition results from naturalistic exposure in situations where caregivers naturally scaffold development (Tomasello & Brooks, 1999), whereas classroom environments for second or foreign language teaching can distort the patterns of exposure, function, medium, and social interaction (Ellis & Laporte, 1997). Third, it differs in transfer from L1: Adult SLA builds on preexisting L1 knowledge (Kellerman, 1995; MacWhinney, 1992; Odlin, 1989). Nevertheless, the L1 acquisition sequence—from formula, through low-scope pattern, to construction—seems also to apply in child and naturalistic SLA (Ellis, 1996; Hakuta, 1976; McLaughlin, 1995; Wong-Fillmore, 1976) and is a reasonable default in guiding the investigation of the ways in which exemplars and their type and token frequencies determine the second language acquisition of structure (Bardovi-Harlig, 2002; Bybee & Hopper, 2001; Ellis, 1996, 2002a, 2002b).

Knowledge of language is a huge collection of memories of previously experienced utterances. These exemplars are linked, with like kinds being related in such a way that they resonate as abstract linguistic categories, schema, and prototypes. The power, creativity, and systematicity of language emerges; it is another example of D'Arcy Thomson's observation On Growth and Form: "Everything is what it is because it got that way." Linguistic regularities emerge as central tendencies in the conspiracy of the database of memories for utterances. This is the linguistic construction kit. Traditional descriptive and pedagogical grammars relate well to these theories of acquisition both in their induction and in their descriptive grain, which focuses on constructions as recurrent patterns of linguistic elements that serve some well-defined linguistic function.

FORM–MEANING RELATIONS ARE PROBABILISTIC

Counting from 1 to 10 is early content in most second and foreign language courses and an ESL or EFL student is soon secure in the knowledge of what "wʌn" means. But should they be so sure? Consider the following wʌns: "That's wʌn for the money, two for the show, three to get ready"; "To love wʌnself is the beginning of a lifelong romance"; "wʌnnce upon a time..."; "Alice in wʌnderland"; "wʌn the battle, lost the war"; "How to win life's little games without appearing to try—wʌnUpmanship"; "the human brain is a wʌnnderful thing." These are different "ones". Form–meaning associations are multiple and probabilistic, and fluent language processing exploits prior knowledge of utterances and of the world in order to determine the most likely interpretation in any given context. This usually works very well and the practiced comprehender is conscious of just one interpretation—Alice in wʌn sense and not the other. But to achieve this resolution, the language processing mechanism is unconsciously weighing the likelihoods of all candidate interpretations and choosing among them. Thus, there is a lot more to the perception of language than meets the eye or ear. A percept is a complex state of consciousness in which antecedent sensation is supplemented by consequent ideas that are closely combined to it by association. The cerebral conditions of the perception of things are thus the paths of association irradiating from them. If a certain sensation is strongly associated with the attributes of a certain thing, then that thing is almost sure to be perceived as a consequence of that sensation. But where the sensation is associated with more than one reality, unconscious processes weigh the odds, and what is perceived is the most probable thing: "all brain-processes are such as give rise to what we may call FIGURED consciousness" (James, 1890, p. 82). Accurate and fluent language perception, then, rests on the comprehender having acquired the appropriately weighted range of associations for each element of the language input.

Language learning is the associative learning of representations that reflect the probabilities of occurrence of form–function mappings. Frequency is thus a key determinant of acquisition because 'rules' of language, at all levels of analysis from phonology, through syntax, to discourse, are structural regularities that emerge from learners' lifetime analysis of the distributional characteristics of the language input. Learners have to FIGURE language out. It is these ideas that underpin the last 30 years of investigations of cognition using connectionist and statistical models (Elman et al., 1996; McLeod, Plunkett, & Rolls, 1998; Rumelhart & McClelland, 1986), the competition model of language learning and processing (Bates & MacWhinney, 1987; MacWhinney, 1987, 1997), and proper empirical investigations of the structure of language by means of corpus analysis (Biber, Conrad, & Reppen, 1998; Biber, Johansson, Leech, Conrad, & Finegan, 1999; Sinclair, 1991).

Fluent language processing is intimately tuned to input frequency and probabilities of mappings at all levels of grain: phonology and phonotactics, reading, spelling, lexis, morphosyntax, formulaic language, language comprehension, grammaticality, sentence production, and syntax. It relies on this prior statistical knowledge. Consider an example or two from each domain just to get an idea of the size of the relevant database. What follows is a very small sample from the range of published psycholinguistic demonstrations of learners' implicit statistical knowledge of language.

Orthographics

One of the earliest proofs, a defining study of psycholinguistics, was the demonstration by Miller, Bruner and Postman (1954) that people are sensitive to varying degrees of approximation to their native language. When young adults were shown strings of 8 letters for just a tenth of a second, they could, on average, report 53% of strings made up of letters randomly sampled with equal probabilities (zero-order approximations to English such as "CVGJCDHM"). They could report 69% of strings where the letters were sampled according to their individual frequencies in written English (first-order approximations like "RPITCQET"), 78% of second order approximation strings which preserve common bigram sequences of English (e.g., "UMATSORE"), and 87% of fourth order approximating strings made up of common tetragrams in English (like "VERNALIT"). Clearly, the participants' span of apprehension of more regular orthographic sequences was greater than for less regular ones. The advantage of first-order over zero-order demonstrates that perceptual systems are sensitive to the fact that some letters occur in written language more often than others and pattern-recognition units for letters have their thresholds tuned accordingly. The advantage of second-order over first-order shows that perceptual systems are tuned to the expected frequency of bigrams. The advantage of fourth order over second order demonstrates that they are tuned to orthographic chunks four letters long. These chunking effects extend upward through the levels of the representational hierarchy, and rest assured that in 1954 the undergraduate participants in the Miller et al. study would have been able to report rather more than the first eight letters of the string "One, two, three o'clock, four o'clock, rock."

Phonotactics

People are very good at judging whether or not nonwords are native-like and young children are sensitive to these regularities when trying to repeat nonwords (Treiman & Danis, 1988). Phonotactic competence simply emerges from using language, from the primary linguistic data of the lexical patterns that a speaker knows (Bailey & Hahn, 2001). Frisch, Large, Zawaydeh, and Pisoni (2001) asked native speakers to judge nonword stimuli for whether they were more or less like English words. The nonwords were created with relatively high or low probability legal phonotactic patterns as determined by the logarithm of the product of probabilities of the onset and rime constituents of the nonword. The mean wordlikeness judgments for these nonword stimuli had an extremely strong relationship with expected probability ($r = .87$). An emergentist account of phonotactic competence is thus that any new nonword is compared to the exemplars that are in memory: The closer it matches their characteristics, the more wordlike it is judged. The gathering of such relevant distributional data starts in infancy. Saffran, Aslin, and Newport (1996) demonstrated that 8 month old infants exposed for only 2 minutes to unbroken strings of spoken nonsense syllables (e.g., 'bidakupado') are able to detect the difference between three-syllable sequences that appeared as a unit and sequences that also appeared in their learning set but in random order. These infants managed this learning on the basis of statistical analysis of phonotactic sequence data, right at the age when their caregivers start to notice systematic evidence of their recognizing words.

Lexical Recognition and Production

The recognition and production of words is a function of their frequency of occurrence in the language. For written language, high frequency words are named more rapidly than low frequency ones (Balota & Chumbly, 1984; Forster & Chambers, 1973), they are more rapidly judged to be words in lexical decision tasks (Forster, 1976), and they are spelled more accurately (Barry & Seymour, 1988). Auditory word recognition is better for high frequency than low frequency words (Luce, 1986; Savin, 1963). Kirsner (1994) showed that there are strong effects of word frequency on the speed and accuracy of lexical recognition processes (in speech perception, reading, object naming, and sign perception) and lexical production processes (speaking, typing, writing, and signing), in children and adults, in L1 and in L2.

Abstraction is an automatic consequence of aggregate activation of high frequency exemplars, with regression toward central tendencies as numbers of highly similar exemplars increase. Thus, there is a single voice advantage. Words repeated in the same voice are better recognized than those in a different voice. Moreover, this advantage is greater for low frequency words: "old" words that have been frequently experienced in various places by a variety of speakers inspire "abstract" echoes, obscuring context and voice elements of the study trace (Goldinger, 1998, p. 255).

Phonological Awareness

Children's awareness of the sounds of their language, particularly at the segmental levels of onset-rime and phoneme, is important in their acquisition of literacy (Ellis & Large, 1987; Goswami & Bryant, 1990). It is an awareness that develops gradually. De Cara and Goswami (2002) show that 4- to 7- year-old children are better able to identify the word with the odd sound in the Bradley and Bryant (1983) odd-one-out task when the spoken stimuli were from dense phonological neighborhoods where there are lots of words that share these rhymes (e.g., "bag, rag, jack"), rather than when the stimuli came from sparse ones (e.g., "pig, dig, lid"). The children were also better in short-term memory span tasks at remembering nonword triples from dense phonological neighborhoods like "cham, shen, deek" than triples like "deeve, chang, shem" derived from sparse ones. These phonological neighborhood density effects are driven by vocabulary age, not by chronological age. Metsala and Walley (1998) proposed a Lexical Restructuring Hypothesis of these effects whereby, as vocabulary increases, more and more similar words are acquired; this drives an increasingly well-specified representation of these words in terms of subunits like onset and rime, and is an effect that occurs first in dense phonological neighborhoods. It is the learner's knowledge of individual lexical items that drives the abstraction process.

Spoken Word Recognition

The speech signal unfolds over time and processes of word recognition begin with the very onset of speech. The initial phoneme of a word activates the set of all words in the lexicon which begin that way. Hearing 'w', a large cohort of English words are activated—*wad, ouija, way, wow, Wyoming*. Then, as the speech signal unfolds, and more information is received, "wʌ", the set is narrowed down, removing no-longer viable candidates like *waddled, waffle,* and *wage*. But the candidate set is still substantial, including *worry, worrying, worryingly, wondrous,* and *wonder,* besides *one*. This explains neighborhood effects in speech recognition, whereby word recognition is harder when there are lots of words that begin in the same way. Out of context, a particular word can only be identified once the uniqueness point reached has been reached. Hearing "waI@," this would already be at the uniqueness point, since the only possible completion is *Wyoming*. But hearing "wʌn", the uniqueness point hasn't yet been reached: There is still scope for our being *wonder-struck*. In the cohort model of speech recognition (Marslen-Wilson, 1990), activation in the cohort varies so that items are not simply "in or out." Rather, higher frequency words get more activation from the same evidence than do low frequency words. This assumption provides a means for accounting for lexical similarity effects, whereby a whole neighborhood of words is activated but the higher frequency words get more activation: Listeners are slower at recognizing low frequency words with high frequency neighbors because the competitors are harder to eliminate (Lively, Pisoni, & Goldinger, 1994). Such effects demonstrate that the language processing system is sensitive both to the frequency of individual words and to the number of words that share the same beginnings (at any length of computation).

Reading and Spelling

Language learners are sensitive to the frequencies and consistencies of mappings that relate written symbols and their sounds. To the extent that readers are able to construct the correct pronunciations of novel words or nonwords, they have been said to be able to apply sublexical "rules" that relate graphemes to phonemes (Coltheart, Curtis, Atkins & Haller, 1993; Patterson & Morton, 1985) or larger orthographic units to their corresponding rimes or syllables (Ehri, 1998; Glushko, 1979; Goswami, 1999; Treiman, Mullennix, Bijeljac-Babic & Richmond-Welty, 1995). For the case of adults reading English, words with regular spelling-sound correspondences (like *mint*) are read with shorter naming latencies and lower error rates than words with exceptional correspondences (cf. *pint*) (Coltheart, 1978). Similarly, words that are consistent in their pronunciation in terms of whether this agrees with those of their neighbors with similar orthographic body and phonological rime (*best* is regular and consistent in that all *-est* bodies are pronounced in the same way) are named faster than inconsistent items (*mint* is regular in terms of its grapheme-phoneme conversion, GPC, rule, but inconsistent in that it has *pint* as a neighbor) (Glushko, 1979). The magnitude of the consistency effect for any word depends on the summed frequency of its friends (similar spelling pattern and similar pronunciation) in relation to that of its enemies (similar spelling pattern but dissimilar pronunciation) (Jared, McRae, & Seidenberg, 1990). Adult naming latency decreases monotonically with increasing consistency on this measure (Taraban & McClelland, 1987). Because of the power law of learning, these effects of regularity and consistency are more evident with low frequency words than with high frequency ones where performance is closer to asymptote (Seidenberg, Waters, Barnes, & Tanenhaus, 1984).

Morphosyntax

Morphological processing, like reading and listening, shows effects of neighbors and false friends where, even within the regular paradigm, regular inconsistent items (e.g. *bake-baked* is similar in rhyme to neighbors *make-made*, and *take-took*, which have inconsistent past tenses) are produced more slowly than entirely regular ones (e.g., *hate-hated, bate-bated, date-dated*) (Daugherty & Seidenberg, 1994; Seidenberg & Bruck, 1990). Ellis & Schmidt (1998) measured production of regular and irregular forms as learners practiced an artificial second language where regularity and frequency were factorially combined. Accuracy and latency data demonstrated frequency effects for both regular and irregular forms early in the acquisition process. However, as learning progresses, the frequency effect on regular items diminished while it remained for irregular items—a classic frequency by regularity interaction that is a natural result in connectionist models of morphological ability of simple associative learning principles operating in a massively distributed system abstracting the statistical regularities of association using optimal inference (MacWhinney & Leinbach, 1991; Plaut, McClelland, Seidenberg, & Patterson, 1996; Plunkett & Juolla, 2001).

Formulaic Language

Just as individuals learn the common sequences of sublexical components of their language, the tens of thousands of phoneme and letter sequences large and small, so also they learn the common sequences of words. Formulae are lexical chunks that result from binding frequent collocations. Large stretches of language are adequately described by finite-state-grammars, as collocational streams where patterns flow into each other. Sinclair (1991, p. 110) summarized this as the Principle of Idiom: "A language user has available to him or her a large number of semi-preconstructed phrases that constitute single choices, even though they might appear to be analyzable into segments. To some extent this may reflect the recurrence of similar situations in human affairs; it may illustrate a natural tendency to economy of effort; or it may be motivated in part by the exigencies of real-time conversation." Rather than its being a rather minor feature, compared with grammar, Sinclair suggested that for normal texts, the first mode of analysis to be applied is the idiom principle, as most of text is interpretable by this principle. People process collocates faster and they are more inclined therefore to identify them as a unit (Schooler, 1993). These processing effects are crucial in the interpretation of meaning: It is thus that an idiomatic meaning can overtake a literal interpretation, and that familiar constructions can be perceived as wholes.

Language Comprehension

The Competition Model (Bates & MacWhinney, 1987; MacWhinney, 1987, 1997) emphasizes lexical functionalism where syntactic patterns are controlled by lexical items. Lexical items provide cues to functional interpretations for sentence comprehension or production. Some cues are more reliable than others. The language learner's task is to work out which are the most valid predictors. The Competition Model is the paradigmatic example of constraint-satisfaction accounts of language comprehension. Consider the particular cues that relate subject-marking forms to subject-related functions in the English sentence, *The learner counts the words*. They are preverbal positioning (*learner* before *counts*), verb agreement morphology (*counts* agrees in number with *learner* rather than *words*), sentence initial positioning, and use of the article *the*. Case-marking languages, unlike English, would additionally include nominative and accusative cues in such sentences. The corresponding functional interpretations include actor, topicality, perspective, givenness, and definiteness. Competition Model studies analyze a corpus of exemplar sentences that relate such cue combinations with their various functional interpretations, thus to determine the regularities of the ways in which a particular language expresses, for example, agency. They then demonstrate how well these probabilities determine (a) cue use when learners process that language, and (b) cue acquisition—the ease of learning an inflection is determined by its cue validity, a function of how often an inflection occurs as a cue for a certain underlying function (cue availability) and how reliably it marks this function (cue reliability) (MacWhinney, 1997).

For illustration of some more particular cues in sentence comprehension, consider the utterance *"The plane left for the..."* Does *plane* refer to a geometric element, an airplane, or a tool? Does *left* imply a direction, or is it the past tense of the verb leave in active or in passive voice? Odds on that your interpretation is along the lines in *The plane left for the East Coast*, and that you would feel somewhat led up the garden path by a completion such as *The plane left for the reporter was missing*. But less so by *The note left for the reporter was missing* (Seidenberg, 1997). Why? Psycholinguistic experiments show that fluent adults resolve such ambiguities by rapidly exploiting a variety of probabilistic constraints derived from previous experience. There is the first order frequency information: *plane* is much more frequent in its vehicle than its other possible meanings, and *left* is used more frequently in active rather than passive voice. Thus, the ambiguity is strongly constrained by the frequency with which the ambiguous verb occurs in transitive and passive structures, of which reduced relative clauses are a special type (MacDonald, 1994; MacDonald, Pearlmutter, & Seidenberg, 1994; Trueswell, 1996). On top of this, there are the combinatorial constraints: *plane* is an implausible modifier of noun *left*, so *plane left* is not a high probability noun phrase, and is thus less easy to comprehend as a reduced relative clause than *note left* because it is much more plausible for a note to be left than to leave. Thus, how an utterance is interpreted is also constrained by combinatorial lexical information (MacDonald, 1994; Tabossi, Spivey- Knowlton, McRae, & Tanenhaus, 1994; Trueswell, Tanenhaus & Garnsey, 1994).

Studies of sentence processing show that fluent adults have a vast statistical knowledge about the behavior of the lexical items of their language. They know the strong cues provided by verbs, in English at least, in the interpretation of syntactic ambiguities. Fluent comprehenders know the relative frequencies with which particular verbs appear in different tenses, in active vs. passive and in intransitive vs. transitive structures, the typical kinds of subjects and objects that a verb takes, and many other such facts. This knowledge has been acquired through experience with input that exhibits these distributional properties and through knowledge of its semantics. This information is not just an aspect of the lexicon, isolated from "core" syntax; rather, it is relevant at all stages of lexical, syntactic, and discourse comprehension (McKoon & Ratcliffe, 1998; Seidenberg & MacDonald, 1999). Frequent analyses are preferred to less frequent ones.

There is no scope here for further review of psycholinguistic effects. See Altman (1997, 2001), Ellis (2002a), Gernsbacher (1994), and Harley (1995) for more complete treatment of these phenomena at all levels of language processing, in comprehension and production, in first and second language, from semantics, through syntax and grammaticality, right down to the tuning of infants' iambic/trochaic bias in their language-specific production of prosody. But what is here is surely enough to illustrate that the language construction kit is huge indeed, involving tens of thousands of pieces, large and small, and mappings across several input and output modalities and to semantic and conceptual systems. And all of these associations are frequency tuned. The mechanism underlying such counting is to be found in the plasticity of synaptic connections rather than abacuses or registers, but one way or another, a learner figures language out by counting frequencies of occurrence and mapping.

SLA INVOLVES THE IMPLICIT LEARNING OF THE STRENGTHS OF THESE ASSOCIATIVE MAPPINGS

Implicit and explicit learning are quite different styles of learning, varying in the degree to which acquisition is driven by conscious beliefs, as well as in the extent to which they give rise to explicit verbalizable knowledge. Although both modes of learning apply to differing extents in all learning situations, there is now a considerable body of psychological research on the dissociation between these two forms of learning (Berry & Dienes, 1993; Cleeremans, Destrebecqz, & Boyer, 1998; Ellis, 1994; Reber, 1993; Schmidt, 1994; Stadler & Frensch, 1998). Implicit learning is acquisition of knowledge about the underlying structure of a complex stimulus environment by a process that takes place naturally, simply and without conscious operations. Explicit learning is a more conscious operation where the individual makes and tests hypotheses in a search for structure. Knowledge attainment can thus take place implicitly (a nonconscious and automatic abstraction of the structural nature of the material arrived at from experience of instances), explicitly through selective learning (the learner searching for information and building then testing hypotheses), or, because people can communicate using language, explicitly via given rules (assimilation of a rule following explicit instruction).

What of the frequency information that a language learner requires for effective and efficient language processing, is it acquired implicitly or explicitly? The answer is clear from introspection. It does not seem like people spend their time counting the units of language. Instead, when they use language, they are conscious of communicating. Yet, in the course of conversation, people naturally acquire knowledge of the frequencies of the elements of language and their mappings. As Hasher and Chromiak (1977) explained it as follows:

> That we can rank order events with as seemingly little meaning as bigrams suggests that the processing of frequency may fall into the domain of what Posner & Syder (1975) have called "automatic processes." That is, of processes which the organism runs off both without any awareness of the operation, with no intention of doing so, and with little effort, in the sense that the tagging of frequency has little impact on one's ability to simultaneously attend to other aspects of a situation, such as the interpretation of an ongoing conversation.

This knowledge, at the very core of communicative competence, is acquired on the job of language processing. The activation of existing mental structures (representing letters, letter clusters, sounds, sound sequences, words, word sequences, grammatical constructions, etc.), whatever the depth of processing or the learner's degree of awareness as long as the form is attended to for processing, will result in facilitated activation of that representation in subsequent perceptual or motor processing. Each activation results in an increment of facilitated processing. It is a power function that relates improvement and practice, rather than a linear one, but it is a process of counting and tuning nonetheless (Ellis, 2002a). Whatever else traditional grammar books, teachers, or other explicit pedagogical instruction can give toward effective language learning, it is not this frequency information. The only source is usage, in naturalistic communication.

WHERE INPUT FAILS TO BECOME INTAKE IN SLA

Yet, if that was all there was to it, then second language acquisition would be as effective as first language acquisition, and would routinely proceed to an endpoint of fluent and proficient success for all individuals who engage naturalistically in communication in their L2. But this is not the case. It is a defining concern of second language research that there are certain aspects of language to which second language learners commonly prove impervious, where input fails to become intake.

Schmidt's paradigm case, Wes, was very fluent, with high levels of strategic competence but low levels of grammatical accuracy. He was described as being interested in the message, not the form, and as being impatient with correction. In discussing Wes' unconscious naturalistic acquisition of ESL in the five years since coming to America, Schmidt (1984) reported the following:

> If language is seen as a medium of communication, as a tool for initiating, maintaining and regulating relationships and carrying on the business of life, then W has been a successful language learner...If language acquisition is taken to mean (as it usually is) the acquisition of grammatical structures, then the acquisition approach may be working, but very slowly. Using 90% correct in obligatory contexts as the criterion for acquisition, none of the grammatical morphemes counted has changed from unacquired to acquired status over a five year period. (p. 5)

Schmidt concluded his report of Wes with a call for research on the proposition that "in addition to communicative effort, cognitive effort is a necessary condition for successful adult SLA" (Schmidt, 1984, p. 14). Clearly, he was suggesting a cognitive effort above and beyond the implicit learning that I have been describing so far. Later, Schmidt (1990) proposed in his noticing hypothesis that a conscious involvement, explicit learning, was required for the conversion of input to intake: It is necessary that the learner notice the relevant linguistic cues.

This idea has rightly become a cornerstone of second language research. A strong form of the noticing hypothesis is that attention must be paid to some aspect of the stimulus environment and that aspect must be noticed before a mental representation of it can first be formed. This is broadly correct, although with two provisos. The first is the strong form of the implicit tallying hypothesis expanded here—that once a stimulus representation is firmly in existence, that stimulus need never be noticed again; yet, as long as it is attended for use in the processing of future input for meaning, its strength will be incremented and its associations will be tallied and implicitly catalogued. The second is that implicit learning is clearly sufficient for the successful formation of new chunks from the binding of adjacent or successive items that are experienced repeatedly.

The noticing hypothesis subsumes various ways in which SLA can fail to reflect the input: failing to notice cues because they are not salient, failing to notice that a feature needs to be processed in a different way from that relevant to L1, failing to acquire a mapping because it involves complex associations that cannot be acquired implicitly, or failing to build a construction as a result of not being developmentally ready in terms of having the appropriate representational precursors. Such failings reflect limits of implicit learning, working memory, or representational precursors.

Failing to Notice Cues Because They Are Not Salient

Although some grammatical form–meaning relationships are both salient and essential to understanding the meaning of an utterance (e.g., Spanish interrogatives *qué* 'what?' and *quién* 'who?'), others, such as grammatical particles and many inflections like that third person singular *-s* in English, are not. Inflections marking grammatical meanings such as tense are often redundant because they are usually accompanied by temporal adverbs that indicate the temporal reference. The high salience of these temporal adverbs leads L2 learners to attend to them and to ignore the grammatical tense verb morphemes.

This is a prime motivation for explicit instruction. Thus, for example, processing instruction (VanPatten, 1996) aims to alter learners' default processing strategies, to change the ways in which they attend to input data, thus to maximize the amount of intake of data that occurs in L2 acquisition. Likewise, Terrell (1991), whose view of language learning echoes construction grammar in its emphasis on individual meaning-form relationships rather than grammatical rules, characterized explicit grammar instruction as "the use of instructional strategies to draw the students' attention to, or focus on, form and/or structure" (p. 53). His "binding/access framework" postulated that learners' primary motivation is to understand language, and therefore that the acquisition of grammatical form comes as a result of establishing a connection between form and meaning. He recommended instruction as a way of increasing the salience of inflections and other commonly ignored features by first pointing them out and explaining their structure, and second by providing meaningful input that contains many instances of the same grammatical meaning–form relationship.

Perseveration and Transfer: Failing to Notice That a Feature Needs to be Processed in a Different New Way

Why is it that adults can still learn and adapt many skills, yet the ability to adapt the perception and production of speech appears to diminish in adulthood? If an English infant is open to the */r/ /l/* phonemic contrast, why do natives of Japanese, where there is only a single alveolar liquid phoneme, fail to acquire the */r/ /l/* contrast when learning ESL, despite high frequencies in the input? Perceptual Magnet Theory (Kuhl & Iverson, 1995) suggests that in such cases the phonetic prototypes of the native language act like magnets, or, in neural network terms, attractors (Cooper, 1999; van Geert, 1993, 1994), distorting the perception of items in their vicinity to make them seem more similar to the prototype. Neural commitment and behavioral entrenchment leads thus to perseveration: The L2 learner's neocortex has already been tuned to the L1, incremental learning has slowly committed it to a particular configuration, and it has reached a point at which the network can no longer revert to its original plasticity (Elman et al., 1996, p. 389). Nevertheless, successful remediation is still possible using exaggerated stimuli. McCandliss, Conway, Fiez, Protopapas, and McClelland (1998) reported that the English */r/ /l/* discrimination learning could be induced in Japanese L1 speakers who were presented with exaggerated stimuli that they could discriminate from the outset. Contrasts such as "rock" vs. "lock" were computer synthesized into continua and the contrast was exaggerated by extending their outer limits. Participants started with these discernible poles and then, as eight stimuli in succession were correctly identified, the discrimination was made progressively more difficult. This use of exaggerated stimuli and adaptive training led to rapid learning, whereas the use of difficult stimuli with no adaptive modification produced little or no benefit. In terms of noticing, the provision of exaggerated input made the learner notice and become aware of a contrast that previously went unheard. Learners need to be made to notice in order to make processing avoid attractors once optimized for L1 but that now serve as magnets to local minima.

Failing to Acquire a Mapping Because it Involves Complex Associations that Cannot be Acquired Implicitly

The tuning of perceptual systems to bigram frequencies and phonotactic sequences suggests that there can be implicit learning of sequential associations that have not been noticed. Careful research on implicit grammar and sequence learning confirms this to be the case (for reviews, see Berry & Dienes, 1993; Cleeremans, et al., 1998; Reber, 1993; Seger, 1994; Stadler & Frensch, 1998). Two separate unitized and preexisting representations that occur repeatedly in the same sequence, again and again, can accrete into one chunk even if their conjunction is not noticed. Hebb (1961) demonstrated that, when people were asked to report back random 9 digit sequences in a short-term memory task, if, unbeknownst to the participants, every third list of digits was repeated, memory for the repeated list improved over trials faster than memory for non-repeated lists. The Hebb Effect is the central mechanism of exemplar-based, implicit chunking accounts of linguistic form (Ellis, 2003; Gobet et al., 2001; Peruchet & Pacteau, 1990; Redington & Chater, 1996; Servan-Schreiber & Anderson, 1990). The key determinants of implicit learnability here are adjacency and many repetitions.

However, associations that are more complex than adjacency or immediate succession in artificial grammar learning experiments seem to require more conscious explicit learning and hypothesis testing to acquire. Ellis, Lee, and Reber (1999) provided evidence that this is the case for some long distance discontinuous dependencies in language acquisition. Cohen, Ivry, and Keele (1990) and Curran and Keele (1993) showed that although unique sequences can be acquired implicitly in artificial grammar learning experiments, ambiguous sequences require more attentional forms of learning. Likewise, Gomez (1997) demonstrated that learning can occur without awareness in cases of lesser complexity such as learning first order dependencies in artificial languages, but more complex learning, such as that involved in second order dependencies or in transfer to stimuli with the same underlying syntax but new surface features, is linked to explicit learning.

Developmental Readiness and Sequences of Acquisition

The issue of fixed sequences of acquisition is another core feature of SLA research: There appear to be common developmental sequences of certain syntactic structures despite different learner L1 backgrounds, different exposures to language, and different teaching regimes. Although frequency and salience seem to play a large role in determining some aspects of these sequences (Goldschneider & DeKeyser, 2001), the aspects of language that fit into this category suggest additional explanatory factors in terms of complexity and developmental readiness. The role of chunking in these processes is discussed in Ellis (1996, 2001, 2003). The basic idea here is that complex structures are built of prior structures: A new construction can only be acquired if the learner has already acquired the relevant representational building blocks or if they have sufficient working memory capacity, phonological short-term memory span, or other aspects of general language processing resource, to be able to use the structure. In Lego analogy, how can learners realize that a portal comprises an arch and two pillars while the notion of an arch is still foreign to them? Pienemann's (1985) Teachability Hypothesis is a good example of a theory that denies any possibility that instruction can alter the natural route of development of developmental features: "Instruction can only promote language acquisition if the interlanguage is close to the point when the structure to be taught is acquired in the natural setting" (Pienemann, 1985, p. 37). His Processability Theory (Pienemann, 1998) makes formal predictions regarding the structures that can be processed at a given level of second language learning based on psychological mechanisms that underlie interlanguage and proposes a hierarchy of second language acquisition processing procedures in the framework of lexical-functional grammar. Another well-developed theory of this type is O'Grady's (1997, 1998, 1999, 2003) General Nativist theory of syntactic representations, which addresses issues of learnability and development as a consequence of an innate endowment for language that does not include an inborn grammar per se, but instead consists of more general processing mechanisms and principles such as the general computational features (a) a propensity to operate on pairs of elements and (b) a propensity to combine functors with their arguments at the first opportunity (a storage-reducing "efficiency" strategy).

In all of these types of cases, implicit learning is not enough for the consolidation of a new construction, and explicit learning is additionally necessary in order for input to become intake.

EXPLICIT LEARNING IN SLA

A central and long-standing theme in second language research has concerned the interface between explicit and implicit knowledge. Krashen's (1985) Input Hypothesis was a noninterface position positing that although adults can both subconsciously acquire languages and consciously learn about language, nevertheless subconscious acquisition dominates in second language performance, learning cannot be converted into acquisition, and conscious learning can be used only as a Monitor (i.e., an editor to correct output after it has been initiated by the acquired system).

The phenomena gathered in section three lend support to the importance of implicit/subconscious acquisition of language. But those reviewed in section four show clearly that this is not enough. How then might explicit learning be involved in SLA?

First, it may be involved in the beginnings. The initial registration of a language representation may well require attention and conscious identification. Schmidt's noticing hypothesis has already been introduced:

> Noticing is used here as a technical term to refer only to registration of the occurrence of a stimulus event in conscious awareness and subsequent storage in long term memory, not the detection of form/meaning relationships or inductive formation of hypotheses or other processes that may lead to the organization of stored knowledge into a linguistic system. (Schmidt, 1994, p. 179)

Implicit learning is specialized for incremental cumulative change—the tuning of strengths of preexisting representations, and the chunking of contiguous or sequential existing representations. Otherwise, new associations are best learned explicitly. Attention is required in order to bind features to form newly integrated objects. Attention carves out for conscious experience the correct subset of conjunctions amidst the mass of potential combinations of the features present in a scene. Attentional focus is the solution to Quine's (1960) "gavagai" problem that single words cannot be paired with experiences because they confront experience in clusters. Imagine a second language community who says "gavagai" when confronted by a rabbit. Other things being equal, it is natural to translate the word as "rabbit", but why not translate it as, say, "undetached rabbit-part" because any experience that makes the use of "rabbit" appropriate would also make that of "undetached rabbit-part" appropriate. But guided attention, focused by sharing the gaze and actions of another, scaffolded by interaction that creates some focus on form or consciousness-raising, makes salient the appropriate features. Explicit, episodic memory systems then rapidly and automatically bind together disparate cortical representations into a unitary representation of these new conjunctions of arbitrarily paired elements (Squire, 1992)—a unitary representation that can then be recalled by partial retrieval cues at a later time. Thus, attention and explicit memory are key to the formation of new pattern recognition units.

Similar processes are involved in the formation of new categories that may subdivide what was previously served by a single attractor in L1 (as in the use of exaggerated input being used to promote acquisition of the */r/ /l/* distinction), or more generally in situations where the old ways of processing are no longer relevant or optimal and where the input needs to be perceived in new ways. Only when new representations for pattern recognition are formed and subsequently used in processing can their frequencies, along with the probabilities of their functional mappings, be updated by implicit learning processes. This is the major mechanism by which attention affects implicit learning, as is discussed by Boyland (1998), who illustrated these same processes occurring in vision in the experiments of Pevtzow and Goldstone (1994). People who are shown a figure such as Fig. 3.1a are usually quicker at finding the embedded parallelogram (as in Fig. 3.1b) and triangle (as in Fig3.1c) than at finding the forked stick (as in Fig. 3.1d) and turtle shell (as in Fig. 3.1e). However, if they have been previously involved in a categorization task involving a wide range of composite figures but where a criterial feature is shaped as in Fig. 3.1d, then the figure is more easily segmented into Fig. 3.1d plus Fig. 3.1e, rather than the usual parallelogram plus triangle. People thus learn to decompose complex objects based on their experience of component

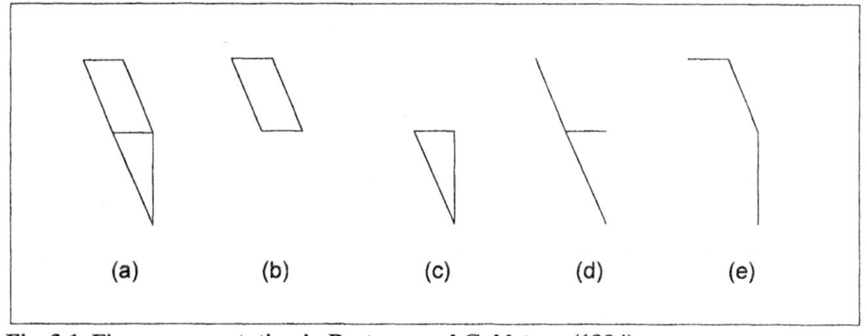

Fig. 3.1. Figure segmentation in Pevtzow and Goldstone (1994).

parts: Categorization training influences how a stimulus is parsed. Once individuals are trained to see the object in that way, that is the way they see it (or that is the way they first see it), and those are the features whose strengths are incremented on each subsequent processing episode. Such categorization training in language instruction may come from the provision of prior pedagogical rules or explanations, exaggerated input, or orienting instructions to focus on particular elements of form and increase their salience.

And the data show that these forms of attentional focus are effective and that language acquisition can be speeded by such provision. Reviews of the experimental and quasi-experimental investigations into the effectiveness of L2 instruction (e.g., Ellis & Laporte, 1997; Hulstijn & DeKeyser, 1997; Lightbown, Spada & White, 1993; Long, 1983; Spada, 1997), particularly the Norris and Ortega (2000) comprehensive meta-analysis of the last 20 years' empirical work, demonstrate that focused L2 instruction results in large target-oriented gains, that explicit types of instruction are more effective than implicit types, and that the effectiveness of L2 instruction is durable. This is not to say that just providing learners with pedagogical rules will make them into fluent language users. Far from it (Krashen, 1985; Krashen & Terrell, 1983), because then the learner neither gets the exemplars nor the tuning. Pedagogical rules are only properly effective when demonstrated in operation with a number of illustrative exemplars of their application (Ellis, 1993).

The real stuff of language acquisition is the slow acquisition of form–function mappings and the regularities therein. This, like other skills, takes tens of thousands of hours of practice, which cannot be substituted for by provision of a few declarative rules. Communicative approaches give input, time-on-task, and opportunity for relating form and function. All of this is necessary for developing the associations necessary for language learning. Naturalistic environments provide motivation and plenty of opportunity for output practice as well. These are situations that guarantee sufficient quantity of language and proper involvement in the communicative functions of language. But without any focus on form or consciousness raising (Sharwood-Smith, 1994), formal accuracy is an unlikely result: Relations that are not salient or essential for understanding the meaning of an utterance are otherwise only picked up very slowly, if at all (Schmidt, 1990; Terrell, 1991). Focus on forms alone can teach some declarative rules of grammar, but at its worst can be accompanied by too little time on the task of language use itself. But focus on form instruction, which is rich in communicative opportunities and also makes salient the associations between structures that the learner is already at a stage to be able to represent and functions, can facilitate language acquisition (Doughty & Williams, 1998; Long, 1991).

The communicative functions of language motivate the learner to the task. Noticing lays out the problem. Consciousness-raising can speed its solution. Figuring provides the final tally of native levels of fluency and idiomaticity.

BRAIN PROCESSES, COMPLEMENTARY MEMORY SYSTEMS, AND INTERFACE: TOWARD A COGNITIVE NEUROSCIENCE OF NOTICING

These are some of the psycholinguistic processes involved in second language acquisition. They can be viewed from many perspectives, focusing variously on learner, language, input, sociolinguistic context, cognitive representations and processes, or brain. There are important insights to be had about these psycholinguistic processes from current work in cognitive science (including the use of connectionist models of learning and representation) and neuroscience (including cognitive neuropsychology and brain imaging).

Humans have two separable but complementary memory systems (Squire & Kandel, 1999). *Explicit memory* refers to situations where recall involves a conscious process of remembering a prior episodic experience; it is tapped by tasks like recall and recognition where the individual is consciously aware of the knowledge held. *Implicit memory* is where there is facilitation of the processing of a stimulus as a function of a prior encounter with an identical or related stimulus but where the subject at no point has to consciously recall the prior event; it is tapped by tasks involving perceptual priming or procedural skills—people do not have to remember when they last juggled to have improved as a result of the practice. Implicit and explicit memory are clearly dissociable: Bilateral damage to the hippocampus and related limbic structures results in profound anterograde amnesia, a failure to consolidate new explicit memories, along with a temporally graded retrograde amnesia. Amnesic patients cannot learn new names or concepts or arbitrary paired-associates, and they cannot remember any episode more than a few minutes after it has happened. But amnesic patients show normal implicit memory abilities. They learn new perceptual and motor skills, and they show normal priming effects, they evidence normal classical conditioning.

Thus, the hippocampus and related structures serve explicit memory, one-trial learning that the Quinean for rabbit is *gavagai*, declarative learning (e.g., of verbal rules like "i before e except after c"), an autobiographical record of specific episodes. Then there are the memory systems of the neocortex, including relatively peripheral primary sensory-input and motor-output systems, secondary association areas, as well as more central, highly interconnected frontal areas. The neocortical system underpins implicit learning and is the locus of the frequency effects discussed earlier. Whenever a stimulus is presented to the senses, say a visually presented word, it produces a pattern of activity in the appropriate sensory system. This, in turn, gives rise to activity in the more central parts of the neocortical system, including those perhaps representing the visual appearance, the meaning, the sound of the word; and this in turn may give rise to an overt response, such as reading the word aloud. Any such event, any experience, produces a distributed pattern of activity in many parts of the cognitive system, and the information processing that people do occurs through the propagation of this activation through networks of neurons whose connection strengths have been tuned by prior experience. The neocortex underpins both the perception and the implicit memory of past experiences. Individuals perceive the world through their memories of the world. Implicit memory is the result of small changes that occur in the synapses among the neurons that participate in this processing of the event. These small changes tend to facilitate the processing of the item if it is presented again at a later time. But the changes made on any given processing episode or event in the neocortex, as in the connectionist simulations of this implicit learning, are very subtle, and as such are insufficient to serve as the basis for forming adequate associative links between arbitrarily paired items that have never occurred together before, or new concepts, or new episodic records.

It is by bringing together the role of the hippocampus in consolidation, the differences between one-off episodic learning and gradual implicit learning, and observations of nonnatural catastrophic interference in connectionist networks, that McClelland (1998, 2001; McClelland, McNaughton, & O'Reilly, 1995) developed a cognitive neuroscience theory of the complementary interactions of hippocampal and neocortical learning systems. This suggests that memories are first registered via synaptic changes in the hippocampus involving a sparse pattern of activity in which the individual neurons represent specific combinations or conjunctions of elements of the event that gave rise to the pattern of activation. These changes support reinstatement of recent memories in the rich and highly distributed networks of activation in the neocortex, the neocortical synapses change a little on each reinstatement, and remote memory is based on accumulated changes. Models that learn via changes to connections help explain this organization. These models discover the structure in ensembles of items if learning of each item is gradual and interleaved with learning about other items. This suggests that the neocortex learns slowly to discover the structure in ensembles of experiences. The hippocampal system permits rapid learning of new items without disrupting this structure, and reinstatement of new memories interleaves them with others to integrate them into structured neocortical memory systems.

Further research into these complementary memory systems, as well as into the unique contributions of the attentional systems of the prefrontal cortex in binding features to form newly integrated object representations, and how neuronal synchrony is related to perceptual integration, buildup of coherent representations, attentional selection, and awareness (Cleeremans, 2003; Humphreys, Duncan & Treisman, 1999) gives promise for understanding the cognitive neuroscience of the learning processes of noticing, figuring, and tuning that support second language acquisition. These issues lie at the heart of cognitive science and language acquisition both.

REFERENCES

Altman, G. T. M. (1997). *The ascent of Babel.* Oxford, England: Oxford University Press.

Altman, G. T. M. (2001). The language machine: Psycholinguistics in review. *British Journal of Psychology, 92*, 129–170.

Bailey, T. M., & Hahn, U. (2001). Determinants of wordlikeness: Phonotactics or lexical neighborhoods? *Journal of Memory and Language, 44*, 568–591.

Balota, D. A., & Chumbley, J. L. (1984). Are lexical decisions a good measure of lexical access. The role of word frequency in the neglected decision stage. *Journal of Experimental Psychology: Human Perception and Performance, 10*, 340–357.

Bardovi-Harlig, K. (2002). A new starting point? Investigating formulaic use and input in future expression. *Studies in Second Language Acquisition, 24*, 189–198.

Barry, C., & Seymour, P. H. K. (1988). Lexical priming and sound-to-spelling contingency effects in nonword spelling. *Quarterly Journal of Experimental Psychology, 40*, 5–40.

Bates, E., & MacWhinney, B. (1987). Competition, variation, and language learning. In B. MacWhinney (Ed.), *Mechanisms of language acquisition* (pp. 157–193). Hillsdale, NJ: Lawrence Erlbaum Associates.

Berry, D. C., & Diennes, Z. (1993). *Implicit learning: Theoretical and empirical issues.* Hove, England: Lawrence Erlbaum & Associates.

Biber, D., Conrad, S., & Reppen, R. (1998). *Corpus linguistics: Investigating language structure and use.* Cambridge, England: Cambridge University Press.

Biber, D., Johansson, S., Leech, G., Conrad, S., & Finegan, E. (1999). *Longman grammar of spoken and written English.* Harlow Essex, England: Pearson Education Limited.

Boyland, J. T. (1998). How developing perception & production contribute to a theory of language change: Morphologization < expertise+listening < development. *Chicago Linguistic Society, 34*, (1), main session, M. C. Gruber, D. Higgins, K. S. Olson, and T. Wysocki (Eds.) pp. 27-38.

Bradley, L., & Bryant, P. E. (1983). Categorising sounds and learning to read: A causal connection. *Nature, 310*, 419–421.

Bybee, J., & Hopper, P. (Eds.). (2001). *Frequency and the emergence of linguistic structure.* Amsterdam: Benjamins.

Cleeremans, A., Destrebecqz, A., & Boyer, M. (1998). Implicit learning: News from the front. *Trends in Cognitive Sciences, 2*, 406–416.

Cleeremans, A. (Ed.) (2003). *The unity of consciousness: binding, integration, and dissociation.* Oxford, England: Oxford University Press.

Cohen, A., Ivry, R. I., & Keele, S. W. (1990). Attention and structure in sequence learning. *Journal of Experimental Psychology: Learning, Memory, and Cognition, 16*, 17–30.

Coltheart, M. (1978). Lexical access in simple reading tasks. In G. Underwood (Ed.), *Strategies of information processing.* New York: Academic Press.

Coltheart, M., Curtis, B., Atkins, P., & Haller, M. (1993). Models of reading aloud: Dual-route and parallel-distributed-processing approaches. *Psychological Review, 100*, 589–608.

Cooper, D. (1999). *Linguistic attractors: The cognitive dynamics of language acquisition and change.* Amsterdam: Benjamins.

Croft, W. (2001). *Radical construction grammar: Syntactic theory in typological perspective.* Oxford, England: Oxford University Press.

Curran, T., & Keele, S. W. (1993). Attention and non-attentional forms of sequence learning. *Journal of Experimental Psychology: Learning, Memory, and Cognition, 19*, 189–202.

Daugherty, K. G., & Seidenberg, M. S. (1994). Beyond rules and exceptions: A connectionist approach to inflectional morphology. In S.D. Lima, R.L. Corrigan, and G. K. Iverson (Eds.), *The reality of linguistic rules* (pp. 353–388). Amsterdam: Benjamins.

De Cara, B., & Goswami, U. (2002). Statistical analysis of similarity relations among spoken words. *Behavioral Research Methods and Instrumentation, 34*, 416-423.

Doughty, C., &Williams, J. (Eds.). (1998). *Focus on form in classroom second language acquisition.* Cambridge, England: Cambridge University Press.

Ehri, L. C. (1998). Word reading by sight and by analogy in beginning readers. In C. Hulme & R.M. Joshi (Eds.), *Reading and spelling: Development and disorders* (pp. 87–111). Mahwah, NJ: Lawrence Erlbaum Associates.

Ellis, N. C. (1993). Rules and instances in foreign language learning: Interactions of explicit and implicit knowledge. *European Journal of Cognitive Psychology, 5*, 289–318.

Ellis, N. C. (Ed.). (1994). *Implicit and explicit learning of languages*. London: Academic Press.

Ellis, N. C. (1996). Sequencing in SLA: Phonological memory, chunking, and points of order. *Studies in Second Language Acquisition, 18*, 91–126.

Ellis, N. C. (2001). Memory for language. In P. Robinson (Ed.), *Cognition and second language instruction.* Cambridge, England: Cambridge University Press.

Ellis, N. C. (2002a). Frequency effects in language acquisition: A review with implications for theories of implicit and explicit language acquisition (Target article). *Studies in Second Language Acquisition, 24*, 143–188.

Ellis, N. C. (2002b). Reflections on frequency effects in language acquisition: A response to commentaries. *Studies in Second Language Acquisition, 24*, 297–339.

Ellis, N. C. (2003). Constructions, chunking, and connectionism: The emergence of second language structure. In C. Doughty & M. H. Long, (Eds.), *Handbook of Second Language Acquisition* (pp. 33-68). Oxford, England: Blackwell.

Ellis, N. C., & Laporte, N. (1997). Contexts of acquisition: Effects of formal instruction and naturalistic exposure on second language acquisition. In A.M.B. de Groot & J.F. Kroll (Eds.), *Tutorials in bilingualism: Psycholinguistic perspectives* (pp. 53–83). Mahwah, NJ: Lawrence Erlbaum & Associates.

Ellis, N. C., & Large, B. (1987). The development of reading: As you seek so shall you find. *British Journal of Psychology, 78*, 1–28.

Ellis, N. C., Lee, M. W., & Reber, A.R. (1999). *Phonological working memory in artificial language acquisition.* Manuscript submitted for publication.

Ellis, N. C., & Schmidt, R. (1998). Rules or associations in the acquisition of morphology? The frequency by regularity interaction in human and PDP learning of morphosyntax. *Language and Cognitive Processes, 13*, 307–336.

Elman, J. L., Bates, E. A., Johnson, M. H., Karmiloff-Smith, A., Parisi, D., & Plunkett, K. (1996). *Rethinking innateness: A connectionist perspective on development.* Cambridge, MA: Bradford.

Fillmore, C. J., & Kay, P. (1993). *Construction grammar coursebook* (Chaps. 1 through 11, Reading Materials for Ling. X20). University of California, Berkeley.

Forster, K. (1976). Accessing the mental lexicon. In R. J. Wales & E. Walker (Eds.), *New approaches to language mechanisms* (pp. 257–287). Amsterdam: North Holland.

Forster, K., & Chambers, S. (1973). Lexical access and naming time. *Journal of Verbal Learning and Verbal Behavior, 12*, 627–635.

Frisch, S. F., Large, N. R., Zawaydeh, B., & Pisoni, D. B. (2001). Emergent phonotactic generalizations in English and Arabic. In J. Bybee & P. Hopper (Eds.), *Proceedings of the symposium on frequency effects and emergent grammar* (pp. 159–180). Amsterdam: Benjamins.

Gernsbacher, M. A. (1994). *A handbook of psycholinguistics*. Hillsdale, NJ: Academic Press.

Glushko, R. J. (1979). The organization and activation of orthographic knowledge in reading aloud. *Journal of Experimental Psychology: Human Perception and Performance, 5*, 674–691.

Gobet, F., Lane, P. C. R., Croker, S., Cheng, P. C-H., Jones, G., Oliver, I., & Pine, J. M. (2001). Chunking mechanisms in human learning. *Trends in Cognitive Science, 5*, 236–243.

Goldberg, A. E. (1995). *Constructions: A construction grammar approach to argument structure*. Chicago: University of Chicago Press.

Goldinger, S. D. (1998). Echoes of echoes? An episodic theory of lexical access. *Psychological Review, 105*, 251–279.

Goldschneider, J. M., & DeKeyser, R. M. (2001). Explaining the "natural order of L2 morpheme acquisition" in English: A meta-analysis of multiple determinants. *Language Learning, 51*, 1–50.

Gomez, R.L. (1997). Transfer and complexity in artificial grammar learning. *Cognitive Psychology, 33*, 154–207.

Goswami, U. (1999). Causal connections in beginning reading: The importance of rhyme. *Journal of Research in Reading, 22*, 217–240.

Goswami, U., & Bryant, P.E. (1990). *Phonological skills and learning to read*. Hillsdale, NJ: Lawrence Erlbaum & Associates.

Hakuta, K. (1976). A case study of a Japanese child learning ESL. *Language Learning, 26*, 321–352.

Harley, T. A. (1995). *The psychology of language: From data to theory*. Hove, Sussex: Erlbaum (UK) Taylor & Francis.

Hasher, L., & Chromiak, W. (1977). The processing of frequency information: An automatic mechanism? *Journal of Verbal Learning and Verbal Behavior, 16*, 173–184.

Hebb, D. O. (1961). Distinctive features of learning in the higher animal. In J. F. Delafresnaye (Ed.), *Brain mechanisms and learning* (pp. 37–46). Oxford, England: Blackwell.

Hulstijn, J., & DeKeyser, R. (Eds.). (1997). [Special issue devoted to Testing SLA theory in the research laboratory]. *Studies in Second Language Acquisition, 19*.

Humphreys, G. H., Duncan, J., & Treisman, A. (Eds.) (1999). *Attention, space, and action: Studies in cognitive neuroscience*. Oxford, England: Oxford University Press.

James, W. (1890). *The principles of psychology* (Vol. 2). New York: Holt.

Jared, D., McRae, K., & Seidenberg, M. S. (1990). The basis of consistency effects in word naming. *Journal of Memory & Language*, 29, 687–715.

Kellerman, E. (1995). Crosslinguistic influence: Transfer to nowhere? *Annual Review of Applied Linguistics, 15*, 125–150

Kirsner, K. (1994). Implicit processes in second language learning. In N. Ellis (Ed.), *Implicit and explicit learning of languages* (pp. 283–312). London: Academic Press.

Krashen, S. D. (1985) *The input hypothesis: Issues and implications*. London: Longman.

Krashen, S., & Terrell, T (1983). *The natural approach: Language acquisition in the classroom.* Oxford, England: Pergamon.

Kuhl, P. K. & Iverson, P. (1995). Linguistic experience and the "perceptual magnet effect". In W. Strange (Ed.), *Speech perception and linguistic experience: Issues in cross-language research* (pp. 121–154). Baltimore: York Press.

Langacker, R. W. (1987). *Foundations of cognitive grammar: Vol. 1: Theoretical prerequisites.* Palo Alto, CA: Stanford University Press.

Lieven, E. V. M., Pine, J. M., & Dresner Barnes, H. (1992). Individual differences in early vocabulary development: Redefining the referential-expressive dimension. *Journal of Child Language, 19*, 287–310.

Lightbown, P. M., Spada, N., & White, L. (Eds.) (1993). [Special issue devoted to the role of instruction in second language acquisition.]. *Studies in Second Language Acquisition, 15.*

Lively, S. E., Pisoni, D.B., & Goldinger, S.D. (1994). Spoken word recognition. In M.A. Gernsbacher (Ed.), *Handbook of psycholinguistics* (pp. 265–318). San Diego, CA: Academic Press.

Long, M. H. (1983). Does second language instruction make a difference? A review of research. *TESOL Quarterly, 17*, 359–382.

Long, M. H. (1991). Focus on form: A design feature in language teaching methodology. In K. de Bot, R. Ginsberg, & C. Kramsch (Eds.), *Foreign language research in cross-cultural perspective* (pp. 39–52). Amsterdam: Benjamins.

Luce, P. A. (1986). A computational analysis of uniqueness points in auditory word recognition. *Perception and Psychophysics, 39*, 155–158.

MacDonald, M. C. (1994). Probabilistic constraints and syntactic ambiguity resolution. *Language & Cognitive Processes, 9*, 157–201.

MacDonald, M. C., Pearlmutter, N.J., & Seidenberg, M.S. (1994). The lexical nature of syntactic ambiguity resolution. *Psychological Review, 101*, 676–703.

MacWhinney, B. (Ed.) (1987). *Mechanisms of language acquisition.* Hillsdale, NJ: Lawrence Erlbaum & Associates.

MacWhinney, B. (1992). Transfer and competition in second language learning. In R.J. Harris (Ed.), *Cognitive processing in bilinguals* (pp. 371–390). Amsterdam: North Holland.

MacWhinney, B. (1997). Second language acquisition and the competition model. In A.M.B. de Groot & J.F. Kroll (Eds.), *Tutorials in bilingualism: Psycholinguistic perspectives* (pp. 113–144). Mahwah, NJ.: Lawrence Erlbaum & Associates.

MacWhinney, B., & Leinbach, J. (1991). Implementations are not conceptualizations: Revising the verb learning model. *Cognition, 40*, 121–157.

Marslen-Wilson, W. D. (1990). Activation, competition, and frequency in lexical access. In G. T. M. Altmann (Ed.), *Cognitive models of speech processing* (pp. 148–172). Cambridge, MA: MIT Press.

McCandliss, B. D., Conway, M., Fiez, J. A., Protopapas, A., & McClelland, J. L. (1998). Eliciting adult plasticity: Both adaptive and non-adaptive training improves Japanese adults' identification of English /r/ and /l/. *Society for Neuroscience Abstracts, 24*, 1898.

McClelland, J. L. (1998). Complementary learning systems in the brain: A connectionist approach to explicit and implicit cognition and memory. In R. M. Bilder and F. F. LeFever (Eds.), *Neuroscience of the mind on the centennial of Freud's project for a Scientific Psychology. Annals of the New York Academy of Sciences, 843*, 153–169.

McClelland, J. L. (2001). Failures to learn and their remediation: A Hebbian account. In J. L. McClelland and R. S. Siegler (Eds), *Mechanisms of cognitive development: Behavioral and neural perspectives. Carnegie Mellon symposia on cognition* (pp. 97-121). Mahwah, NJ: Lawrence Erlbaum Associates.

McClelland, J. L., McNaughton, B. L., & O'Reilly, R. C. (1995). Why there are complementary learning systems in the hippocampus and neocortex: Insights from the successes and failures of connectionist models of learning and memory. *Psychological Review, 102*, 419-437.

McLaughlin, B. (1995). Fostering second language development in young children: Principles and practices. *National Center For Research On Cultural Diversity And Second Language Learning: Educational practice report: 14*. Retrieved from http://www.ncbe.gwu.edu/miscpubs/ncrcdsll/epr14.htm

McKoon, G., & Ratcliff, R. (1998). Memory-based language processing: Psycholinguistic research in the 90s. *Annual Review of Psychology, 49*, 25–42.

McLeod, P., Plunkett, K., & Rolls, E. T. (1998). *Introduction to connectionist modeling of cognitive processes*. Oxford, England: Oxford University Press.

Metsala, J. L., & Walley, A. C. (1998). Spoken vocabulary growth and the segmental restructuring of lexical representations: Precursors to phonemic awareness and early reading ability. In J. L. Metsala & L. C. Ehri, (Eds.). *Word recognition in beginning literacy* (pp. 89–120). Mahwah, NJ: Lawrence Erlbaum Associates.

Miller, G. A., Bruner, J. S., & Postman, L. (1954). Familiarity of letter sequences and tachistoscopic identification. *Journal of General Psychology, 50*, 129–139.

Norris, J., & Ortega, L. (2000). Effectiveness of L2 instruction: A research synthesis and quantitative meta-analysis. *Language Learning, 50*, 417–528.

Odlin, T. (1989). *Language transfer*. Cambridge, England: Cambridge University Press.

O'Grady, W. (1997). *Syntactic development*. Chicago: University of Chicago Press.

O'Grady, W. (1998). The acquisition of syntactic representations: A general nativist approach. In W. Ritchie & T. Bhatia (Eds.), *Handbook of language acquisition* (pp. 157–193). New York: Academic Press.

O'Grady, W. (1999). Toward a new nativism. *Studies in Second Language Acquisition, 21*, 621–633.

O'Grady, W. (2003). The radical middle: Nativism without Universal Grammar In C. Doughty & M. H. Long (Eds.), *Handbook of Second Language Acquisition* (pp. 43-62). Oxford, England: Blackwell.

Patterson, K. E., & Morton, J. C. (1985). From orthography to phonology: An attempt at an old interpretation. In K.E. Patterson, J.C. Marshall, & M. Coltheart (Eds.), *Surface dyslexia: Neuropsychological and cognitive studies of phonological reading* (pp. 335–359). Mahwah, NJ: Lawrence Erlbaum & Associates.

Perruchet, P., & Pacteau, C. (1990). Synthetic grammar learning: Implicit rule abstraction or explicit fragmentary knowledge? *Journal of Experimental Psychology: General, 119*, 264–275.

Pevtzow, R., & Goldstone, R. L. (1994). Categorization and the parsing of objects. *Proceedings of the Sixteenth Annual Conference of the Cognitive Science Society*. (pp. 717–722). Hillsdale, New Jersey: Lawrence Erlbaum Associates.

Pienemann, M. (1985). Learnability and syllabus construction. In K. Hyltenstam & M. Pienemann (Eds.), *Modeling and assessing second language acquisition* (pp. 23–75). Clevedon, England: Multilingual Matters.

Pienemann, M. (1998). *Language processing and second language development: Processability theory*. Amsterdam: Benjamins.

Pine, J. M., & Lieven, E. V. M. (1993). Reanalyzing rote-learned phrases: individual differences in the transition to multi-word speech. *Journal of Child Language, 20*, 551–571.

Pine, J. M., & Lieven, E. V. M. (1997). Slot and frame patterns in the development of the determiner category. *Applied Psycholinguistics, 18*, 123–138.

Pine, J. M., Lieven, E. V. M., & Rowland, C. F. (1998). Comparing different models of the development of the English verb category. *Linguistics, 36*, 807-830.

Plaut, D.C., McClelland, J. L., Seidenberg, M. S., & Patterson, K. (1996). Understanding normal and impaired word reading: Computational principles in quasi regular domains. *Psychological Review, 94*, 523–568.

Plunkett, K., & Juola, P. (2001). A connectionist model of English past tense and plural morphology. In M.H. Christiansen & N. Chater (Eds.). *Connectionist psycholinguistics* (pp. 106–117). Westport, CT: Ablex.

Posner, M. I., & Syder, C. R. (1975). Attention and cognitive control. In G.H. Bower & J.T. Spence (Eds.), *Psychology of learning and motivation* (Vol. 3). New York: Academic Press.

Quine, W. V. O. (1960). *Word and object*. Cambridge, MA: MIT Press.

Reber, A. S. (1993). *Implicit learning and tacit knowledge: An Essay on the Cognitive Unconscious*. New York: Oxford University Press.

Redington, M. & Chater, N. (1996). Transfer in artificial grammar learning: A reevaluation. *Journal of Experimental Psychology: General, 125*, 123–138.

Rumelhart, D. E., & McClelland, J. L. (Eds.). (1986). *Parallel distributed processing: Explorations in the microstructure of cognition: Vol. 2: Psychological and biological models*. Cambridge, MA.: MIT Press.

Saffran, J. R., Aslin, R. N., & Newport, E. L. (1996). Statistical learning by 8-month-old infants. *Science, 274*, 1926–1928.

Savin, H. B. (1963). Word-frequency effects and errors in the perception of speech. *Journal of the Acoustic Society of America, 35*, 200–206.

Schmidt, R. (1984). The strengths and limitations of acquisition: A case study of an untutored language learner. *Language, Learning and Communication, 3*, 1–16.

Schmidt, R. (1990). The role of consciousness in second language learning. *Applied Linguistics, 11*, 129–158.

Schmidt, R. (1994). Implicit learning and the cognitive unconscious: Of artificial grammars and SLA. In N. Ellis (Ed.), *Implicit and explicit learning of languages* (pp. 165–210). London: Academic Press.

Schooler, L. J. (1993). *Memory and the statistical structure of the environment*. Unpublished doctoral dissertation, Carnegie Mellon University.

Seger, C. A. (1994). Implicit learning. *Psychological Bulletin, 115*, 163–196.

Seidenberg, M. S. (1997). Language acquisition and use: Learning and applying probabilistic constraints. *Science, 275*, 1599–1603.

Seidenberg, M. S., & Bruck, M. (1990, November). *Consistency effects in the generation of past tense morphology*. Paper presented at the 31st Meeting of the Psychonomic Society. New Orleans, LA, USA.

Seidenberg, M. S., & MacDonald, M. C. (1999). A probabilistic constraints approach to language acquisition and processing. In M. H. Christiansen, N. Chater, & M. S. Seidenberg (Eds.), Connectionist models of human language processing: Progress and prospects [Special issue] .*Cognitive Science, 23*, 415–634.

Seidenberg, M. S., Waters, G. S., Barnes, M. A., & Tanenhaus, M. K. (1984). When does irregular spelling or pronunciation influence word recognition? *Journal of Verbal Learning and Verbal Behavior, 23*, 383–404.

Servan-Schreiber, E., & Anderson, J. R. (1990). Learning artificial grammars with competitive chunking. *Journal of Experimental Psychology: Learning, Memory and Cognition, 16*, 592–608.

Sharwood-Smith, M. (1994).The unruly world of language. In N. Ellis (Ed.), *Implicit and explicit learning of languages* (pp. 33–44). London: Academic Press.

Sinclair, J. (1991). *Corpus, concordance, collocation*. Oxford, England: Oxford University Press.

Spada, N. (1997). Form-focused instruction and second language acquisition: A review of classroom and laboratory research. *Language Teaching. 30.*

Squire, L. R. (1992). Memory and the hippocampus: A synthesis from findings with rats, monkeys, and humans. *Psychological Review, 99.* 195–231.

Squire, L. R., & Kandel, E. R. (1999). *Memory: From mind to molecules.* New York: Scientific American Library.

Stadler, M. A., & Frensch, P. A. (Eds.). (1998). *Handbook of implicit learning.* Thousand Oaks, CA: Sage.

Tabossi, P., Spivey-Knowlton, M. J., McRae, K., & Tanenhaus, M. K. (1994). Semantic effects on syntactic ambiguity resolution: Evidence for a constraint-based resolution process. In C. Umilta & M. Moscovitch (Eds.), *Attention and performance 15: Conscious and nonconscious information processing* (pp. 589–615). Cambridge, MA: MIT Press.

Taraban, R., & McClelland, J. L. (1987). Conspiracy effects in word pronunciation. *Journal of Memory & Language, 26,* 608–631.

Terrell, T. (1991). The role of grammar instruction in a communicative approach. *Modern Language Journal, 75* , 52–63.

Tomasello, M. (1992). *First verbs: A case study of early grammatical development.* Cambridge, England: Cambridge University Press.

Tomasello, M. (Ed.) (1998). *The new psychology of language: Cognitive and functional approaches to language structure.* Mahwah, NJ: Lawrence Erlbaum & Associates.

Tomasello, M. (2000). The item based nature of children's early syntactic development. *Trends in Cognitive Sciences, 4,* 156–163.

Tomasello, M., & Bates, E. (2001). *Language development: The essential readings.* Oxford, England: Blackwell.

Tomasello, M., & Brooks, P. (1999). Early syntactic development: A construction grammar approach. In M. Barrett (Ed.), *The development of language.* London: University College London Press.

Treiman, R., & Danis, C. (1988). Short-term memory errors for spoken syllables are affected by the linguistic structure of the syllables. *Journal of Experimental Psychology: Learning, Memory and Cognition, 14,* 145–152.

Treiman, R., Mullennix, J., Bijeljac-Babic, R., & Richmond-Welty, E. D. (1995). The special role of rimes in the description, use, and acquisition of English orthography. *Journal of Experimental Psychology: General, 124,* 107–136.

Trueswell, J. C. (1996). The role of lexical frequency in syntactic ambiguity resolution. *Journal of Memory & Language, 35,* 566–585.

Trueswell, J. C., Tanenhaus, M. K., & Garnsey, S. M. (1994). Semantic influences on parsing: Use of thematic role information in syntactic ambiguity resolution. *Journal of Memory & Language, 33,* 285–318.

van Geert, P. (1993). A dynamic systems model of cognitive growth: Competition and support under limited resource conditions. In L. B. Smith & E. Thelen (Eds.), *A dynamic systems approach to development: Applications* (pp. 265–331). Cambridge, MA: MIT Press.

van Geert, P. (1994). *Dynamic systems of development: Change between complexity and chaos.* New York: Harvester Wheatsheaf.

VanPatten, B. (1996). *Input processing and grammar instruction in second language acquisition.* Norwood, NJ: Ablex.

Wong-Fillmore, L. (1976). *The second time around.* Unpublished doctoral dissertation, Stanford University.

CHAPTER 4
Context and Second Language Acquisition

Susan M. Gass
Michigan State University

One incontrovertible fact that scholars in the field of second language acquisition can agree on is that language is not learned in isolation. What is not clear is what the role of context is as learners move forward to learn forms, to learn meanings, and to make the necessary connections between those forms and meanings. This chapter explores the context of acquisition, focusing on the linguistic context in the narrow sense of the word (e.g., syntax, morphology).[1]

Nearly 20 years ago Gass & Madden (1985) published the first book dealing with input in second language acquisition. Given the history of the field of second language acquisition, the role of input, shunned in the years subsequent to the behaviorist era, had never received much attention until that time. In the following years, the role of input, which is of course central to any discussion of context and form–meaning connections, has endured and yet is still not entirely clear. Today's research world, as the chapters in this volume illustrate, is dealing with greater theoretical and methodological sophistication and a greater focus on psycholinguistic aspects of form–meaning relationships than in the 1980s. Further, theories depending on input–output relationships are emerging and becoming prominent, an area not of central concern in earlier research climates.

To understand the early lack of uniform acceptance of the topic of input, recall Chomsky's remarks in 1986 at the Boston University Child Language Conference. As Snow (1994) reminded us, Chomsky "characterized all child language research as falling into one of three categories: wrong, trivial, and absurd. Needless to say, he put attempts to relate aspects of acquisition to the input squarely in the third category." Undoubtedly, Chomsky would have characterized second language input research in the same vein, if he had even recognized the field of second language acquisition.

Today's research climate is in some sense different from what it was in the 1980s and in some sense is not. Those who take a Universal Grammar (UG) perspective on second language learning have tended to ignore the environment and the context in which learning takes place, perhaps adhering to the old argument that children can just feed on the scraps of language thrown at them by adults because the primary guiding principle for acquisition is innateness. Others, for example Elaine Klein (chap. 8 in this vol.) argue that a better

[1] Funding for part of this project was provided by a federal grant to establish a National Foreign Language Resource Center at Michigan State University, grant nos. P229A60012, P229A990012, and P229A020001. The author is grateful to helpful comments by Bill VanPatten and Jessica Williams. They questioned some of my initial claims and helped me clarify my thinking on certain points. All errors that remain are, unfortunately, my own.

understanding of how the environment interacts with prior knowledge is necessary, where prior knowledge is meant to include knowledge of the L1, other L2s, and universal principles of language. This position is a juxtaposition that is crucial to the ultimate understanding of the myriad influences on the development of second language knowledge.

The approach to the study of language and in particular to second language acquisition described here does not always include a well-developed role for context (see Gass, 1998, for elaboration on this point). It is possible to study aspects of language and aspects of second language acquisition devoid of context. That is not to say that contextual features do not play a role in acquisition, for they do. Their role, however, can at times be overblown and there is a time and place for context and a time and place for contextless study, the difference being highly dependent on the research paradigm and hence on the research questions being addressed. And perhaps most important, the relevance of context must be shown empirically (see Tarone & Liu, 1995). It is not sufficient to say that rich contextual information is relevant to acquisition, it is necessary to show precisely in what way rich contextual information relates to the creation of new second language knowledge. One way that this is currently being studied is in work on study abroad. The typical view is that a study abroad context is superior to learning a language in the classroom in a foreign language environment. Recent work, however, points to the fact that this view is overly simplistic and that there is a complex interaction between learning context and learner internal readiness. Segalowitz and Freed (in press) indicated that despite the fact that a greater number and variety of opportunities exist in a second language (i.e., study abroad) environment, one has to also consider the linguistic and cognitive readiness of learners.

Comments in this chapter are somewhat restricted and focus on the information that learners extract from the input in their attempt to use their internal processing capabilities to interpret the language of the input.

HISTORICAL SYNOPSIS OF THE ROLE OF CONTEXT

The beginnings of the role of input or context may be found in the realm of child language acquisition. Work on language addressed to nonproficient learners (generally children) has been approached from two primary directions. One was by anthropological linguists who looked at what they called "baby talk," the special register used to talk to young child learners. This speech genre was related to the language used when speaking to nonproficient speakers, most notably non-native speakers (NNSs). This relationship, although generally attributed to Ferguson (1964), actually goes further back to Hockett (1958), who in the 1950s noted the similarity between talking to non-native speakers and so-called "baby-talk," although he did little more than mention this relationship. The work of Ferguson (1971) was certainly groundbreaking in linking a number of these special registers.

A second group of researchers, those interested in language learning per se, attempted to tie input and actual language production, as can be seen in early work by Brown and Bellugi (1964) in which one of the proposed processes of acquisition was related to adult expansion of a child's utterance.

Within the short history of second language studies, there have been two predominant strands of research: One strand is concerned with internal representation of language knowledge and the other is concerned with the social context of language learning. Snow (1994) made it clear that even for those, at least in the field of child language learning, who are more concerned with "in the head" analyses of output, there has always been attention to the input, minimally because there would be a desire to eliminate any child utterances that could only be characterized as imitation and not a true reflection of linguistic knowledge and hence of a developing linguistic system. For second language research, particularly with adults, UG research, the most common example of so-called "in the head" research, has tended to pay less attention to the input than is the case in child language research. One reason for this is that the type of data that can be collected in second language contexts are quite different than what can be collected in child language research. For the most part, child language data come from spontaneous utterances in context. The context is therefore an integral part of the data record. For adults, data may be gathered through forced elicitation methods (e.g., acceptability judgments) where no input information is available and no input information is part of the data record. Hence, the context of learning and of data elicitation can be backgrounded and in many research reports is even unavailable (see Polio & Gass, 1997). In other words, given the methodological tools available to second language researchers, it is possible to abstract language away from the context. Of course, there are noticeable exceptions even within a UG paradigm, for example, the input flood work of Trahey and White (1993) where the focus was explicitly on positive evidence (the input provided to the learner).

CONTEXT ACROSS THEORIES

In talking about the role of context in the acquisition of a second language, we first consider context across theories. The discussion reviews some of the positions in which context does and does not play a role in second language learning and then focuses on attention as that mechanism that unites the linguistic context with internal processing. The final section briefly describes two empirical studies that address these issues.

In the early part of the 20th century, conceptualizations or theories of how languages were learned (both first and second) relied heavily on the input provided to the learner. This was particularly the case within the behaviorist period of language study, a research tradition that can reasonably be seen as falling outside of the "modern era" of language acquisition research. Within the behaviorist orthodoxy, language acquisition was seen to rely entirely on the input that a child received because, within that framework, a child was seen to learn by imitation and correction. In this view, language learning is heavily reliant on the concept of stimulus–response and the consequent concept of habit formation, with the linguistic context being the stimulus.

The same mechanistic view of language learning can be seen in some of the work focusing on second language acquisition in the mid-1900s. Fries (1957), recognizing the importance of basing pedagogical materials on principles of language learning, echoed the prevailing view of language learning—that of habit formation based on associations stemming from the input. In these early approaches to understanding both first and second language acquisition, input was of paramount importance because the input formed the basis of what was imitated and, therefore, the basis on which so-called language habits were created. Following the effective demise of behaviorism also came the minimization of the role of input. Mental activity that became the focus rather than the context of learning.

The topic of input within what may be called the modern era gained steam in second language research from a number of directions: Corder's (1967) discussion of input and intake; research on foreigner talk in the 1970s (e.g., Ferguson, 1971); and Long's (1980) discussion of input and interaction, a topic that had begun to receive prominence from the work of Wagner-Gough and Hatch (1975) in the mid-1970s.

However, not all theories of SLA have treated or even now treat context with equal enthusiasm. At one extreme is the UG approach, discussed earlier, where the question is one of learnability: How can certain kinds of knowledge be learned without explicit teaching or even without direct exposure? In fact, the term "Poverty of the Stimulus" suggests some sort of impoverished input. The claim is that, at least children, have an innate capacity for language. This is not to say that the input does not provide crucial information, as perhaps in triggering certain types of new knowledge, but the context or input is trivial in the sense that language is obviously not learned in a vacuum; there is always some context involved in the learning process, but the context does not figure prominently. Thus, within this framework, the input provides language specific information that interacts with innate structures that an individual (child or adult) brings to the language learning situation. The goal of researchers is to isolate language as a system in an effort to understand what aspects of that system come from an innate source.

Other approaches, for example that offered by Ellis (2002) on frequency effects, rely on the context to provide the input from which learners can extract abstractions. No innate mechanism needs to be posited. He claimed that learners are able to abstract linguistic units and patterns through frequent exposure to the input. But, the primary device for learners is their own ability and capacity to extract such patterns and create abstractions. In other words, the context provides the crucial data from which learners build grammars and a study of the linguistic context is essential to a verification of these claims. Other nonlinguistic contextual issues (e.g., sociolinguistic status of interlocutor) do not figure in this theoretical framework (but see responses in *Studies in Second Language Acquisition* [2002], *24*[2]).

Still other approaches (e.g., variationist approaches) do rely on contextual features to understand how learners use contextual information to build knowledge. Researchers such as Preston (1989), Tarone (1988), Young

(1991), and Zuengler (1989), argued that it is necessary to understand all contextual information in order to understand the variation seen in learners' grammars. In fact, Tarone and Liu (1995) presented data showing that the role of interlocutor is crucial in understanding the appearance of different forms in learner output and for understanding the rate and route of acquisition.

The input/interaction framework perhaps falls in the middle of these positions, as interlocutor status, for example, might play a role in the quantity and quality of interaction and input. What is intended in the input/interaction framework is that through focused negotiation work, learners' attentional resources may be oriented to a particular discrepancy between what they "know" about the second language and what is reality vis-à-vis the target language or an area of the second language about which the learners have little or no information. Learning may take place during the interaction or negotiation may be an initial step in learning; it may serve as a priming device (Gass, 1997) thereby representing the setting of the stage for learning rather than being a forum for actual learning. As already mentioned, learning may take place as part of an interaction or as the Example 1 suggests. Example 1 from Mackey (1999) illustrates recognition of a new lexical item as a result of negotiation of that word. This example illustrates how the learner may have used the conversation as a resource to learn the new phrase *reading glasses*.

1. From Mackey (1999)

NS: There's there's a pair of reading glasses above the plant.

NNS: A what?

NS: Glasses reading glasses to see the newspaper?

NNS: Glassi?

NS: You wear them to see with, if you can't see. Reading glasses.

→ NNS: Ahh ahh glasses to read you say reading glasses.

NS: Yeah.

In Example 2, an extended negotiation appears to be unnecessary. Here the NNS recognizes immediately that she is lacking a word and is most likely seeking conversational help:

2. Personal observation (homeowner talking to a gutter cleaner)

NNS: Puede venire en tres o cuattro semanas cuando están más uh uh árboles (Can you come in 3 or 4 weeks when there are more uh uh trees.)

NS: hojas (leaves)

NNS: sí, ah sí más hojas (yes, ah yes, more leaves)

In an input/interaction framework, understanding the interactional context assumes great importance, although some details of context often are necessarily backgrounded.

A view essentially incompatible with a UG approach is the Firth and Wagner (1997, 1998) position. They argued against what they perceived to be the mentalistic orientation of SLA in favor of the social and contextual orientations to language, arguing that second language acquisition studies have gone too far to the side of focusing on learners' mental activities (see responses by Gass, 1998; Kasper, 1997; Long, 1997; Poulisse, 1997).

In sum, the preceding discussion was intended to show that there is a wide range of positions in SLA that view the role of context and input in different ways and attach varying degrees of significance to the context in which learning takes place and in which language is produced.

MEDIATING BETWEEN CONTEXT AND LEARNER INTERNAL PROCESSES: ATTENTION

Whatever position is taken on the role of contextual information, there needs to be a mechanism that unites the context with internal mental activity of learners. Much recent research has begun to argue that attention is just such a concept. Long's (1996) statement of the Interaction Hypothesis makes this particular suggestion. According to Long, in dealing with the Interaction Hypothesis,

> *negotiation for meaning*, and especially negotiation work that triggers *interactional* adjustments by the NS or more competent interlocutor, facilitates acquisition because it connects input, internal learner capacities, particularly **selective attention**, and output in productive ways. (pp. 451–452, emphasis added)

He went on:

> it is proposed that environmental contributions to acquisition are mediated by selective attention and the learner's developing L2 processing capacity, and that these resources are brought together most usefully, although not exclusively, during *negotiation for meaning*. Negative feedback obtained during negotiation work or elsewhere may be facilitative of L2 development, at least for vocabulary, morphology, and language-specific syntax, and essential for learning certain specifiable L1-L2 contrasts. (p. 414)

This sets the groundwork for investigating just what learners pay attention to and when. Schmidt (2001), in his review of attention, stated that

> the essential claim...is that the concept of attention is necessary in order to understand virtually every aspect of second language acquisition, including the development of interlanguages over time, variation within interlanguage at particular points in time, the development of second language fluency, the role of individual differences such as motivation, aptitude and learning strategies in second language learning, and the ways in which interaction, negotiation for meaning, and all forms of instruction contribute to language learning. (p.3)

Robinson (2003), in his review of attention and memory, outlined three stages of processing at which attention is relevant: auditory/visual intake, decisionmaking (e.g., allocation of attention to competing demands), and "monitoring via sustained attention." He went on to claim that these stages correspond with selection of information, capacity of resources and effort needed to sustain attention. With regard to context, the significant issue is Robinson's first stage, selection of information. What do people pay attention to? And when? Attention mediates internal processing with the ambient language and is essential to understanding how individuals extract meaning and form from the context, and ultimately how they connect the two. Such a connection is a process rather than a static phenomenon. The beginning of the process is not unlike the beginning of the processes involved in language learning, in general. For example, there first needs to be a recognition that there is something that needs to be learned. This corresponds to the initial selection of information in Robinson's terms.

In the past few years, there have been a number of empirical studies dealing with attention. It is not the intention here to review them in depth, but rather to present some highlights.

Although not an empirical study of attention, Tomlin and Villa (1994) examined the role of attention in SLA from the perspective of cognitive psychology, proposing three components to attention: alertness, orientation, and detection. Alertness refers to the overall "readiness to deal with incoming stimuli or data" (p. 190) and relates to the rate at which information is selected for further processing. Orientation directs attentional resources to a particular bit of information while excluding other information thereby facilitating detection. Detection is defined as the "cognitive registration of sensory stimuli" (p. 192). It is "the process that selects, or engages, a particular and specific bit of information" (p. 192).

Leow's (1998) study of the differential effects of Tomlin and Villa's (1994) three attentional functions (i.e., alertness, orientation, and detection) found evidence for the crucial role of detection in acquisition. In addition to a crucial role for detection in acquisition, his results showed that orientation can facilitate or inhibit further processing, depending on whether or not information occurs as expected. He supported Tomlin and Villa (1994) further by arguing that although alertness and/or orientation may facilitate detection, they are not crucial for L2 intake unless detection occurs (p. 147).

Simard and Wong (2001) argued against Tomlin and Villa's theoretical treatment and Leow's supporting empirical study. Their main claim was that the three attentional functions (i.e., alertness, orientation, and detection) and awareness are not generalizable to the second language acquisition context. A more reasonable approach is to view these functions "as coexisting and interacting in graded levels" (p. 119). There are numerous factors that may determine the extent to which they are activated (e.g., nature of the task, the linguistic structure in question, individual differences, and modality; Wong, 2001).

But if attention is a mechanism that relates the external context to learning, additional questions should be posed. The remainder of this chapter asks two relevant, if not central, questions: Attention to what? Attention when?

ATTENTION TO WHAT?

Robinson (2003) defined attention as "the process that encodes language input, keeps it active in working and short-term memory, and retrieves it from long-term memory." The treatment of attention subscribed to here does not deal with the latter part of his definition, that is, the part related to memory structure. The concern here is with that part of a theory of second language acquisition that has been termed a transition theory (see Gregg, 2001)—that is, how does movement from Point A to Point B take place? Numerous studies have looked at attention, and there appears to be an implicit assumption that language is language, and attention, whatever its role may turn out to be, affects language in general without teasing apart the various components of language. This was brought to light in a somewhat different way by both VanPatten (1994) and Schwartz (1993). VanPatten (1994, p. 31) made the suggestion that "perhaps different aspects of language are processed and stored differentially." He went on to refer to arguments by Schwartz (1993), who suggested that syntax, lexicon, and morphology are learned differently. Similarly Schmidt (1995, p. 14) proposed that "different aspects [of language] may require more or less of it [attention]" and more recently reiterated this when he argued that the field of SLA "requires research within SLA itself, focused on different domains of language" (2001, p. 24).

Clearly, there is theoretical import to the question of the input–intake relationship that depends on different parts of language. Schwartz's (1993) work on negative data,[2] which can serve as an attention-driving function, is not relevant to the development of an underlying knowledge system (i.e., competence). Within Schwartz's framework, the syntactic system grows rather

[2] Negative data are data that explicitly inform learners of what is not possible in the language being learned.

than being learned. Important for the purpose of the discussion of differential effects of attention, Schwartz claimed that the lack of usefulness of negative data for the learning of syntax does not necessarily extend to other areas of language (e.g., lexicon, morphology) "as no clustering is posited in these areas" (p. 159). Assuming that there is differential learning, as the aforementioned scholars have suggested, and if attention is a major factor in learning, then it stands to reason that the effect of attention will be different for different parts of language.

This thinking was the starting point of a study by Gass, Svetics, and Lemelin (2003). The study investigated the acquisition of Italian by native speakers of English with reference to different levels of abstractness, complexity, and native language–target language differences. These were investigated by considering a syntactic structure [question formation] (complex and abstract), a morphosyntax structure [direct and indirect object placement] (complex, not abstract), and five lexical items (neither complex nor abstract). The participants were 34 English speakers enrolled in first-, second-, and third-year Italian as foreign language courses at a large midwestern university.

There were two conditions: [+ focused attention] and [– focused attention]. Each participant was given input on all three language areas, but they differed in which language area (syntax, morphosyntax, lexicon) they were in a [+ focused attention] condition and in which language area they were in a [-focused attention] condition. The entire procedure was conducted on computer. Each experimental procedure had three parts: input, rule/synonym, and practice. The [+ focused attention] condition had structures, forms, or vocabulary items underlined in the input condition (a story) and were presented with a rule explaining the rule/structure or information on guessing from context for the vocabulary items. In the [–focused attention] condition, there was no underlining and participants were told to find a synonym for a distractor (i.e., not the target word) in a sentence that was presented in the rule/synonym part of the [+focused attention] condition.

Each participant took a pretest and immediate posttest. For syntax and morphosyntax, it was an acceptability judgment task with corrections of those sentences judged unacceptable. For the lexicon, it was a translation task from Italian into English.

To briefly summarize the results, with the exception of syntax, learning occurred with or without attention.[3] In the area of syntax, learning occurred only with focused attention. In comparing the three language areas, in the [+focused] groups the greatest learning took place in syntax/morphology and the least in

[3] The issue of attention, of course, becomes complicated when it is recognized that our operational definition of attention involved manipulation of the experimental setting. The possibility that learners, because of their own individual needs and interests, paid attention to something despite the fact that their attention was not drawn there as part of the experiment cannot be ruled out. This differs from "unattended learning" which Schmidt (2001) dismissed as "limited in scope and relevance for SLA" (p. 1). The manipulation was designed to limit this possibility to the extent possible (see Leow, 2001, and Williams, 2001).

lexicon. For the [–focused] groups, the ordering was the reverse (lexicon → morphology → syntax). Thus, learners make better use of focused attention in more complex areas. In other areas, particularly vocabulary, where there is little complexity or abstractness, learners can avail themselves of internal resources to a greater extent.

With regard to proficiency level, there was, in general, a diminished role for focused attention. As learners gain greater knowledge of the language, they can use their own internal resources to "figure out" aspects of the L2. High proficiency learners benefited from focused attention only on syntax. This finding is consistent with the notion of complexity/abstractness and illustrates the interaction between proficiency and focused attention. Higher level learners may be ready to benefit from focused attention on complex structures. The increasing effect of attention on syntax is suggestive of the increasing extent to which learners are "ready" to learn the particular structure in question. In other words, their increasing sophistication on complex parts of language allows for attention to be a relevant learning mechanism.

To put these results in the context of form–meaning connections, it could be argued that the lexicon was the only obvious area of investigation where form–meaning connections had to be made (i.e., improvement was measured by a translation test, which by its very nature involves both forms and meanings). For both syntax and morphosyntax, all that was being asked for was information about form (acceptability judgment). Thus, attention seemed to be least important for the area that required form–meaning connections. This is not surprising if there is the understanding of what learners can and cannot pay attention to: It is possible to pay attention to form; it is not possible to pay attention to meaning without an additional process of inferencing, a process that must include context.

ATTENTION WHEN?

The second study to report on deals with the different timing of contextual information presented to learners (Alvarez-Torres & Gass, 2002). This study examined the differential effects of order and type of information presented to learners. It dealt with four types of presentation of information: input only presentation, interaction only presentation, input followed by interaction, and interaction followed by input. The study involved 102 third-semester learners of Spanish at a large midwestern university. We looked at vocabulary and two grammatical structures: gender agreement and *estar* + location. These are areas of Spanish that are both high frequency and difficult to acquire, perhaps, as VanPatten (1987) suggested, due to their low communicative value and lack of presence in the learners' L1. These are also areas that, in a pilot study, proved to be appropriately difficult for our level of learner.

Table 4.1. Summary of Results from "Attention When" Study

	Interaction + Input	Input + Interaction	Interaction Only	Input Only
Vocabulary	2nd	1st	3rd	4th
Gender	1st	2nd	4th	3rd
Estar	1st	4th	3rd	2nd

As mentioned earlier and consistent with previous work within the input/interaction framework, interaction was viewed as an attention-drawing device with input providing the context that can provide confirmatory information for learner hypotheses (see Gass, 1997).

It was predicted that learning would be greatest when interaction preceded input because it is during interaction that learners' attention is drawn to something and then input can provide follow-up information to the learner. It was further predicted that the least effective of the conditions would be the input only presentation because there would be little to draw learners' attention to specific areas of language. A final prediction related to the combination of conditions; those with both input and interaction would fare better than those with one or the other, but not both. The results are summarized in Table 4.1.

For the gender agreement and estar + location, the first prediction was accurate, the interaction + input showed greatest improvement. For vocabulary, the interaction followed by input group was second highest, but not the highest (highest was input + interaction). For the second predication (that the input only group would show the least amount of learning), it was only with vocabulary that this was this borne out. The third prediction (that a combination would be best) was borne out in all areas but *estar* where one of the combination groups (input + interaction) showed the least improvement. In both of the studies reported in this chapter, morphosyntax seems to behave differently than other parts of language. With particular regard to interaction, as an attention-driving device, it appears that for the learning of morphosyntax, more than pure noticing may be necessary. This may be because morphosyntactic feedback is more difficult to perceive given that there is more to pay attention to. In fact, Mackey, Gass, and McDonough (2000) showed that feedback on morphosyntactic errors was less likely to be perceived as morphosyntactic correction than feedback on other parts of language.

CONCLUSIONS

VanPatten (chap. 2 in this vol.) argues that "input is necessary for acquisition, defined as the development of an underlying mental representation." Certainly, input is necessary, but interaction plays an important role for acquisition because it facilitates the attentional link that is crucial to understanding how learners extract information from the environment and use it in the development of their second language grammars. However, in and of themselves, they may be less important than in combination. This is very similar to Van Patten's conclusion about the roles of input and of output. Acquisition, in his view, is input dependent. As stated earlier, there can be no acquisition without input. Output is similarly important, but is not a sine qua non. However, as shown in the second study described here, the combination leads to greater learning than either one alone. What seems to be emerging is that there are numerous factors that guide second language acquisition. They can be investigated in isolation and their significance can be determined, but they should also be investigated as interacting and converging factors to truly see how they operate in the learning of a second language.

As many have said before, selective attention is a crucial mechanism in the development of second language knowledge. Importantly, it is what links the context with internal learning mechanisms. But part of the controversy as to whether it is essential for learning may be obscured by the fact that no one has looked carefully enough at the contributing factors to attention of which there are many. To just take the examples dealt with in this chapter, it is necessary to understand the what of attention—that is, what parts of language can be attended to and can benefit from focal attention—and to pay attention to the when of attention. For example, is it in conjunction with large doses of input, the so-called input-flooding that Trahey and White (1993) investigated with regard to positive and negative evidence? Is it the same at all proficiency levels? What sort of input is necessary? Is input through interaction necessary? Is input through specific explanation necessary? But, this too, is only a drop in the bucket.

In sum, this chapter goes beyond the questions of whether or not context is relevant and begins to examine the nature of the role of the environment. An initial attempt was made to understand what internal mechanisms are necessary for linkage with the linguistic context. These are just some of the questions that need to be addressed as the field moves forward.

REFERENCES

Alvarez-Torres, M., & Gass, S. (2002). Input and interaction: Attention when? Paper presented at the AILA, Singapore.

Brown, R., & Bellugi, U. (1964). Three processes in the child's acquisition of syntax. *Harvard Educational Review, 34*, 133–151.

Corder, S. P. (1967). The significance of learners' errors. *International Review of Applied Linguistics, 5*, 161–170.

Ellis, N. C. (2002). Frequency effects in language processing: A review with implications for theories of implicit and explicit language acquisition. *Studies in Second Language Acquisition, 24*, 143–188

Ferguson, C. (1964). Baby talk in six languages. *American Anthropologist, 66*, 103–114.

Ferguson, C. (1971). Absence of copula and the notion of simplicity: A study of normal speech, baby talk, foreigner talk and pidgins. In D. Hymes (Ed.), *Pidginization and Creolization of Languages*. Cambridge: Cambridge University Press.

Firth, A., & Wagner, J. (1997). On discourse, communication and (some) fundamental concepts in SLA research. *Modern Language Journal, 81*, 285–300.

Firth, A., & Wagner, J. (1998). SLA property: No trespassing! *Modern Language Journal, 82*, 91–94.

Fries, C. (1957). Foreword. In R. Lado (Ed.), *Linguistics across cultures.* Ann Arbor: University of Michigan Press.

Gass, S. (1988). Integrating research areas: A framework for second language studies. *Applied Linguistics, 9*, 198–217.

Gass, S. (1997). *Input, interaction and the second language learner*. Mahwah, NJ: Lawrence Erlbaum Associates.

Gass, S. (1998). Apples and oranges: Or, why apples are not orange and don't need to be. *Modern Language Journal, 81*, 83–90.

Gass, S., & Madden, C. (1985). *Input in second language acquisition*, Rowley, MA: Newbury House.

Gass, S., Svetics, I., & Lemelin, S. (2003). Differential effects of attention. *Language Learning, 53*, 3.

Gregg, K. (2001). Learnbility and second language acquisition theory. In P. Robinson (ed.), *Cognition and second language instruction* (pp. 152–180). Cambridge, England: Cambridge University Press.

Hockett, C. (1958). *A course in modern linguistics*. New York: Macmillan.

Kasper, G. (1997). "A" stands for acquisition. *Modern Language Journal, 81*, 307–312.

Leow, R. (1998). Toward operationalizing the process of attention in SLA: Evidence for Tomlin and Villa's (1994) fine-grained analysis of attention. *Applied Psycholinguistics, 19*, 133–159.

Leow, R. (2001). Attention, awareness and foreign language behavior. *Language Learning, 51* (suppl. 1), 113–155.

Long, M. (1980). *Input, interaction and second language acquisition*. Unpublished doctoral dissertation, University of California, Los Angeles.

Long, M. (1996). The role of the linguistic environment in second language acquisition. In W. C. Ritchie & T. K. Bhatia (Eds.), *Handbook of second language acquisition* (pp. 413–468). San Diego, CA: Academic Press.

Long, M. (1997). Construct validity in SLA research. *Modern Language Journal, 81*, 318–323.

Mackey, A. (1999). Input, interaction and second language development: An empirical study of question formation in ESL. *Studies in Second Language Acquisition, 21*, 557–587.

Mackey, A., Gass, S., & McDonough, K. (2000). Do learners recognize implicit negative feedback as feedback? *Studies in Second Language Acquisition, 22*, 471–497.

Polio, C., & Gass S. (1997). Replication and Reporting: A commentary. *Studies in Second Language Acquisition, 19*, 499–508.

Poulisse, N. (1997). Some words in defense of the psycholinguistic approach. *Modern Language Journal, 81*, 324–328.

Preston, D. (1989). *Sociolinguistics and second language acquisition*. Oxford, England: Blackwell.

Robinson, P. (2003). Attention and memory during SLA. In C. Doughty & M. Long (Eds.), *Handbook of research in second language acquisition*. Oxford, England: Blackwell.

Schmidt, R. (1995). Consciousness and foreign language learning: A tutorial on the role of attention and awareness in learning. In R. Schmidt (Ed.), *Attention and awareness in foreign language learning*. (pp. 1–63). Honolulu, HI: University of Hawaii Press.

Schmidt, R. (2001). Attention. In P. Robinson (Ed.), *Cognition and second language instruction*. Cambridge, England: Cambridge University Press.

Schwartz, B. (1993). On explicit and negative data effecting and affecting competence and linguistic behavior. *Studies in Second Language Acquisition, 15*, 147–163.

Segalowitz, N. & Freed, B. (in press) Context, contact and cognition in second language learning. *Studies in Second Language Acquisition*.

Sharwood Smith, M. (1993). Input enhancement in instructed SLA: Theoretical bases. *Studies in Second Language Acquisition, 15,* 165–179.

Simard, D., & Wong, W. (2001). Alertness, orientation and detection: The conceptualization of attentional functions in SLA. *Studies in Second Language Acquisition, 23,* 103–124.

Snow, C. (1994). Beginning from baby talk: Twenty years of research on input and interaction. In C. Gallaway & B. Richards (Eds.) *Input and interaction in language acquisition* (pp. 3–12). Cambridge, England: Cambridge University Press.

Tarone, E. (1988). *Variation in interlanguage.* London: Edward Arnold.

Tarone, E., & Liu, G. (1995). Situational context, variation, and second language acquisition theory. In G. Cook & B. Seidlhofer (Eds.), *Principle and practice in applied linguistics: Studies in honour of H. G. Widdowson* (pp. 107–124). Oxford, England: Oxford University Press.

Tomlin, R., & Villa, V. (1994). Attention in cognitive science and second language acquisition. *Studies in Second Language Acquisition, 16,* 183–203.

Trahey, M., & White, L. (1993). Positive evidence and preemption in the second language classroom. *Studies in Second Language Acquisition, 15,* 181–204.

VanPatten, B. (1987). Classroom learner's acquisition of ser and estar: Accounting for developmental stages. In B. VanPatten, T. Dvorak, & J. F. Lee (Eds.), *Foreign language learning: A research perspective* (pp. 61–75).Cambridge, MA: Newbury House.

VanPatten, B. (1994). Evaluating the role of consciousness in second language acquisition: Terms, linguistic features & research methodology. *AILA Review 11,* 27–36.

Wagner-Gough, K., & Hatch, E. (1975). The importance of input in second language acquisition studies. *Language Learning, 25,* 297–308.

Williams, J. (2001). Learner-generated attention to form. *Language Learning 51*(suppl. 1), 303–346.

Wong, W. (2001). Modality and attention to meaning and forming the input. *Studies in Second Language Acquisition, 23,* 345–368.

Young, R. (1991). *Variation in interlanguage morphology.* New York: Peter Lang.

Zuengler, J. (1989). Performance variation in NS–NNS interactions: Ethnolinguistic difference, or discourse domain? In S. Gass, C. Madden, D. Preston, & L. Selinker (Eds.), *Variation in second language acquisition: Discourse and pragmatics* (pp. 228–244). Clevedon, England: Multilingual Matters.

CHAPTER 5
A Multiple-Factor Account for Form–Meaning Connections in the Acquisition of Tense-Aspect Morphology

Yasuhiro Shirai
Cornell University

This chapter proposes an explanation for a universal tendency observed in the acquisition of tense-aspect morphology, summarized in what is known as the Aspect Hypothesis (AH; Andersen & Shirai, 1994; Bardovi-Harlig, 2000), which claims that learners create restricted form–meaning relationships at the early stages of acquiring L2 tense-aspect morphology. Specifically, learners strongly associate past tense and perfective aspect forms with punctual and telic verbs, imperfective aspect forms with atelic verbs, and progressive aspect forms with activity verbs. It is argued that learners form–meaning mapping is based on multiple factors such as input frequency, learning environment, L1 influence, and learner characteristics. The reason why so many studies converge on the predicted acquisitional pattern is that various factors work in concert, pushing learners' form–meaning mappings in the same direction. For example, the prototype past (i.e., past tense with telic verbs) is frequent in the input, and the learners' L1s tend to have a similar prototype.

In addition to the aforementioned factors that shape learners' semantic representation (i.e., form–meaning mapping), elicitation procedures (i.e., task) contribute to specific patterns of distributions across studies. It is suggested that production data involving longitudinal or cross-sectional data, whether they are free production or elicited production, often go against the AH, with learners showing stronger prototypical association at later stages rather than the earliest stages, whereas paper-and-pencil tests often show patterns consistent with the hypothesis. It is suggested that the degree of rote-learned forms in learner data largely determines the degree of congruence with the hypothesis.

The investigation into tense-aspect acquisition in SLA regarding the AH provides an important empirical database through which to learn about the mechanism of form–meaning connections in SLA. The tense-aspect morphology is a quintessential grammatical form, and this morphology has been found to be associated with aspectual classes organized around semantic features such as dynamicity, telicity, and punctuality. This is arguably the linguistic area most extensively investigated in terms of form–meaning connection in SLA.[1] Therefore, it is important to reevaluate the AH from the perspective of how and why this form–meaning connection is created by learners.

[1] There are other areas of SLA that have amassed extensive empirical evidence such as NPAH, negation, and question formation, but they do not necessarily address the "meaning" with which the form is associated.

The chapter is structured as follows. First, it gives a brief summary of the predictions of the AH in first and second language acquisition. Second, it reviews studies of L2 English, evaluating whether each study supports the hypothesis, and it presents a generalization regarding acquisitional patterns.

Finally it discusses why some studies support the hypothesis better than others.

THE ASPECT HYPOTHESIS IN L2 ENGLISH

The discussion begins with a brief review of the AH, which predicts specific sequences of the development of tense-aspect markers in relation to inherent aspect categories (for a more comprehensive review, see Andersen & Shirai, 1996; Bardovi-Harlig, 2000, chap. 4; Slabakova, 2001, chap. 4). Vendler's (1957) semantic categories of verbs—state, activity, accomplishment, and achievement—are shown in Fig. 5.1.

State terms (e.g., love) describe a situation that is viewed as continuing to exist unless some outside situation makes it change. Activity terms (e.g., run) describe a dynamic and durative situation that has an arbitrary endpoint (i.e., it can be terminated at any time). In contrast, Accomplishment terms (e.g., make a chair) describe a situation that is dynamic and durative, but has a natural endpoint after which the particular action cannot continue (i.e., it is telic). Finally, Achievement terms (e.g., arrive) describe an instantaneous and punctual situation, which can be reduced to a point on a time axis.

States are [-dynamic], [-telic], [-punctual]; Activities are [+dynamic], [-telic], [-punctual]; Accomplishments are [+dynamic], [+telic], [-punctual]; Achievements are [+dynamic], [+telic], [+punctual] (Andersen, 1989, 1991). This inherent aspect classification based on the temporal schemata of the situation nicely predicts the aspectual meanings that aspectual markers (e.g., 'be V-ing' in English) carry (Smith, 1997).

The predictions of the AH, which are based on the comprehensive review of L1 and L2 acquisition of tense-aspect markers, are as follows (Shirai, 1991, pp. 9-10, slightly modified, see also Andersen and Shirai, 1996):

State	________________	love, contain, know
Activity	~~~~~~~~~~	run, walk, play
Accomplishment	~~~~~~~~~~ X	make a chair, walk to school
Achievement	X	die, drop, win the race

Fig. 5.1 Schematic representation of four inherent aspect classes (Andersen, 1990).

1. Past marking[2] first appears on achievement/accomplishment verbs, and is eventually extended to activity and stative verbs.
2. In languages that encode the perfective/imperfective distinction, imperfective past appears later than perfective past, and imperfective past marking begins with stative verbs, extending next to activity verbs, then to accomplishment verbs, and finally to achievement verbs.
3. In languages that have progressive aspect, progressive marking begins with activity verbs, then extends to accomplishment and achievement verbs.
4. Progressive markings are not incorrectly overextended to stative verbs.

This chapter focuses mostly on generalizations 1 and 3, which are most relevant to the acquisition of English. (Regarding Predition 4, see Li & Shirai, 2000, chap. 4, pp. 75–79). An idealized pattern of development, for both L1 and L2 acquisition, is summarized in Fig. 5.1 (Shirai, 1995).

In Fig. 5.2, the cell numbered 1 is the earliest in development, and the acquisition of the morphological marking spreads from this prototype to the peripherals (2 through 4). To test whether the predicted developmental sequences are consistently observed, this chapter reviews case studies, cross-sectional studies, and longitudinal studies in the acquisition of English as L2. These studies have specifically reported quantitative data regarding progressive and past marking in connection with lexical aspect. Even though the predictions of the hypothesis are applicable to any natural language, the primary focus is on English in this chapter, because in order to understand the conditions under which the hypothesis is or is not supported, it is necessary to control for the target language.

In terms of form–meaning connection, if the aspect hypothesis is supported, it can be assumed that L2 learners initially make a semantic representation that is restricted compared to the native speaker norm, and then later learners expand their semantic boundaries.

	State		Activity		Accomplishment		Achievement
(Perfective) Past	4	←	3	←	2	←	1
Progressive	?	←	1	→	2	→	3
Imperfective Past	1	→	2	→	3	→	4

Fig. 5.2. Predicted order of development of morphology from prototypes to nonprototypes.

[2] In tenseless languages, such as Chinese, a perfective/completive marker first emerges with telic/punctual verbs (see Erbaugh, 1978).

Table 5.1. Research on L2 English Acquisition that Addressed the Aspect Hypothesis

	N	Learner Characteristics, L1	task
Single-Level Studies			
Wenzell (1989)	2	untutored, SL, adult, Russian	oral interview
Robison (1990)	1	untutored, SL, adult, Spanish	oral interview
Huang (1993, 1999)	5	tutored, SL, adult, Chinese	oral interview
Salaberry (2000)	14	tutored, FL, adult, Spanish	film retell (oral/written)
Cross-Sectional Studies			
Robison (1995)	30	tutored, FL, adult, Spanish	oral interview
Bardovi-Harlig & Bergström (1996)	23	tutored, SL, adult, mixed L1	film retell (written)
Bardovi-Harlig (1998)	37	tutored, SL, adult, mixed L1	film retell (oral/written)
Bardovi-Harlig (1992)	30	tutored, SL, adult, mixed L1	cloze-type test
Bardovi-Harlig & Reynolds (1995)	182	tutored, SL, adult, mixed L1	cloze-type test
Collins (2002)	70 108	tutored, FL, adult, French	cloze-type test
Longitudinal Studies			
Rohde (2002)	4	untutored, SL, child, German	natural interaction
Lee (2001)	2	untutored, SL, adolescent, Korean	natural interaction Frog story
Rocca (2002)	3	tutored, SL, child, Italian	natural interaction film retell (oral) picture story book
Gavruseva (2002)	1	untutored, SL, child, Russian	natural interaction
Housen (1995)	6	tutored, FL, child, French/Dutch	conversation

The discussion first reviews small-scale studies that do not involve learners from different proficiency levels, then cross-sectional studies, and finally longitudinal studies. Table 5.1 summarizes the studies reviewed here.

Single-Level Studies

Wenzell (1989) investigated the stative-dynamic distinction and its relationship with past marking in conversational data from two of the three Russian learners of English. One informant's 36 past forms (token count) were limited to dynamic verbs (which Wenzell called active); there was no occurrence of stative verbs with past tense. Another informant used 96 past forms, among which 67 were dynamic verbs, and only 4 were stative verbs. (For the rest, stative-dynamic values were not reported.) This finding supports the AH, which predicts that past tense morphology is less likely to be used with stative verbs than with dynamic verbs.

Robison's (1990) case study of an untutored learner from El Salvador (L1 Spanish) looked at the correlation between morphology and two semantic oppositions: stative versus dynamic, and punctual versus durative. He found that punctual verbs were more likely to be given past marking than durative verbs (21 vs. 7, by token counts). He also found that dynamic verbs received more past markings than stative verbs. In fact, no stative verbs received past marking, whereas 28 dynamic verbs did. These results are highly consistent with the predictions of the AH.

Huang (1993, 1999) investigated the interlanguage of five Chinese learners of English living in the United States. In conversational interviews, all learners used past marking most frequently with achievements (61%–89%, average 80%, token counts). Four out of the five learners used progressive *-ing* most frequently with activity verbs (58%–100%). One learner, however, used it more evenly, 1 token for state, 2 for activities, and 2 for achievements, without showing any association with particular classes of verbs. This learner used fewer progressive forms than the other learners (5 tokens, as compared to 10–20 tokens used by the other learners). Except for this learner, whose use of progressive is too limited for any conclusion, Huang's study is consistent with the predictions of the AH.

Salaberry (2000) analyzed oral and written movie narratives elicited from 14 EFL learners in Uruguay (L1 Spanish). He suggested that the results "seem to go against the prediction of the lexical aspect hypothesis," citing the data from two learners. One learner left 12 out of 14 telic verbs unmarked for past, even though all of the five statives were marked for past. However, all these stative verbs were copula, which is known to be past-marked often (Kumpf, 1984) and should not be compared on a par with lexical verbs (see Shirai & Kurono, 1998, pp. 269–271, for further discussion). Unfortunately, Salaberry's quantitative data (his Tables 4 and 5) only reported which verb classes (telic, activity, stative) were used how many times in the narrative, and did not report which verb classes were inflected for past tense. Therefore, his claim that his study showed a trend that goes against the AH cannot be evaluated.

Cross-Sectional Studies

Production Data (Oral/Written). Robison's (1995) cross-sectional study is an oral interview study that includes learners from four different proficiency groups, and therefore shows more clearly the spread of morphological marking from the prototype to the nonprototypes. He used conversational data for his analyses, although he classified the learners into four proficiency groups on the basis of the correct use of verb morphology in obligatory contexts in their writing samples. The percentages of progressive marking used with activities from Level I (lowest) to Level IV (highest) were: 57% → 70% → 79% → 80%. The percentages of past marking used with achievements[3] were: 43% → 60% →

[3] Robison (1995) introduced new categories: punctual states (e.g., notice, realize) and punctual activities (e.g., jump, knock). Because these are classified as achievements in other studies, the number of achievements here is based on the total of punctual states, punctual activities, and punctual events.

54% → 55%.[4] These results show that (a) at any given time, the prototype progressive/past has the highest percentage of use compared with non-prototypes, which is consistent with the AH, and (b) less advanced L2 learners are not necessarily more restricted to the prototypes than more advanced learners, which goes against the AH.

Bardovi-Harlig and Bergström's (1996) cross-sectional study reported results similar to Robison's (1995) cross-sectional study, although they used written narratives based on a film-retell task as data. The percentages of progressive marking used with activities from Level 1 to Level 4 were: 63% → 84% → 100% → 52%. The percentages of past marking used with achievements were: 62% → 59% → 67% → 61%.[5] Thus, the most frequent verb classes are activities for progressive and achievements for past, a result consistent with the AH. However, the association is not necessarily stronger at the lower levels of proficiency, and it is strongest at Level 3, which goes against the AH. Also noteworthy is the fact that for each level, the association of past marking and lexical aspect is in the order of achievement → accomplishment → activity, which is consistent with the prediction,[6] for progressive, the order is activity → accomplishment → achievement → state, for each level.[7]

Bardovi-Harlig's (1998) cross-sectional study also shows the same trend. Here, data from a reanalysis in Bardovi-Harlig (2002) is used to facilitate comparison with other studies reviewed here. The analysis of written film-retell narratives reveals that at any level, the highest past-marked category was achievement verbs, and the highest progressivized category was activity verbs. However, the ratio of achievement verbs among past-marked verbs for written narrative from lowest to highest levels of proficiency was 62% → 52% → 60% → 54% → 66% → 54% → 53%, and that for progressive marking for activity verbs was 64% → 100% → 80% → 86% → 96% → 67% → 75%. Thus, in neither case was the spread from lower level to higher level observed. (The results from the oral narrative showed the same trend.)

Paper-and-Pencil Test. Bardovi-Harlig (1992) reported a cross-sectional study of ESL students (n=135) at Indiana University using a cloze-type passage in which learners were asked to change the base forms of verbs into appropriate

[4] These percentages were calculated on the basis of Robison's (1995, p. 354) Table 1, which reported token counts. In the reanalysis of the frequency data presented here, an across-category analysis is used throughout (Bardovi-Harlig, 2002; Shirai, 1991), reanalyzing studies not originally presented in this analysis for ease of comparison. This issue is addressed further in the discussion.

[5] These percentages were calculated on the basis of Bardovi-Harlig and Bergström's (1996, p. 316) Table 4, which reports token counts.

[6] In their study, state verbs consistently outnumbered activity verbs except for Level I; the learners produced more state verbs than activity verbs with past inflections. This is probably because their analysis included copula. Copula is very frequent early in development and its inclusion seems to have inflated the frequency of past-marked states. Otherwise, the trend is consistent with the prediction. Most other studies did not include copula because copula in English has suppletive past forms that are very different from regular and irregular past.

[7] There was one exception: At Level 4, the association of progressive with states (3.3%) was higher than with achievements (2.1%), but the difference is minimal.

Table 5.2. Percent Accuracy for Verb Types in Obligatory Simple Past Contexts in Bardovi-Harlig (1992)

	State (live)	Activity (work, stay)	Achievement (tell, die)
Level 1	31.6%	35.1%	63.2%
Level 2	50.0%	48.3%	82.5%
Level 3	25.0%	54.2%	78.2%
Level 4	48.3%	60.9%	88.0%
Level 5	75.8%	78.8%	87.9%
Level 6	66.7%	70.4%	86.1%

morphological forms in context. She provided detailed results concerning the items where simple past tense was obligatory, which makes a reanalysis possible. The AH predicts that learners will find it hardest to apply a simple past marker to states, but easiest to apply it to achievements. Table 5.2 shows the accuracy rate for three lexical aspect classes, calculated on the basis of her Tables 3 to 8. (Her test items did not include any accomplishment verbs.)

As is clear from the table, the prediction is borne out. At all levels, it is more difficult to inflect state verbs for past tense than activity verbs (with the exception of Level 2, where states had a slightly higher past marking rate than activities, by 1.7%), and it is easiest for learners to apply past inflection to achievement verbs.

Bardovi-Harlig and Reynolds (1995), in a similar cross-sectional study (n=182), also found that achievements and accomplishments, which they called "events," showed a consistently higher past marking rate in obligatory past contexts than activities and states. This supports the AH. However, in this study, learners at Levels 4 and 5 clearly showed a higher past marking rate for states than for activities. This result appears to go against the prediction of the AH, but Collins' (2002) replication studies showed that that is not necessarily the case.

Collins (2002), in her Study 1, replicated Bardovi-Harlig and Reynolds (1995) with Francophone university students (n=70) learning English in Québec. Although Collins did not report actual percentages, it is clear from her results that at all levels, telic verbs (achievements and accomplishments) are easier to inflect for past than atelic verbs (i.e., states and activities), and there were statistically significant differences. This supports the AH. However, stative verbs consistently had a higher rate of simple past marking at all 6 levels than activity verbs, which seemingly goes against the prediction, as does the case of Levels 4 and 5 learners in Bardovi-Harlig and Reynolds (1995). However, Collins noted that item analysis revealed that the low rate of past marking on activities was mostly due to three items (snow, dance, and sing), which were in background clauses and quite acceptable with progressive. Therefore, many learners chose progressive inflection rather than past inflection. In other words, even though these items were intended to be obligatory past context, they were not. This was confirmed in her Study 2, in which more than 90% of 30 native controls accepted the progressive form for these three items in addition to the past tense form. Indeed, the revised cloze test in her Study 2 (n=108) excluded these three items, and found that state verbs had lower past marking rate than activities. Collins' replications show that Bardovi-Harlig and Reynolds' results are actually consistent with the AH.[8]

Longitudinal Studies

Rohde (1996) analyzed data from two German children acquiring English in the United States, and found that their use of past tense was strongly associated with achievement verbs. This association was particularly conspicuous for the regular past (*-ed*) for the 6-year-old child: Only achievement verbs during the first 4 months of recording received *-ed* marking; in the fifth month, non-achievement verbs (in this case, states) appeared with past marking. For the 9-year-old, the trend was not that clear, but only achievements received *-ed* marking in the first month, and during the next 3 months, achievements still received by far the most frequent *-ed* marking; in the fifth month, other verbs appeared. Overall, the development of regular past is consistent with the AH. However, irregular past showed some deviation from the prediction. In the first month, both achievement verbs and non-achievement verbs (i.e., state verbs) appeared for both children. Overall, however, achievements were the most frequent category.

Rohde also found that the earliest progressive marking was strongly associated with achievements as well as activities, and for the 9-year-old, achievements showed the highest association with progressive inflections during the first 2 months. He suggested that children were using progressive with achievements to express future tense (e.g., "I'm stealing." "Why is John not coming?"). This goes against the AH, which predicts that progressive morphology is initially associated with activity verbs to denote action in progress.

Rohde (2002), building on his 1996 study, discussed various types of non-targetlike uses of verbal morphology by four German children acquiring English in a naturalistic setting. Rohde claimed that the analysis of his data does not necessarily support the prediction of the AH. Especially problematic for the AH was the finding that state verbs had a very high past marking rate in obligatory past context for all four children (80%–100%). Although the state verbs in his data included be copula/auxiliary, the same tendency is observed by Housen (2002), who excluded *be* but still arrived at a similar conclusion. Rohde and Housen, therefore, both provided important counterexamples to the AH.

Another longitudinal study, by Lee (2001), examined the acquisition of progressive and past morphology with lexical aspect by two Korean learners of English in Hawaii. Table 5.3, calculated from her Tables 6 to 9, shows the

[8] In fact, Collins' Study 2, after removing the 'noise' found in Bardovi-Harlig and Reynolds (1995), such as three activity items and the possible effect of instruction on past progressive, constitutes the strongest support for the AH.

pattern of development for the two learners (a 10-year-old boy and a 14-year-old girl). The data were based on token counts to facilitate comparison with other studies, although she also reported type count.

The table indicates that (a) there are the predicted associations between telic verbs and the past tense marking, and between activity verbs and the progressive marking, and (b) the spread from prototype to non-prototype is not transparent. Such a spread might be argued for the past tense marking for the 14-year-old learner, but not for the 10-year-old, and not for the progressive for either child.

Rocca (2002) analyzed longitudinal data from three Italian children learning English in England, as part of the bidirectional study in which she also analyzed three L1 English learners of Italian. In the 6-month longitudinal studies that analyzed production data (spontaneous conversation about past events, film retell, and insertion of verbs in a picture story with missing verbs) from three children (ages 7 and 8), she found clear support for the AH. The percentages of prototypical combinations (i.e., telic verbs with past and activity verbs with progressive) are shown in Table 5.4.

For both past and progressive forms, the typical association is stronger at earlier stages, and then gradually weakens over time. This is clearly consistent with the AH. She also found support for the hypothesis in the L2 Italian data. She stated, "This bidirectional study supports the AH in that the spread of verb morphology appears to be influenced by the lexical aspect of the predicate. This bias is more evident in the L2 English children than in the L2 Italian children" (p. 275).

Table 5.3. Percentages of Lexical Aspect by Morphological Marking (Lee, 2001)

	T1	T2	T3	T4	T5	T6	T7	T8	T9	T10	T11	T12
Past Marking with Telic Verbs												
14-year-old	100	83	78	75	83	77	53	48	69	54	58	50
10-year-old	NA*	0	60	50	63	67	63	50	58	63	49	39
Progressive Marking with Activity Verbs												
14-year-old	100	50	80	80	57	50	57	100	100	78	77	77
10-year-old	0	NA	75	71	83	89	71	100	83	88	65	77

Note. T1=Time 1, T2=Time 2, etc.

*No occurrence of the past marking.

Table 5.4. Percentages of Lexical Aspect by Morphological Marking in Rocca (2002)

	T1	T2	T3	T4	T5	T6	T7	T8	T9	T10	T11	T12	T13	T14	T15
Past Marking with Telic Verbs															
	100	100	100	96	96	88	98	82	88	78	79	78	75	76	77
Progressive Marking with Activity Verbs															
	92	67	95	94	80	85	68	83	96	84	64	73	61	47	61

Gavruseva's (2002) findings are also clearly consistent with the AH. In a longitudinal study of an 8-year-old Russian girl acquiring English in the United States that replicated the Shirai and Andersen (1995) L1 study, she found that past tense marking and progressive marking are predominantly associated with achievement verbs and activity verbs respectively, and the association is stronger at earlier stages than later stages of development.

Housen (1995) reported on a longitudinal study of the acquisition of verb morphology by English L2 learners in Belgium (grades 3-5 in primary school) of two different L1 groups (French and Dutch). He collected spontaneous speech data (with some structured activity included) on five occasions with 5-month intervals, resulting in data from Time 1 to Time 5. Although his L1 French group did not do as well as the Dutch L1 group, all of them made some progress over time in their use of tense-aspect morphology as measured by TLU (Stauble, 1984). The findings are presented in Table 5.5.

The pattern of acquisition of past tense and progressive morphology showed considerable individual variation. Here, past morphology includes both past tense (e.g., fell) and past participle (e.g., fallen) forms. The latter was often produced by the French L1 group because perfective past in French (i.e., passé composé) has formal similarity to present perfect in English (see Housen, 1995, for details).[9]

Table 5.5. Percentages of Lexical Aspect by Morphological Marking in Housen (1995)

French L1 Children	T1	T2	T3	T4	T5	Dutch L1 Cchildren	T1	T2	T3	T4	T5
SAH						FLU					
Past Marking with Telic Verbs	100	78	81	53	57	Past Marking with Telic Verbs	83	69	61	70	67
Progressive Marking with Activity Verbs	100	86	59	50	80	Progressive Marking with Activity Verbs	76	43	63	59	64
LEN						EVA					
Past Marking with Telic Verbs	0	100	100	100	65	Past Marking with Telic Verbs	67	55	59	48	64
Progressive Marking with Activity Verbs	48	47	22	9	38	Progressive Marking with Activity Verbs	63	66	63	55	55
MAG						EMA					
Past Marking with Telic Verbs	60	63	82	100	85	Past Marking with Telic Verbs	83	71	63	68	67
Progressive Marking with Activity Verbs	73	82	36	50	67	Progressive Marking with Activity Verbs	61	51	32	36	53

[9] Housen had additional categories of "semi-state" (e.g., sit) and "punctual activity" (e.g., jump), which in other studies are classified as activities and achievements, respectively, and therefore are included in those categories in this reanalysis.

The only learner that clearly follows the predicted pattern of development is SAH, the lowest level learner among all six children. Although there is a predicted association, the predicted spread from the prototypes to nonprototypes is not clearly observed for the five other children.

Housen (2002) reported a more detailed analysis of the longitudinal data from EMA, a 9-year-old Dutch speaker. He suggested that although the development of progressive marking supported the prediction of the AH, the prediction for past tense was not supported clearly. First, state verbs were given past marking at the early stages, much more than expected, and second, type analysis, as opposed to token analysis, did not support the early association of past and achievement, given that frequent use of a few achievement verbs (i.e., said and got) inflated the token count of achievement verbs. Pointing out that early state verbs are mostly irregular verbs, Housen argued that the AH for past tense may be valid for regular past only, whereas a different processing mechanism is involved for irregular past, which is more prone to rote learning than regular past. This is a plausible scenario, which is also observed by Rohde (1996), and further research is needed to test this hypothesis, but it should be pointed out that such a tendency was not found for L1 acquisition—both regular and irregular past were restricted to achievements (Shirai, 1991).

To summarize, the following generalizations can be derived from the previous studies of the acquisition of tense-aspect morphology and lexical aspect in English as a second language:

1. Learners tend to use the prototypical combinations (past with punctual/telic verbs, and progressive with activity verbs) most frequently.
2. The development from prototype to nonprototype is not always observed in the cross-sectional and longitudinal studies that used oral or written production data. In fact, for many cases the prototypical association is stronger for the intermediate level than for the beginning level.
3. The results from the paper-and-pencil tests on the use of past tense forms in obligatory contexts are generally consistent with the prediction of the AH, including the developmental claim (i.e., lower level learners more constrained by inherent aspect).

Apparently, these generalizations are not completely consistent with the patterns from L1 acquisition, which showed the sequence of development from prototypes (i.e., achievement verbs for past marking and activity verbs for progressive marking) to nonprototypes, as Shirai and Andersen (1995) showed. The next section, discusses this discrepancy.

DISCUSSION

This section attempts to make sense of the difference between the findings for L1 acquisition and for L2 acquisition of tense-aspect morphology. A consistent finding from L1 acquisition is that children acquiring English initially start with the prototype and then gradually expand the application of the inflections to non-prototypes (Bloom, Lifter, & Hafitz, 1980; Olsen, Weinberg, Lilly, & Drury, 1998; Shirai, 1991; Shirai & Andersen, 1995). This, however, was not always found in L2 acquisition. Although most of the L2 English studies reviewed here are consistent with the AH in that the prototypical combinations are more frequent than nonprototypical combinations at any particular level of development, the cross-sectional studies and longitudinal studies that analyzed production data did not support the hypothesized spread from prototype to nonprototypes (Bardovi-Harlig & Bergström, 1996; Lee, 2001; Robison, 1995; Rohde, 1996, especially for progressive). These studies indicate that the associations often strengthen as learners' proficiency level increases, in sharp contrast to the one-way relaxation of the initial restriction to the prototype observed in spontaneous production data of L1 English. In contrast, the cross-sectional studies in which the learners were tested for their ability to supply past tense for obligatory contexts in discrete point tasks did show data consistent with the AH. These studies almost always find the predicted accuracy order of achievement/accomplishment → activity → state for each proficiency group, and the accuracy rate increases as the proficiency level increases[10]; that is, lower level learners are more constrained by inherent aspect (Bardovi-Harlig, 1992; Bardovi-Harlig & Reynolds, 1995; Collins 2002).

I suggest the following scenario: The difference between L1 and L2 acquisition comes from the higher rote memory capacity of L2 learners who use memorized forms in early acquisition. In L1 and L2 acquisition, learners use both rote learning and analytic learning (Bates, Bretherton, & Snyder, 1988; Bloom et al., 1980; Karmiloff-Smith, 1986; Krashen & Scarcella, 1978; MacWhinney, 1978; Peters, 1983). Some researchers suggest that L2 learners with a higher memory capacity tend to rely more on the data-driven, rote-learning strategy in acquisition (Hakuta, 1974; Huang & Hatch, 1978; Klein, Dietrich, & Noyau, 1995). For example, Huang and Hatch (1978) reported that their 5-year-old Chinese learner acquiring English in the United States produced long sentences such as "It's time to eat and drink" as memorized phrases when his productive language was still lacking correct use of copula (e.g., "This... kite."). In conversation and writing tasks for L2 learners, where learners occasionally need to produce forms beyond their capacity, they sometimes access the form that is easily available to them (probably through rote memory). Because high frequency forms are easily activated in the learner's mental lexicon, learners tend to produce such forms more frequently. Thus, the weaker association between past and achievements or between progressive and activities observed with L2 learners at lower proficiency levels is due to the use of these high frequency forms that learners access and produce without really knowing or controlling the semantics of the morphological forms associated with them. In

[10] One exception is the learners in Bardovi-Harlig (1992), whose accuracy rates were lower at Level 6 than at Level 5. This is because the learners started to use more advanced constructions such as past progressive, present perfect, and past perfect. These new forms began to compete with the correct simple past form (as indicated in the tables in the original study).

other words, early on these forms are produced haphazardly before the actual form–meaning relationship is solidified.

Robison (1995) reported an example that supports this interpretation. He stated that an unexpectedly high correlation between achievement and progressive marking was due to the form going—a high frequency form in the input. He revealed that "the elevated application of -ing to punctual events thus appears to be artificially induced. With increasing proficiency level, this spurious inflation reverses to a deficit" (Robison, 1995, p. 357). Thus, L2 learners can easily produce inflected forms due to their higher memory capacity even when they are not sure about the semantics of the inflections.

However, this scenario cannot explain why in cross-sectional studies involving production data the prototypical association becomes stronger as the learner's proficiency increases. I argue that the increasing association is the result of developing form–meaning mapping based on L2 input, which is biased in the direction predicted by the hypothesis (the Distributional Bias Hypothesis, Andersen, 1993; Andersen & Shirai, 1994). Going beyond the initial haphazard production of the forms, learners begin to notice the association between past and telic meaning, and progressive and activity meaning. The haphazard production of past and progressive forms will decrease as a function of increasing proficiency, and as a result, relatively speaking, the ratio of prototypical use of these forms will increase.[11]

In contrast to production data, discrete-point paper-and-pencil tests of verb form manipulation yielded results consistent with the Aspect Hypothesis. In paper-and-pencil tests, it is not likely that a high frequency, rote-learned form is haphazardly produced because the communicative pressure is much weaker and the learner has much more time and the attention is not on meaning, but on form. Thus, the results may reflect the learners' semantic representations of tense-aspect morphology more directly.

A MULTIPLE-FACTOR ACCOUNT

The research reviewed here on the acquisition of English as L2 is consistent with the hypothesis that progressive markers are associated with activity verbs, and that past tense form is associated with achievement verbs, thus supporting the universal status of the prediction of the AH. However, some studies do not show a gradual spread from prototypical use to non-prototypical use, thus calling into question the developmental claim of the AH; that is, the phrases "learners first" or "at early stages" might need to be reconsidered.

How can the common trend and the deviation from it be explained? Because SLA is a complex process involving linguistic, cognitive, and social

[11] Note that in some studies reviewed here, prototypical combinations decrease again at the highest levels of proficiency (e.g., progressive marking in Bardovi-Harlig, 1998). This may be because the learners became more native-like as their proficiency increases and become more flexible in the use of inflection (see Salaberry, 1999, for similar results for Spanish L2).

factors interacting, it is probably most accurate to posit a multiple-factor account for the universal tendencies (and deviation) in tense-aspect acquisition. Although they are not mutually exclusive, two types of factors likely contribute to the acquisitional patterns: learner internal factors and learner external factors (Shirai, 2000, 2002; also Rohde, 2002). Learner internal factors include (a) universal predispositions on the part of learners, and (b) individual differences. The former is represented by the Language Bioprogram Hypothesis proposed by Bickerton (1980) or Basic Child Grammar proposed by Slobin (1985). Individual differences in past tense acquisition in L1 are reported by Bloom and Harner (1989), where some children do not follow the path predicted by the AH.[12] In L2 acquisition, another learner internal factor, (c) the learner's first language, appears to play an important role. Needless to say, (a) contributes to universal tendencies, whereas (b) and (c) contribute to the diversity. If universal factors are strong (i.e., if learners are equipped with a prelinguistic mapping bias), then there is a strong tendency to converge on the predicted pattern of acquisition. Whereas if (b) and (c) are strong, there will be much diversity across learners, although in the case of (c) such diversity will obtain only across learners with different L1s.

The learner external factors include (a) input and interaction both in L1 and L2 acquisition, and (b) instructional factors in the case of L2 acquisition, although (a) and (b) cannot be totally distinct in L2 because instruction more or less determines the type of input and interaction learners have. Regarding input, Shirai (1994) found that in L1 acquisition of English the difference in parental input clearly influences how children used progressive marking with state verbs. Regarding instructional effects, unfortunately there is no study that has seriously tested the effects of instruction on tense-aspect acquisition, especially concerning predictions 1–4 stated earlier.

These learner external factors appear to contribute to the predicted acquisition patterns. Input distribution in English appears to be congruent with the prediction of the AH, showing high correlations between telic verbs and past marking, and between activity verbs and progressive marking (Andersen, 1993; Andersen & Shirai, 1996; Rohde, 2002; Shirai & Andersen, 1995). In the case of instruction, most teachers' intuition is to teach the progressive marking with the action in progress meaning first, which results in higher concentration of progressive with activity verbs. This then may contribute to early acquisition of activity verbs (Shirai, 1997a). Thus, as far as the acquisition of English is concerned, universal factors, input factors, and instruction factors may all work together to produce the acquisition pattern predicted by the AH. Future research should address the issue of which factors are more important than others, and which are possibly unnecessary.

[12] Bloom and Harner (1989, p. 211) noted the case of a child, whose earliest use of past marking was not restricted to telic verbs, because of her conservatism in the area of verb inflections; that is, she did not use verb inflections until other aspects of her language were relatively well-developed, and once she started using the past tense form, it was already used with atelic verbs.

Regarding the role of L1, it is interesting to note that the pattern of development of Rocca's L1 Italian learners is highly consistent with the AH, especially in the development of past tense marking. Even though the acquisition of inflectional morphology is not heavily influenced by L1 transfer, there still is a strong effect of L1 (see Andersen, 1983; Sasaki, 1987; Shirai, 1992; Terauchi, 1994),[13] and therefore it is not surprising that L2 learners use L1 tense-aspect marking as a reference point in making form–meaning associations in L2 learning of similar markers. It should be noted here that among the four comparable child L2 longitudinal studies reviewed here, Italian and French have a clear perfective past marker, whereas Korean, German, and Dutch all have more full-fledged deictic past tense marking, which is further grammaticized along the perfective path (Bybee, Perkins, & Pagliuca, 1994). This may have contributed to the clear adherence to the AH by the Italian L1 children because Italian has a very strong perfective value, which attracts telic predicates. Of the L1 French children, SAH closely followed the prediction, whereas the other two learners did not. In the case of LEN, however, the first 3 recordings had only one or two tokens of past marked verbs, and when past marking was productive, at Time 4, all such verbs were telic, and therefore the result is consistent with the AH. Only MAG is a clear deviation from the pattern.

Regarding the progressive, the effect of L1 is unclear. Rohde (1996) found that early progressive was associated with achievements. His data may suggest that older children learning L2 English use the progressive marker with achievement verbs as a convenient modal marker for expressing intention in interactional contexts.[14] Because this kind of productive use of progressive with achievement verbs is not reported elsewhere, it is possible to suspect that this may be related to the lack of progressive marker in the learner's L1 (German). However, another study from a Russian learner, whose L1 lacks progressive marking, does not report such data and is clearly consistent with the AH (Gavruseva, 2002). Three other similar acquisition studies (child L2) reviewed here all involve L1s that have progressive markers (French, Dutch, Italian, Korean), but do not support the developmental prediction of the AH. Therefore, the lack of progressive marking may not be the factor that determines the compliance with the AH with respect to progressive marking. In any case, further research is necessary to explore the effect of L1.

[13] These studies argue for the contribution of L1 in the morpheme acquisition and accuracy orders by Japanese learners of English, which goes against Krashen's (1978) Natural Order Hypothesis. In particular, Terauchi (1994) reviewed all the available morpheme studies of Japanese L1 learners and showed that Japanese learners have good correlation among themselves, but not with Krashen's (1978) natural order. One exception to this trend was Makino (1981), which is often cited as support for Krashen's natural order.

[14] Rohde is not necessarily correct that these data suggest that tense is more important than aspect in L2 acquisition. Shirai and Kurono (1998) argued that most of the progressive achievements in Rohde's data are modal uses to indicate intention. Furthermore, whether such uses encode tense or modality may be impossible to determine given that the distinction between tense and modality is not discrete but continuous (especially future tense and modality of intention), as suggested by grammaticization theory (Bybee, et al., 1994).

Although these factors may effectively determine how learners create form–meaning mapping in tense-aspect acquisition, the additional factor of elicitation procedure (i.e., task) may also contribute to the variation, which is always a difficulty in interpreting L2 data. In L1 acquisition, where studies of English showed the clear spread from the prototype to nonprototypes, it may be the case that because natural interaction does not require children to perform beyond their capacity, their semantic representation may be more directly reflected. In contrast, L2 learners, as already discussed, often have to perform beyond their capacity by using rote-learned forms, and that may affect the degree of adherence to the prediction of the AH.

In terms of the process of form–meaning connections that learners make, if the previous scenario based on English acquisition data is correct, it can be assumed that both L1 and L2 learners make prototypical form–meaning associations (i.e., past tense form with [+telic] and [+punctual], progressive form with [-telic] and [+dynamic]) right from the beginning, but this is not necessarily observed in the case of L2 production data because L2 learners have a tendency to use rote-learned expressions regardless of the semantic representation, especially at the lower stages of developing proficiency. This restricted semantic representation will gradually approximate that of native speakers by gradual relaxation of the restriction to prototypical associations. The semantic association created by learners may be mediated by learners' L1.

Before claiming the validity of this scenario, however, it is still necessary to ask the fundamental question concerning the nature of data as a window to learners' semantic representations. Because L2 production tasks may not accurately access learners' semantic representation, it is necessary to test of this scenario further by using online experiments that may directly reflect learners' semantic representation (to be discussed later). This means developing cross-sectional and, if possible, longitudinal studies to test whether learners' meaning of past and progressive morphology is actually restricted at the lower level of proficiency and later approximates that of native speakers.

CONCLUSIONS: BEYOND ENGLISH DATA

This chapter reviews research on the L2 acquisition of English tense-aspect morphology to determine whether the prediction of the AH is supported by empirical studies available so far. The review suggests that the hypothesis is supported by most studies, but its developmental component—namely, the prediction that beginning learners are more restricted by inherent aspectual value than more advanced learners—may need to be revised, because cross-sectional and longitudinal studies that involve production data do not necessarily show such a restriction, or at least not to the extent that L1 data do. It is suggested that such deviation by the beginning learners comes from haphazard production of frequent forms based on rote learning because studies using paper-and-pencil tests do constitute supporting evidence for the developmental aspect of the hypothesis.

Regarding the role of L1 transfer, Japanese acquisition presents an interesting picture. As noted by Shirai and Kurono (1998) and Li and Shirai (2000, chap. 6), the Japanese imperfective marker *-te i-* denotes not only progressive but also resultative aspect, and if some universal predisposition is at work, learners should acquire progressive meaning, which is obtained (mainly) with activity verbs, more easily than resultative meaning, which is obtained with achievement verbs, because the latter is predicted to be, and in fact is, associated with past tense morphology. Most studies reviewed in Li and Shirai show the imperfective *-te i-* to be associated with activity verbs to denote progressive meaning. However, more recent research on Russian L1 learners of Japanese L2 found that they do not necessarily have an advantage for progressive meaning. Russian does not mark progressive aspect grammatically, whereas all the learners from earlier studies had an L1 that does mark progressive aspect grammatically. This possibility needs to be tested further to investigate the role of L1 in tense-aspect acquisition (see Shirai, 2002, for further discussion).

This chapter, which began as a section in Li and Shirai (2000), was originally prompted by Salaberry's (1999) L2 Spanish study, which clearly showed that the predicted prototypical association of perfective past and telic verbs strengthened with increased proficiency. Indeed, the review of English studies revealed that some production studies go against the developmental claim of the AH. One wonders, however, why Ramsay's (1990) cross-sectional study in L2 Spanish did show much stronger adherence to the AH. Shirai (1997b) argued that this difference is due to the low level of monitor use in Ramsay's study, which excluded apparent monitor overusers from the analysis. Shirai (1997b) further suggested that Salaberry's English L1 learners, in retelling a plot of a silent film, tried to map the semantics of L1 simple past tense marker onto L2 preterit morphology without its aspectual value, hence the initial lack of association of Spanish preterit with telic verbs. To test this hypothesis, a comprehensive review of L2 Spanish studies is also in order, focusing on the relationship between the level of monitor use and the adherence to the prediction of the AH.

So what can be said about the current state of the AH? It has been suggested that the acquisition pattern predicted by the AH is a universal of language acquisition (e.g., Shirai & Kurono, 1998). If "universal" is taken to mean "without exception," then the universal claim needs to be modified. However, the AH can still be treated as a universal tendency (McLaughlin, 1987, pp. 84–85) which most learners follow,[15] and the position here is that the prediction is still valid in the sense that it predicts semantic development of tense-aspect morphology, which may or may not be directly reflected in spontaneous production.

[15] See Gass and Selinker (2001, p. 151) for a discussion concerning counterexamples to universal predictions. They suggested that L2 acquisition is so complex that only when exceptions outweigh the rule should the prediction be modified.

One way to elicit the learner's semantic representation is online experiments. If learners' representation of pastness is semantically constrained, then there should be faster reaction times and higher accuracy for telic verbs than for atelic verbs in judgment tasks involving past tense. Collins and Segalowitz (2002) performed an experiment with judgment tasks involving simple past sentences, and found partial support for the AH. Similar studies can be performed for activity verbs and progressive markers. Also, conspicuously missing from L2 aspect research are comprehension studies. These studies may have an advantage in assessing learners' semantic representations more directly than the production tasks and offline written tests that are typically used in L2 research.

Finally, an important methodological issue must be considered. Bardovi-Harlig (2002) discussed two different analyses that have been used in the study on aspect: within-category analysis and across-category analysis. *Within-category analysis*, used in Bardovi-Harlig (1998) and elsewhere, asks how many tokens of each aspectual category (e.g., achievements, states, etc.) receives past marking, whereas *across-category analysis*, which is used in this chapter, asks how much of past marking consists of which aspectual category. She claimed that within-category analysis is more sensitive to developmental change than across-category analysis. Bardovi-Harlig's claim is probably true, but the fact remains that in L1 acquisition, the across-category analysis employed by Shirai (1991) clearly showed a developmental effect. Such an effect is missing in many L2 studies involving production data, although not in all (e.g., Rocca, 2002), and this needs to be explained. It appears that the inclusion of base forms in the equation in the within-category analysis is a key factor, because the rate of base forms is something that drastically changes across proficiency levels, which makes the within-category analysis much more sensitive to developmental change. However, further study of the differences between the two analytical methods often used in studies of tense-aspect acquisition is necessary.

ACKNOWLEDGMENTS

I thank Kathleen Bardovi-Harlig, Kevin Gregg, Hiromi Ozeki, Rafael Salaberry, Natsue Sugaya, and the editors of this volume for their helpful comments and discussions. All remaining errors are mine.

REFERENCES

Andersen, R. W. (1983). Transfer to somewhere. In S. M. Gass & L. Selinker (Eds.), *Language transfer in language learning* (pp. 177–201). Rowley, MA: Newbury House.

Andersen, R. W. (1989). La adquisición de la morfología verbal. *Lingüística, 1,* 89–141.

Andersen, R. W. (1991). Developmental sequences: The emergence of aspect marking in second language acquisition. In T. Huebner & C. A. Ferguson (Eds.), *Crosscurrents in second language acquisition and linguistic theories* (pp. 305–324). Amsterdam: Benjamins.

Andersen, R. W. (1993). Four operating principles and input distribution as explanations for underdeveloped and mature morphological systems. In K. Hyltenstam & A. Viborg (Eds.), *Progression and regression in language* (pp. 309–339). Cambridge, England: Cambridge University Press.

Andersen, R. W., & Shirai, Y. (1994). Discourse motivations for some cognitive acquisition principles. *Studies in Second Language Acquisition, 16*, 133–156.

Andersen, R. W., & Shirai, Y. (1996). Primacy of aspect in first and second language acquisition: The pidgin/creole connection. In W. C. Ritchie & T. K. Bhatia (Eds.), *Handbook of second language acquisition* (pp. 527–570). San Diego, CA: Academic Press.

Bardovi-Harlig, K. (1992). The relationship of form and meaning: A cross-sectional study of tense and aspect in the interlanguage of learners of English as a second language. *Applied Psycholinguistics, 13*, 253–278.

Bardovi-Harlig, K. (1998). Narrative structure and lexical aspect: Conspiring factors in second language acquisition of tense-aspect morphology. *Studies in Second Language Acquisition, 20*, 471–508.

Bardovi-Harlig, K. (2000). *Tense and aspect in second language acquisition: Form, meaning, and use.* Oxford, England: Blackwell.

Bardovi-Harlig, K. (2002). Analyzing aspect. In R. Salaberry & Y. Shirai (Eds.), *The L2 acquisition of tense-aspect morphology* (pp. 129–154). Amsterdam: Benjamins.

Bardovi-Harlig, K., & Bergström, A. (1996). The acquisition of tense and aspect in SLA and FLL: A study of learner narratives in English (SL) and French (FL). *Canadian Modern Language Review, 52*, 308–330.

Bardovi-Harlig, K., & Reynolds, D. W. (1995). The role of lexical aspect in the acquisition of tense and aspect. *TESOL Quarterly, 29*, 107–131.

Bates, E. A., Bretherton, I., & Snyder, L. (1988). *From first words to grammar: Individual differences and dissociable mechanisms.* Cambridge, England: Cambridge University Press.

Bickerton, D. (1981). *Roots of language.* Ann Arbor, MI: Karoma.

Bloom, L., & Harner, L. (1989). On the developmental contour of child language: A reply to Smith & Weist. *Journal of Child Language, 16*, 207–216.

Bloom, L., Lifter, K., & Hafitz, J. (1980). Semantics of verbs and the development of verb inflection in child language. *Language, 56*, 386–412.

Bybee, J. L., Perkins, R., & Pagliuca, W. (1994). *The evolution of grammar: Tense, aspect, and modality in the languages of the world.* Chicago: University of Chicago Press.

Collins, L. (2002). The roles of L1 influence and lexical aspect in the acquisition of temporal morphology. *Language Learning, 52*, 43–94.

Collins, L. & Segalowitz, N. (2002, April). *Representing and accessing knowledge in a second language: the case of temporal morphology.* Paper presented at the annual meeting of the American Association for Applied Linguistics, Salt Lake City, UT.

Erbaugh, M. (1978). Acquisition of temporal and aspectual distinction in Mandarin. *Papers and Reports on Child Language Development, 15*, 30–37.

Gass, S., & Selinker, L. (2001). *Second language acquisition: An introductory course.* (2nd ed.). Mahwah, NJ: Lawrence Erlbaum Associates.

Gavruseva, E. (2002). Is there primacy of aspect in child L2 English? *Bilingualism: Language and Cognition, 5*, 109–130.

Hakuta, K. (1974). Prefabricated patterns and the emergence of structure in second language acquisition. *Language Learning, 24*, 287–297.

Housen, A. (1995). *It's about time: The acquisition of temporality in English as a second language in a multilingual educational context.* Unpublished doctoral dissertation, University of Brussels, Brussels, Belgium.

Housen, A. (2002). The development of tense-aspect in English as a second language and the variable influence of inherent aspect. In R. Salaberry & Y. Shirai (Eds.), *The L2 acquisition of tense-aspect morphology* (pp. 155–197). Amsterdam: Benjamins.

Huang, C. (1993). *Distributional bias of verb morphology in native and non-native English discourse.* Unpublished master's thesis, University of California, Los Angeles.

Huang, C. (1999). Tense-aspect marking by L2 learners of English and native English speakers: Inherent lexical aspect and unitary vs. repeated situation types. *Issues in Applied Linguistics, 10*, 113–130.

Huang, J., & Hatch, E. (1978). A Chinese child's acquisition of English. In E. M. Hatch (Ed.), *Second language acquisition: A book of readings* (pp. 118–131). Rowley, MA: Newbury House.

Karmiloff-Smith, A. (1986). Stage/structure versus phase/process in modeling linguistic and cognitive development. In I. Levin (Ed.), *Stage and structure: Reopening the debate* (pp. 164–190). Norwood, NJ: Ablex.

Klein, W., Dietrich, R., & Noyau, C. (1995). Conclusions. In R. Dietrich, W. Klein, & C. Noyau (Eds.), *The acquisition of temporality in a second language* (pp. 261–280). Amsterdam: Benjamins.

Krashen, S. D. (1978). The monitor model for second language acquisition. In R. Gingras (Ed.), *Second language acquisition and foreign language teaching* (pp. 1-26). Arlington: Center for Applied Linguistics.

Krashen, S., & Scarcella, R. (1978). On routines and patterns in language acquisition and performance. *Language Learning, 28,* 151–167.

Kumpf, L. (1984). Temporal systems and universality in interlanguage: A case study. In F. R. Eckman, L. H. Bell, & D. Nelson (Eds.), *Universals of second language acquisition* (pp. 132–143). Rowley, MA: Newbury House.

Lee, E. (2001). Interlanguage development by two Korean speakers of English with a focus on temporality. *Language Learning, 51*, 591–633.

Li, P., & Shirai, Y. (2000). *The acquisition of lexical and grammatical aspect.* Berlin: Mouton de Gruyter.

MacWhinney, B. (1978). Processing a first language: The acquisition of morphophonology. *Monographs of the Society for Research in Child Development 43* (Serial No. 174).

Makino, T. (1981). *Acquisition order of English morphemes by Japanese adolescents.* Tokyo: Shinozaki Shoin.

McLaughlin, B. (1987). *Theories of second language learning.* London: Edward Arnold.

Olsen, M. B., Weinberg, A., Lilly, J., & Drury, J. (1998). Mapping innate lexical features to grammatical categories: Acquisition of English *-ing* and *-ed.* In M. Gernsbacher & S. Derry (Eds.), *Proceedings of the 20th annual conference of the Cognitive Science Society.* Mahwah, NJ: Lawrence Erlbaum Associates.

Peters, A. M. (1983). *The units of language acquisition.* Cambridge, England: Cambridge University Press.

Ramsay, V. (1990). *Developmental stages in the acquisition of the perfective and the imperfective aspects by classroom L2 learners of Spanish.* Unpublished doctoral dissertation, University of Oregon, Eugene.

Robison, R. (1990). The primacy of aspect: Aspectual marking in English interlanguage. *Studies in Second Language Acquisition, 12,* 315–330.

Robison, R. (1995). The Aspect Hypothesis revisited: A cross-sectional study of tense and aspect marking in interlanguage. *Applied Linguistics, 16*, 344–370.

Rocca, S. (2002). Lexical aspect in child second language acquisition of temporal morphology: A bidirectional study. In R. Salaberry & Y. Shirai (Eds.), *The L2 acquisition of tense-aspect morphology* (pp. 245–280). Amsterdam: Benjamins.

Rohde, A. (1996). The aspect hypothesis and the emergence of tense distinctions in naturalistic L2 acquisition. *Linguistics, 34,* 1115–1137.

Rohde, A. (2002). The aspect hypothesis in naturalistic acquisition: What uninflected and non-target-like verb forms in early interlanguage tell us. In R. Salaberry & Y. Shirai (Eds.), *The L2 acquisition of tense-aspect morphology* (pp. 199–220). Amsterdam: Benjamins.

Salaberry, R. (1999). The development of past tense verbal morphology in classroom L2 Spanish. *Applied Linguistics, 20,* 151–178.

Salaberry, R. (2000). The acquisition of English past tense in an instructional setting. *System, 28,* 135–152.

Sasaki, M. (1987). Is Uguisu an exceptional case of "idiosyncratic variation"? Another counterexample to the "natural order" [in Japanese]. *Chugoku-Shikoku Academic Society of Education Research Bulletin, 32,* 170–174.

Shirai, Y. (1991). *Primacy of aspect in language acquisition: Simplified input and prototype.* Unpublished doctoral dissertation, University of California, Los Angeles.

Shirai, Y. (1992). Conditions on transfer: A connectionist approach. *Issues in Applied Linguistics, 3,* 91–120.

Shirai, Y. (1994). On the overgeneralization of progressive marking on stative verbs: Bioprogram or input? *First Language, 14,* 67–82.

Shirai, Y. (1995). Tense-aspect marking by L2 learners of Japanese. In D. MacLaughlin & S. McEwen (Eds.), *Proceedings of the 19th annual Boston University Conference on Language Development,* (Vol. 2, pp. 575–586). Somerville, MA: Cascadilla Press.

Shirai, Y. (1997a). Linguistic theory and research: Implications for second language teaching. In G. R. Tucker & D. Corson (Ed.), *The encyclopedia of language and education, Vol. 4: Second language education* (pp. 1–9). Dordrecht: Kluwer Academic.

Shirai, Y. (1997b, October). *The L2 acquisition of Spanish and the Aspect Hypothesis.* Paper presented at the colloquium "The acquisition of aspect in natural and academic L2 Spanish" at the 17th annual Second Language Research Forum, Michigan State University.

Shirai, Y. (2000, September). The aspect hypothesis: A universal of SLA? Paper presented at the 20th Second Language Research Forum, University of Wisconsin, Madison.

Shirai, Y. (2002). The Aspect Hypothesis in SLA and the acquisition of Japanese. *Acquisition of Japanese as a Second Language, 5,* 42–61.

Shirai, Y., & Andersen, R. W. (1995). The acquisition of tense/aspect morphology: A prototype account. *Language, 71*, 743–762.

Shirai, Y., & Kurono, A. (1998). The acquisition of tense/aspect marking in Japanese as a second language. *Language Learning, 48,* 245–279.

Slabakova, R. (2001). *Telicity in the second language.* Amsterdam: Benjamins.

Slobin, D. I. (1985). Crosslinguistic evidence for the Language-Making Capacity. In D. I. Slobin (Ed.), *The crosslinguistic study of language acquisition, Vol 2: Theoretical issues* (pp. 1157–1249). Hillsdale, NJ: Laurence Erlbaum Associates.

Smith, C. S. (1997). *The parameter of aspect* (2nd ed). Dordrecht: Kluwer Academic.

Stauble, A. (1984). A comparison of the Spanish-English and Japanese-English interlanguage continuum. In R.W. Andersen (Ed.), *Second languages: A cross-linguistic perspective* (pp. 323-353). Rowley, MA: Newbury House.

Terauchi, M. (1994). Keitaiso no syuutoku [The acquisition of morphology]. In SLA Kenkyukai (Ed.), *Daini gengo syuutoku riron ni motozuku saisin no eigo kyooiku* [Current English language teaching based on second language acquisition theory] (pp. 24–48). Tokyo: Taishukan.

Vendler, Z. (1957). Verbs and times. *Philosophical Review, 66*, 143–160.

Wenzell, V. E. (1989). Transfer of aspect in the English oral narratives of native Russian speakers. In H. W. Dechert & M. Raupach (Eds.), *Transfer in language production* (pp. 71–97). Norwood, NJ: Ablex.

II
Evidence and Impact

CHAPTER 6
The Emergence of Grammaticalized Future Expression in Longitudinal Production Data

Kathleen Bardovi-Harlig
Indiana University

Second language tense-aspect systems have proven a fruitful area of study of form–meaning associations. Some studies have demonstrated that second language learners show a mastery of form that exceeds their mastery of target-language form–meaning associations (Bardovi-Harlig, 1992a; Dietrich, Klein, & Noyau, 1995). Other studies have focused on the temporal semantics of interlanguage, either beginning with meaning and investigating what forms learners use to express it (the meaning-oriented approach) or beginning with form and investigating what meanings the forms take on as interlanguage develops (the form-oriented approach; see Shirai, chap. 5 in this vol.). Both approaches have resulted in a growing understanding of form–meaning associations in interlanguage and how they develop and change with continued exposure to the second language. This chapter uses meaning-oriented approach to investigate expressions of futurity.

The future, like the past (which is well-researched in second language acquisition), is displaced temporally from the here and now. Semantically, the reference to "not here, not now" comes about when speech time is displaced from event time. In the past, the time of speech follows the time of the event, or E → S (Reichenbach, 1947). The future can be represented in Reichenbachian terms as speech time preceding event time, or S → E. However, temporality is only one of the concepts that makes up the future. Crosslinguistic research on tense-aspect systems agrees that, unlike the purely temporal relationships of the past and the present, the future also encompasses modality. Modality is often concerned with the speaker's assumptions or assessment of possibilities, and in most cases, it indicates the speaker's confidence (or lack of confidence) in the truth of the proposition expressed; this is epistemic modality (Coates, 1983, 1987; Lyons, 1977; Palmer, 1986; Perkins, 1983). Modality is also concerned with obligation and necessity; this is deontic modality. Both are related to the expression of the future. The modal reading of the future may be due in part to that fact that, as Dahl (1985) noted, "We cannot perceive the future directly or 'remember' it" (p. 103), so that each invocation of the future is also an invocation of modality that includes possibility/probability, intention, and desire or volition (Bybee, 1985). As Dahl (1985) observed,

> Normally, when we talk about the future, we are either talking about someone's plans, intentions or obligations, or we are making a prediction or extrapolation from the present state of the world. As a direct consequence, a sentence which refers to the future will almost always differ also modally from a

> sentence with non-future time reference. This is the reason why the distinction between tense and mood becomes blurred when it comes to the future. (p. 103)

Of the enumerated modal readings associated with the future, linguists agree that the most common crosslinguistically is intentionality (Bybee, 1985; Bybee, Perkins, & Pagliuca, 1994; Dahl, 1985; Fleischman, 1982). In fact, Dahl (1985) included intentionality as part of the prototype of the future, a characterization supported by Bybee et al. (1994). In addition, Dahl's crosslinguistic survey shows that the most typical uses of future involve actions that are planned by the speaker of the sentence. (This turns out to be a salient feature of the future in learner journals.) Thus, in any investigation of the expression of the concept of the future, expect to see a range of modal as well as future expression. This is reflected in child first language acquisition (e.g., Fletcher, 1979; Pawłowska, 1999). In this way, studies on the acquisition of future expand SLA inquiry from the domain of tense-aspect systems to the TMA (tense-mood-aspect) systems investigated in typological studies.

Sequences of Acquisition in the Expression of the Past

The most thoroughly explored area of tense-aspect development is temporal expression related to the past. Past research has identified three main stages of development: pragmatic, lexical, and morphological (Bardovi-Harlig, 2000; Dietrich, et al., 1995; Meisel, 1987). In the earliest stage of temporal expression, the pragmatic stage, there is no explicit reference to time or temporal relations. Learners establish temporal reference in four ways: by relying on the contribution of their fellow speakers (scaffolded discourse), through reference inferred from a particular context (implicit reference), by contrasting events, and by following chronological order in narration (Meisel, 1987; Schumann, 1987). In the lexical stage, reference to the past is first expressed explicitly through the use of lexical expressions, including adverbials (e.g., yesterday, then, and after) and connectives (e.g., and, because, and so) (Meisel, 1987). Following the adverbial-only stage, verbal morphology appears. The morphological stage can itself be viewed as a series of lesser stages as tense marking becomes an increasingly reliable indicator of temporal reference. All learners, instructed as well as uninstructed, go through the pragmatic and lexical stages. Some learners also go through the morphological stage (see Bardovi-Harlig, 2000, chap. 6).

The Target Language: Future in English

It is not uncommon for languages to have multiple means for expressing the future. English is no exception to this observation, but this propensity for multiple futures extends beyond Indo-European languages. As Bybee et al. (1994) argued, this is likely due to the historical development and shifts between the modal and future categories. In addition to a synthetic or *will*-future as in Example 1, many languages have a future derived from a verb of motion, typically come or go as in Example 2. These are called the *go*-future by Bybee and her colleagues. The future is also often expressed by the present with an adverb as in Examples 3–5.

1 I will leave for Spain tomorrow. (will-future)
2 I am going to leave for Spain tomorrow. (go-future)
3 I leave for Spain tomorrow. (futurate: pres + adverb)
4 I am leaving for Spain tomorrow. (pres prog)
5 Maria is to sing in Aida tomorrow night.

As Comrie (1985) pointed out, the use of the present with future reference refers to scheduled events. It rains tomorrow does not normally have future interpretation. Similarly as Bybee et al. (1994) further argued, it is not only the present, but the use of present with a future adverb that act together to report a planned event, because "I fly to Chicago" without the adverb cannot be used to report a planned event.[1]

With two major forms, the *will*-future and the *go*-future, and three minor forms in the target language (including the *is to* construction in Example 5)—plus numerous expressions of intentionality—what do the early stages of expression of futurity look like?

This study addresses the following questions for L2 English:

1. How is futurity expressed in interlanguage?
   (a) Beginning with the concept of futurity as defined in the crosslinguistic semantic literature, what forms are associated with that concept?
   (b) How often are each of the forms used to convey futurity?
2. What is the order of emergence of expressions of futurity relative to each other?
3. What factors or principles might account for the form–meaning associations found in the interlanguage of learners of English?

This study continues the analysis of the interlanguage development of 16 ESL learners. Over the course of many analyses, the development of their system of past-time reference has been described from different perspectives, including form-oriented frameworks documenting the emergence and development of the simple past, past progressive, present perfect, and pluperfect, and from meaning-oriented approaches documenting the use of various linguistic devices, including adverbials, tense-aspect morphology, and other linguistic means to express temporal concepts. (These findings are summarized in Bardovi-Harlig, 2000.) This study was designed to answer the previous

[1] The adverb may occur in an interlocutor's turn as in "What's the plan for tomorrow?" "I fly to Chicago."

questions and as a first step toward a description of the tense-mood-aspect system of these learners that includes future as well as past reference.

METHOD

Sixteen learners representing four language backgrounds (5 Arabic, 6 Japanese, 2 Korean, and 3 Spanish) participated in a longitudinal study; the mean length of observation was 11.5 months, ranging from 7 to 17.5 months. The learners were enrolled in the Intensive English Program, Center for English Language Training at Indiana University. The learners were beginners and placed in the first level of instruction out of 6 levels.[2] They attended classes 23 hours a week, receiving instruction in listening and speaking, reading, writing, and grammar. They were in a mixed language environment (R. Ellis, 1990), receiving instruction in the host environment, with access to the ambient language, although they differed individually in their patterns of contact with native speakers and with other non-native speakers of different first language backgrounds. The learners also showed individual differences in rates of development and eventual proficiency (Bardovi-Harlig, 2000).

The progress of the learners was monitored for the purposes of data collection during each 7 week session that they attended classes. During the observation period, 1,576 written texts and 175 oral texts were collected. The majority of the written texts consisted of journal entries (1,101); an additional 370 texts were compositions, 73 were essay exams, and 32 were elicited narratives based on silent films. The oral texts consisted of 102 guided conversational interviews supplemented by 73 elicited narratives based on silent films and the ensuing conversations.

These language samples are examples of authentic language use, produced by the learners in the course of their ESL studies. The journals, which comprise the majority of the written samples, were completely up to the learners; the topics of the essays and film retells were determined by the teachers and the researcher, respectively, but what learners wrote and how they wrote it was up to them. The same holds true for the oral samples. There were no tasks that controlled the production of any particular form (as opposed to topics). As a result of the topics that the learners wrote or talked about, as well as the number and length of journal entries and compositions completed, the number of tokens of tense-aspect forms varies across learners. This is particularly true of the instances of future expression because the goal of the study for which the longitudinal data were collected was to study the expression of the past.

A second source of data was the teaching logs completed by participating grammar and writing instructors. The teaching logs recorded the topic(s) of instruction, classroom activities, type of feedback, homework, and

[2] See Bardovi-Harlig (2000) for fuller descriptions of the individual learners, especially chapters 3 and 6.

page numbers of lessons in the textbooks, as well as copies of original materials created by the instructors (Bardovi-Harlig, 2000).

ANALYSIS

The accumulated language sample for each learner was analyzed. All future-time contexts were identified independently by two experienced coders (the researcher and her assistant) at 95% interrater reliability. Disagreements were resolved by discussion. The 1,576 written texts included 2,573 future contexts, and the 175 oral texts, 1,170 future contexts.[3] Each predicate that was supplied in future-time contexts was coded for the marking of the verb, lexical markers, and its syntactic environment, analogous to the studies of the past conducted in the same corpus (see Bardovi-Harlig, 1992b, 1994, 2000). These categories were generated by the analysis of the interlanguage rather than by applying target-language categories. Verbal markers included morphology (*will, going to*, present, progressive, base forms), modals (other than *will*; especially, *can, can't*), and verbs that encode the future lexically (henceforth, *lexical futures*, e.g., *want to, have to, like to, hope to*). Lexical markers include adverbials (e.g., *tomorrow, soon, in the future, when I am old*), nouns (*this year, this weekend*), and modal indicators that are syntactically distinct from modals (*maybe, I think*; see Salsbury, 2000). Syntactic environments included main clauses and subordinate contexts created by *if-then*, verbs of cognition (e.g., *think that*), and hope that. Adverb to verb ratios (Bardovi-Harlig, 1992b) were also calculated for the entire sample and for each category. This chapter focuses on the verbal means of expressing the future.

The year was divided into 24 half-month periods with the first sampling period of a month running from the 1st to the 15th of the month (indicated as T3.0, for example) and the second sampling period from the sixteenth to the end of the month (indicated as T3.5). All language samples are identified by a pseudonym, time of production, type of sample, and L1 of the learner.

RESULTS

This section addresses three questions: What expressions are used to express the future? What is the frequency of occurrence of the expressions? What is the order of emergence?

[3] There is a higher concentration of future expressions in the oral texts than in the written texts, suggesting that the frequency of topics may be different in the conversational interviews (even considering the oral film retell tasks) than the journals or compositions that make up the majority of the texts.

Expressions of Futurity and Frequency of Occurrence

The analysis of future-time contexts showed that in these contexts five main categories of verb-level marking occurred (Table 6.1). These are *will, going to,* base/present, progressive, and lexical futures. As discussed in the literature on the past, base and present forms cannot be distinguished from each other in English unless they occur in a third person singular context. The problem of distinguishing base from present is particularly relevant in this corpus where the majority of the future statements are made by the learners about themselves, resulting in the use of first person. Hence, in this corpus, the present and base are treated as a single category, base/present. In addition, from a target-language perspective, there are unexpected uses of other verbal morphology and modals, which were grouped together as "other" in Table 6.1.

As Table 6.1 shows, the dominant form in both the oral and written sample is *will* at 53%, and 60% of all future-oriented utterances, respectively. A distant second are lexical futures used in 22% of the written and 16% of the oral future contexts. This category is dominated by *hope to, want to, have to, like to.* These expressions clearly convey upcoming events and at the same time capture the modal flavor of the future. Occurring only half as often as the lexical futures, *going to* occupies third place for frequency of production in the written corpus.

The distribution of expression of futurity exhibited by the group is also typical of the individual learners (Table 6.2). Table 6.2 lists the learners in the order of the highest to lowest creators of future contexts within a single first language group. *Will* is the dominant form of future expression in the written corpus for all learners except Khaled. Khaled's use of the lexical futures exceeds his use of *will* in writing only. In conversation, *will* is the dominant form for most learners, with lexical futures showing equal or greater use in the production samples of Hiromi, Noriko, and Idechi. Every learner but one (Noriko) attempts at least one token of *going to* in the written and oral corpora combined. As in Table 6.1, Table 6.2 lists the reduced forms of *gonna* and the contraction *'ll* separately from *going to* and *will*, respectively. Only five learners used *gonna* and only in the oral sample. Two learners account for 26 of the 33 tokens. Four learners attempted at least one token of *'ll* in the oral corpus: One of those four who did not use the contraction when speaking (Noriko) had the single highest use rate in the written corpus. She produced a total of 20 written tokens, half of the total 41 used by the group. This suggests that the contractions may not be fully integrated into the grammar as (oral) variants of *going to* and *will*, respectively. For now, they are considered to belong to different categories.

Table 6.1. Expressions of futurity: Group totals for oral and written samples

	Will	*'ll*	*Going to*	*Gonna*	Base/ Pres	Prog	Lexical Future	Other	Total
Written	1370	41	244	0	132	42	559	185	2573
(%)	(53)	(1.5)	(10)	(0)	(5)	(1.5)	(22)	(7)	(100)
Oral	702	32	49	33	98	12	183	61	1170
(%)	(60)	(3)	(4)	(3)	(8)	(1)	(16)	(5)	(100)

Table 6.2. Individual Inventories by Learner

Corpus	Learner	L1	Pred	*Will*	*Going to*	Base	Prog	*Gonna*	*'ll*	Lexical Future	Other
Written	Guillermo	Sp	214	96	25	17	10	0	0	39	27
	Carlos	Sp	212	182	14	1	0	0	4	6	5
	Eduardo	Sp	193	103	30	7	8	0	3	36	6
	Khaled	Ar	269	81	41	20	2	0	0	114	11
	Saleh	Ar	184	137	3	5	1	0	0	28	10
	Abdullah	Ar	130	87	5	5	0	0	0	12	21
	Zayed	Ar	123	104	6	2	0	0	3	0	8
	Hamad	Ar	84	61	4	0	0	0	0	11	8
	Noriko	Jp	222	106	0	13	1	0	20	62	20
	Kazuhiro	Jp	163	67	11	13	2	0	0	57	13
	Hiromi	Jp	154	62	25	7	3	0	8	44	5
	Toshihiro	Jp	139	55	23	5	8	0	2	32	14
	Satoru	Jp	137	54	31	8	1	0	0	30	13
	Idechi	Jp	72	28	1	14	0	0	0	16	13
	Ji-An	Ko	174	77	21	10	6	0	1	50	9
	Sang Wook	Ko	103	70	4	5	0	0	0	22	2
	TOTAL		2573	1370	244	132	42	0	41	559	185
Oral											
	Guillermo	Sp	59	23	0	3	1	0	1	16	15
	Carlos	Sp	212	175	12	2	1	0	1	18	3
	Eduardo	Sp	28	10	7	2	1	3	0	5	0
	Khaled	Ar	80	48	4	1	1	12	7	5	2
	Saleh	Ar	137	121	0	1	0	0	8	5	2
	Abdullah	Ar	130	53	1	53	1	0	1	2	19
	Zayed	Ar	68	50	1	1	0	3	1	9	3
	Hamad	Ar	162	108	7	6	2	14	5	18	2
	Noriko	Jp	44	19	0	3	0	1	0	19	2
	Kazuhiro	Jp	33	14	0	3	0	0	4	11	1
	Hiromi	Jp	72	22	9	1	1	0	1	34	4
	Toshihiro	Jp	18	4	0	0	2	0	0	7	5
	Satoru	Jp	30	11	7	3	1	0	0	8	0
	Idechi	Jp	39	12	0	10	0	0	1	15	1
	Ji-An	Ko	37	16	1	9	1	0	1	7	2
	Sang Wook	Ko	21	16	0	0	0	0	1	4	0
	TOTAL		1170	702	49	98	12	33	32	183	61

Note. Pred = Predicates, Ar = Arabic, Jp = Japanese, Ko = Korean, Sp = Spanish.

Focusing exclusively on the grammaticalized markers of the future that occur in the corpus, namely, *will, going to*, base/pres, and present progressive, reveals an even greater disparity in the rates of use of grammaticalized means. Table 6.3 shows that *will* clearly dominates the grammatical means for expression of future. *Going to* is arguably the only other grammatical form that is acquired specifically for the expression of future. The base form(s) exist with the first verbs in interlanguage, and although the present progressive is acquired very early in interlanguage (the morpheme studies place *–ing* among the earliest morphemes acquired; Krashen 1977), it is rarely used by the learners to express the future (as Table 6.3 shows).

Will outnumbers *going to* 5.5:1 in the written sample, and 14:1 in the oral sample. In comparison, Longman's *Corpus Grammar* (Biber, Johansson, Leech, Conrad, & Finegan, 1999, p. 489, Table 6.6) reports a ratio of about 2.5 *will* to 1 *going to* (or 5,600 to 2,200 occurrences per million words) in conversation in British English, and approximately 1.6 to 1 (4,800 to 3,000 occurrences per million words) in American English conversation (p. 488, Fig. 6.10). This comparison suggests the degree to which *going to* is underrepresented in the interlanguage of these learners.[4]

Returning to the individual learner profiles, Table 6.2 shows that whereas there is widespread use of *will*, the use of *going to* is more restricted. The learners fall naturally into two groups. Eight of the learners used *going to* 11 or fewer times in the written and oral uses combined. Eight learners showed 22 or more uses, ranging from 22 uses (Ji-An) to 45 (Khaled). The group that shows higher rates of use includes learners from each of the first languages represented in the study (Arabic, Japanese, Korean, and Spanish). No learner's use of *going to* reaches the frequency of use of *will*.

The rates of use in this section represent usage totals for the duration of the study. The next section considers the learners' individual longitudinal profiles.

Table 6.3. Grammaticalized Expressions of Futurity: Group Totals for Oral and Written Samples

	Will	*Going to*	Base/Pres	Progressive	Total
Written	1370	244	132	42	1788
(%)	(77)	(14)	(7)	(2)	(100)
Oral	702	49	98	12	861
(%)	(82)	(6)	(11)	(1)	(100)

[4] Studies of production data for child L1 English do not report an acquisition order for *will* and *going to*. However, Broen and Santema (1983) report that children aged 3,6 to 5,5 show no systematic difference in comprehension of *will* and *going to*. The production data of Gee and Savasir (1985) show that two children ages 3,2 to 3,5 showed a predominance of *gonna* over *will* (214 to 112), in contrast to the patterns found in the speech and writing of these adult second language learners and among native speakers in the corpus studies. This may be related as much to the children's social and cognitive development as to their linguistic development.

Order of Emergence

The usage rates show that learners use more tokens of *will* than *going to* overall. What is the order of emergence of these grammaticalized expressions of future? Order of emergence is used to track when learners begin to use a form (Bardovi-Harlig, 2000). Figure 6.1 records the order of emergence of the grammaticalized expressions of futurity for each learner. In order for a form (*will, 'll, going to, gonna*, or progressive as future) to be entered on Fig. 6.1, a learner's production samples had to show that form used in future contexts with at least three distinct verbs (i.e., types rather than tokens). In the case of *going to* and *gonna,* some learners did not reach three distinct uses by the end of the observation period, but did attempt some use of the forms. These cases are indicated as GOING TO or GONNA with a numeral (1 or 2) in parentheses. Thus, learners with limited numbers of *go*-future tokens are included on the grid. The use of three types is more conservative than Pienemann's (1998) use of one token to mark emergence. It is important to bear in mind that emergence is not acquisition: Emergence marks the onset of productive use, not an end point.

Fourteen of the 16 learners clearly show emergence of *will* before the *go*-future. The other two learners (Toshihiro and Hiromi) show emergence within the same 15-day period. One event in particular is worth noting. At T3.0, 6 of the learners had an exam in which they were asked to write a sentence in the future. (This activity is discussed later.) If the first tokens of *going to* occurred in the exam, "going to EXAM" is entered on the grid. Spontaneous uses of *going to* are recorded as they occurred. The use of "0 gonna" (see Hamad, T2.0) indicates the use of gonna without *be*. By this analysis many learners show emergence of a form–meaning association, whereas the usage figures in Table 6.2 show that very few forms other than *will* actually occur. Figure 6.1 illustrates the spread and frequency of going to longitudinally. Figure 6.2 shows that learners begin the use of a new form gradually, and that usage is spread out over many months. It also reports types as well as tokens in order to reflect the range of lexical items with which learners use the *go*-future.

The order of emergence found for these learners was also reported for Lavinia, the single most advanced English learner in the European Science Foundation corpus (Dietrich, et al., 1995). Although the timing of emergence in Lavinia's corpus is somewhat delayed when compared to the present group of learners, the order is the same as the learners in this study. At about 8 months, Lavinia showed an isolated use of *shall.* At 16 months, Klein reported that "future is now often marked by *will* or *shall*" (1995, p. 45). The first occurrence of the prospective *going-to* occurs at month 17, and by the 18th month they report that "there are many forms of the prospective, still in the present (*is-going-to*)" (p. 46).

Learner	Month 0.5	1	1.5	2	2.5	3	3.5	4	4.5	5	5.5	6	6.5	7	7.5
Guillermo Spanish			WILL								GOING TO				PROG AS FUTURE
Carlos Spanish		WILL		GOING TO WRITE	GOING TO									'LL	
Eduardo Spanish	WILL		GOING TO												GONNA
Khaled Arabic	WILL											GOING TO			
Saleh Arabic					WILL	EXAM (WILL)							'LL		
Abdullah Arabic			WILL			EXAM (GOING TO)									
Zayed Arabic				WILL								GOING TO			GONNA
Hamad Arabic				WILL 0 GONNA		EXAM GOING TO							GOING TO GONNA 'LL		
Noriko Japanese		WILL													
Kazuhiro Japanese		WILL			GOING TO										
Hiromi Japanese						WILL/'LL EXAM GOING TO									
Toshihiro Japanese			WILL GOING TO												
Satoru Japanese			WILL												
Idechi Japanese			WILL										GOING TO (1)		
Ji-An Korean		WILL				EXAM GOING TO		GOING TO							
Sang Wook Korean					WILL	EXAM (GOING TO)									

Fig. 6.1. The emergence of grammaticalized future expression, figure continues on next page.

Learner	Month 8	8.5	9	9.5	10	10.5	11	11.5	12	12.5	13	13.5	14	14.5	15
Guillermo Spanish															
Carlos Spanish															
Eduardo Spanish															
Khaled Arabic	GONNA														
Saleh Arabic														GOING TO (1)	T16.5 GOING TO
Abdullah Arabic															
Zayed Arabic		'LL													
Hamad Arabic					GOING TO (2)										
Noriko Japanese															
Kazuhiro Japanese			'LL												
Hiromi Japanese															
Toshihiro Japanese															
Satoru Japanese															
Idechi Japanese															
Ji-An Korean															
Sang Wook Korean															

Fig. 6.1. The emergence of grammaticalized future expression, continued.

Learner	Month 0.5	1.0	1.5	2.0	2.5	3.0	3.5	4.0	4.5	5.0	5.5	6.0	6.5	7.0	7.5
Guillermo Spanish		1									6	2		4	7
Carlos Spanish				5 Oral 1	5	1 Oral 4						1 Oral 3		1 Oral 2	
Eduardo Spanish			7	4	9	4 Oral 1				4		2 Oral 3			Oral 3
Khaled Arabic					2					1	5	Oral 2		3	4
Saleh Arabic						Exam (0)									
Abdullah Arabic						4 Exam (3)									
Zayed Arabic										1	1	2 Oral 2	1		1
Hamad Arabic			Oral 1			2 Exam (2)			Oral 1						
Noriko Japanese															
Kazuhiro Japanese	2				1					3		1		2	1
Hiromi Japanese						7 Exam (5)	3	2	Oral 4	1 Oral 1	9	Oral 1			
Toshihiro Japanese		2	2	3	1					6					
Satoru Japanese						3	1 write			2 (1 write)		Oral 1		2 write Oral 2	6 write Oral 4
Idechi Japanese													1		
Ji-An Korean						5 Exam (3)		8	4		3	1 Oral 1			
Sang Wook Korean						4 Exam (4)									

Fig. 6.2. **The emergence and use of *going to* in number of tokens per half-month, figure continues on next page.**

Learner	8.0	8.5	9.0	9.5	10.0	10.5	11.0	11.5	12.0	12.5	13.0	13.5	14.0	14.5	15.0	Total	Tok	Typ
Guillermo	4	1														W	25	11
Spanish																O	0	0
Carlos		1														W	14	7
Spanish	Oral 2															O	12	10
Eduardo																W	30	17
Spanish																O	7	6
Khaled	1		11	2 write	5	1 write	5	1								W	41	12
Arabic			(10 write)	Oral 1	(2 write)											O	3	3
Saleh														1	T16.5	W	3	3
Arabic															2	O	0	0
Abdullah					1											W	5	3
Arabic												Oral 1				O	1	1
Zayed																W	6	4
Arabic																O	1	1
Hamad				1	1											W	4	4
Arabic										Oral 4				Oral 1		O	7	6
Noriko																W	0	0
Japanese																O	0	0
Kazuhiro				1												W	11	6
Japanese																O	0	0
Hiromi				2	1											W	25	18
Japanese		Oral 1			Oral 2											O	9	6
Toshihiro					1	5	1	2								W	23	15
Japanese																O	0	0
Satoru	3 write	5 write	4 write	3 write	2 write			1 write								W	31	4
Japanese																O	7	5
Idechi																W	1	1
Japanese																O	0	0
Ji-An																W	21	15
Korean																O	1	1
Sang Wook																W	4	4
Korean																O	0	0

Figure 6.2. The emergence and use of *going to* in number of tokens per half-month, continued.

Instruction

To understand the emergence and development of grammaticalized future expression completely, the role of instruction must be considered. In light of the sequence of emergence, the pattern of usage, and the fact that the learners receive instruction in the host environment, it is relevant to ask what instruction contributes to the early emergence and sustained dominance of *will*. From the available data, instructional input seems to be biased toward *going to*, in direct contrast to the pattern found in the acquisitional data.

This brief survey of instructional input is divided into three sections. The first concerns the casual speech of the ESL teachers in the same program as the learners, which although not explicit instruction, does constitute part of the input in the instructional environment. The second section reviews the instructional logs and teaching materials. The third section takes a close look at one teaching activity.

Informal Input. The conversational interviews recorded in the present corpus suggest that the ESL teachers in the program (who also served as native speaker interviewers) use *going to* in some contexts, as in the following examples. As Examples 6 and 7 show, these uses of *going to* by the native speaker interlocutors do not lead to uses of *going to* by the learners. Instead, they maintain their use of *will*:

6 Interviewer: I see. Everyone went to College Mall. Okay. And what are you going to do this weekend?

Kazuhiro: Mmm, I will go to::, oh this weekend? Next-uh Saturday?

Interviewer: Right, uh-huh.

Kazuhiro: Oh, oh, oh, I will go to picnic.

Interviewer: Oh, you're gonna go to a picnic. Where's the picnic? [T.5]

7 Interviewer: What are you going to do for Christmas Break?

Carlos: I will go back to my country on December 8. [T3.0]

Three things are worth noting: The contextualized use of *going to* is available to learners through native speaker talk addressed to the learners, and that positive evidence in the form of casual speech from teachers seems to have little immediate effect on learners as interlocutors.

Instructional Logs. The instructional logs also suggest that *going to* receives instructional focus, and may be favored over *will* in the formal presentations. According to the instructional logs, *be going to* was introduced a full month before *will* in Level 1 (O'Neill et al., 1981, *AKL: Beginning*) and was separated from the introduction of *will* in Level 2 by the program syllabus and the textbook (O'Neill et al., 1978, *AKL: Intermediate*). This textbook series maximizes the differences between *will* and *be going to. Be going to* is introduced as a general future cued by adverbials such as tomorrow and next week. *Will* is introduced in polite requests and offers, then four chapters later as a future form. In contrast, a second textbook used in Level 2 (Azar, 1985, *Fundamentals of English Grammar*) states a general rule that there is no difference between the *will* and *going to* future: "*Be going to* and *will* are the same when they are used to make predications about the future" (p. 51). This is followed by two exceptions: *be going to* is used for a preconceived plan and *will* is used to express willingness or to volunteer. In summary, the general syllabus and instructional logs indicate that *going to* is introduced before *will,* which is the opposite order found in the learner production data.

A Closer Look at Instruction: The Exam. What role does attention to form play for individual learners in the emergence and subsequent use of *going to*? The corpus provides evidence of a natural experiment that addresses just this issue. Six of the learners were enrolled in the same grammar class in the second IEP session (Level 2) during the third month, T3.0. The instructional logs show that the Level 2 grammar class devoted 3 days to the expression of the future (contrasting the use of *going to* which had been previously introduced with *will*) and the writing class also discussed future expression one day the same week. At the beginning of the week the writing class was assigned an in-class essay entitled *Five years from now.* At the end of the week, learners were given a grammar test. One section of the test directed students to "Write a paragraph with at least five sentences telling me what you will do this weekend."

Learners had various responses. One learner, Saleh, used *will* exclusively, as shown in Example 8.

8 Saleh, L1 Arabic, grammar test, 4/6, T3.0

I will go to the Coleg mall.

I will buy anew T.V.

I will go to the move.

I will read a book.

I will go to the pray.

I will lesten to the rido.

I will go to the dowen tawen.

I will sleep.

I will viset my frindes.

I will write my home woork.

Saleh's spontaneous use of *going to* does not begin until T14.5 with a single use in the written corpus followed by two subsequent uses at T16.5. Saleh shows no recorded oral use of *going to*, as shown in Fig. 6.2.

The other learners were slightly more in tune with what strategies to use when they are students in a grammar class: They used the forms that had been introduced in instructional activities immediately prior to the test, even though they were not explicitly cued by the directions. However, the learners differ in whether their use of the *go*-future in the exams marks the emergence of going to in their grammar or the display of a form that is not used spontaneously. One learner, Hamad, showed occasional uses of *going to* and *gonna* between T1.5 and T6.5, with increased use again after T9.5 (Fig. 6.2). Because Hamad was experimenting with *going to* and *gonna* prior to instruction, he is not discussed further here.

For two learners, Hiromi and Ji-An, the use of *going to* marks the emergence of spontaneous use in the corpus more broadly (Fig. 6.2). Hiromi, like Saleh, used only one form; but in contrast to Saleh, who used only *will*, she used only *going to*. The other learners use both *will* and *going to* beginning their paragraphs with *will*, as Ji-An does in Example 9.[5] As Fig. 6.2 shows, Ji-An used 5 tokens of *going to* in the two-week period of the exam.

9 Ji-An, L1 Korean, grammar test, 4-6, T3.0

I will meet my conversation partner at 12:30. I will study the Bible with Korean people on Friday afternoon. When I finish the Bible study, I am going to go discodeck with my friends. My sister and me are going to go Chinese resturent. After we eat lunch, we are going to play bowling in Union.

The other learners, Abdullah and Soon Wook, seem to have been displaying their knowledge of grammar for the test. They both used *going to* on the test, but neither learner used it after the exam. Soon Wook left the program at the beginning of the eighth month without using *going to* again in the corpus, perhaps too early to have shown spontaneous use. Whether his ultimate profile is like Saleh, where no spontaneous tokens of going to were attempted, or like Abdullah, whose spontaneous use was delayed by several months, it is impossible to tell from these data. Abdullah had four uses of *going to* the week that the future is being taught, three on the exam and one use before, then no further uses of *going to* until one written use at T10.0, and one oral use at T13.5. This pattern is not unique to the acquisition of *going to*. Wiberg (in press) also reported that learners of Italian use future forms on exams but do not use them even when prompted by an interlocutor. Such patterns of use support the distinction between explicit and implicit knowledge.

From this summary, it appears that instruction is not the determinant of either the timing of emergence or the (in)frequency of *going to*. *Going to* is introduced early and visited frequently in the first two levels of instruction, and used by the teachers, constituting ample positive evidence for the inclusion of *going to*. The examples show a specific case where explicit practice output had no discernible effect on three fifths of the learners who had not used *going to* or *gonna* before instruction. In fact, the instructional logs paint a similar, although less detailed, picture for more learners. All learners received instruction on *going to* at T1.5. The six learners discussed here received a second round of instruction on the future that included *will* as well as *going to* at T3.0; the remaining 10 learners received the instruction at T2.5. Yet, as many as half do not produce three spontaneous uses of *going to* even after the second instruction at T2.5 or T3.0 (Figs. 6.1 and 6.2).

Learners establish and maintain a system where *will* is dominant. At certain stages of acquisition, learners appear to be able to resist the input provided by instruction (Pienemann, 1989, 1998). Why doesn't repeated instruction and repeated input and exposure change the balance of the interlanguage system? Other factors seem to be at play.

DISCUSSION

This section considers potential determinants of the interlanguage expression of futurity for sequence of emergence and frequency of use, namely, instruction, compositional complexity, the interpretation of *will* as a lexical marker, and the one-to-one principle. This discussion is particularly concerned with half of the learners: the eight who showed 11 or fewer uses of *going to* and Satoru, whose written uses became entirely formulaic.

Formal Complexity

One interpretation of the pattern rests on the formal complexity of the forms under consideration. From a formal perspective, both *will* and *going to* are completely regular. Using *going to* may be a harder task just because it is longer than *will* and so involves more phonological units to be sequenced (cf. N. Ellis, 1996). Learners must also inflect the auxiliary *be*, which may add to the formal complexity of this construction. An appeal to the formal complexity of *going to* relative to *will* might account for the initial order of emergence, but is ultimately unsatisfactory because these same learners do learn compositional tense-aspect forms with past reference (namely, the past progressive, present perfect, and pluperfect, in that order; Bardovi-Harlig, 2000). All 16 learners in this study clearly enter the morphological stage of development. Thus, formal complexity is at best only an explanation for why *will* emerges before *going to*, but not why *going to* is comparatively delayed or infrequent in the production of half of the learners.

Will as a Lexical Marker of Future

An additional factor may be the lexical-before-morphological stage familiar in the stages of acquisition leading to the development of past-time expression. Many studies have reported that learners use lexical means before morphological means to express temporal relations (for extensive reviews see Bardovi-Harlig, 2000; Dietrich et al., 1995). *Will* might have an advantage over *going to* if learners regard it as lexical rather than grammatical. Three facts lead to the suggestion that learners may perceive *will* as a lexical expression: It is a free morpheme, it virtually lacks variants in the learner corpus (there are very few tokens of the phonologically reduced form in the corpus used by only two learners), and it emerges very early. *Will* not only emerges before *going to*, it may be acquired in English much earlier than the morphological future in other languages. In Italian, the only other language for which there is published sequence-of-emergence data relative to other tense-aspect morphology, Giacalone Ramat (1992, p. 305) placed the acquisition of the morphological future well into the development of tense-aspect morphology, as shown in Example 10.[5]

10 Present > (aux +) Past Participle > Imperfect > Future > Conditional > Subjunctive

In contrast to *will*, *going to* behaves more like a morphological future with respect to its later timing. Comparing the emergence of *going to* with the emergence of past morphology for these same learners (namely, the past progressive, present perfect, and the pluperfect; Bardovi-Harlig, 2000) shows that for all learners *going to* emerges after the past progressive but before the pluperfect around the time of the present perfect.

The One-to-One Principle

Although the lexical interpretation of *will* is plausible, it may not be the only factor at play. The dominance of *will* in interlanguage and the difficulty that *going to* has in becoming established may also be due to the one-to-one principle (Andersen, 1984, 1990, 1993). The one-to-one principle states that an interlanguage system "should be constructed in such a way that an intended underlying meaning is expressed with one clear invariant surface form (or construction)" (Andersen, 1984, p. 79). As Andersen (1984) summed up, the one-to-one principle "is a principle of one *form* to one *meaning*"(p. 79, emphasis in original). From the perspective of the association of form and meaning, it is interesting to note that the emergence of *will* before *going to* follows what Leech (1971, p. 64) identified as the "order of importance" of future expressions, suggesting that *will* represents a "neutral" future in English (p. 52).

As specified by the one-to-one principle, *will* is transparent and invariant. There is no morphological variation of *will*, as the concept of morphologically defective modals suggests (i.e., English modals do not take tense morphology). In addition, in the interlanguage of the present learners, there is also very little phonological variation as noted in the general nonuse of the relevant contraction, *'ll*. Thus, the relation of the form *will* to the meaning "future" is firmly established.

For *going to* to take root in the system, it has to have a new meaning that is distinct from "general future," or the learners have to allow multiple forms for a single meaning, or the learners have to reanalyze the meaning

[5] Other studies on the Italian future include Berretta (1990) and Wiberg (in press). Moses (2002) reported on a cross-sectional study of French.

associated with *will.*[6] One hint that learners find a new meaning or meanings for *going to* is in the adverb-verb ratios. The use of adverbs with verbs in the written corpus is lower with *going to* than with *will* or base/present or present progressive futures. *Going to* shows the lowest use of adverbs, with .32, or 3 adverbs for every 10 uses of *going to*; *will* shows .47, or nearly 5 adverbs for every 10 uses of *will*; and base/present and present progressive, forms that are rarely used and have other primary meanings, show the greatest use of future adverbials, .69 and .76, respectively. The lower rate of use of adverbs and lexical markers makes sense if learners have reserved the use of *going to* for what Dahl (1985, 2000) called "in preparation" or impending use. The concept of "immediacy" may be built in to the meaning associated with the form.

The rare use of the progressive as future suggests another illustration of the one-to-one principle. The very low use of present progressive results from the fact that the present progressive is already associated with "ongoing" as its main meaning. Although on the one hand, observers might expect learners to press existing forms into double semantic duty, that is not the case. Following the one-to-one principle, the present progressive largely stays in the realm of the present rather than the future. Many of the earliest progressive futures occur with the lexical verb *go*, as in "I am going to dinner," which suggests that these might be a stepping stone from the "*going to* + verb" form to progressive as future. The use of the progressive as future also has the highest adverb to verb ratio of .69 in the written corpus and .75 in the oral corpus.

Another bit of evidence for how a new form can take hold of part of a meaning associated with another form, in this case how *going to* can carve out a bit of future meaning otherwise claimed by *will*, comes from the use of the formula *I am going to write (about)* (Bardovi-Harlig, 2002). As indicated in Fig. 6.2 by the word "write," 28 of Satoru's 31 written tokens of *going to* are tokens of the *I am going to write about* formula. His first uses of *going to* occurred with three different tokens and types of verbs; after that he began to use *going to* exclusively with the verb *write*. In contrast, his oral use shows 7 tokens, with 5 types in the same time frame. One other learner, Khaled, produced 18 tokens of *going to write* and showed exclusive use of *going to* in the *going to write* formula for about 6 weeks, producing 15 tokens between T9.0 and T10.5. Khaled abandons exclusive use of *going to* in the formula at T11.0 and use resumes with other verbs. Three other learners showed much less dramatic use of the formula that was integrated into their overall production (Guillermo, 6, Eduardo, 6, and Carlos, 5 tokens). (See Bardovi-Harlig, 2002, for a discussion of formulaic use associated with going to in this corpus.)

The formulaic use not only provides a clear form–meaning association in the sense of "in preparation" discussed earlier, it provides a clear discursive

[6] *Going to* may also have to undergo its own semantic expansion, moving from the progressive (and literal) meaning of "go to" as in "I am going to school" to the use as a *go*-future. This should be true cross-linguistically of L2 acquisition for go-futures in general. I am grateful to Yas Shirai for pointing this out to me (personal communication, October 2002).

function. *I am going to write about* occurs at the beginning of essays. This formulaic use is especially consistent with the "immediacy" or "in preparation" reading of the target *going to* construction. The writer who uses this formula typically embarks on the writing of the (body of) the essay in question within a few sentences.

Approaching the interpretation of formulaic use from another perspective, interlanguage can afford the exclusive (if temporary) use of *going to* for *the going to write* formula because the system already has a future form that carries the communicative weight of future meaning. By assigning *going to* to the *going to write* formula and function, learner systems may solve the problem of apparent semantic equivalents.

What the learners in the study seem to establish with the initial uses of *will* is a system of temporal contrast. In the initial stage, *will* indicates future reference in contrast to the past (and various tense-aspect forms that convey different relationships among speech time, event time, and reference time) and the base/present. At this stage of interlanguage, the grammaticalized expression of future seems to lack the modal character described by temporal semanticists as one of the key features of the future. With *will* as the sole marker of the future, there is no grammaticalized marker of modality that may include intentionality, possibility, probability, desire, or volition. If *going to* can be described as encoding events in preparation or other stages of planning (Azar, 1985; Dahl, 2000), then the introduction of *going to* in a later stage represents not only an addition to the repertoire of temporal expression, but also modal expression as well. *Going to* encodes a modal degree of certainty not present in a system that only has *will*. Thus, the expansion of the interlanguage system to accommodate *going to* as it has been described would represent an expansion not only of temporal expression, but a shift from a temporal system to a modal system; that is, a shift from a tense-aspect system to a tense-mood-aspect system. This interpretation is somewhat speculative at this stage of research, but it outlines one direction of further investigation.

CONCLUSIONS

This study focused on the use of two forms to express futurity and considered the reasons for the dominance of *will* over *going to* in the emergent tense-mood-aspect system. Additional areas remain to be studied. In keeping with the meaning-oriented approach, the full spectrum of morphological, lexical, and syntactic means of expression should be considered, as indicated by the original coding of the corpus. Further investigation should show that at least part of the earliest expressions of modality in the future reside in the use of lexical futures by learners; this may result in a relatively early interlanguage stage in which *will* carries the temporal future, but the lexical futures and the adverbials carry the modality.

A second area of investigation is to examine how (or if) the semantic domain of *will* changes when *going to* emerges and becomes established. Ideally, this inquiry should be expanded to include discourse types analogous to the activity types used in the analysis of child language acquisition (cf. Gee & Savasir, 1985; Pawłowska, 1999, for child L1 English; Wiberg, 2002, for adult L2 Italian). Journals written by the learners about themselves and conversations centered around the learners' own activities formed the bulk of the written and oral texts in this study, providing ample opportunity for learners to express intention and volition in addition to future. The texts could be further divided into personal and impersonal texts, or analyzed for reference to first person and others. Text-type plays an important part in the distribution of past-oriented tense-aspect forms, and it may also influence the expression of future.

Although studies like this one shed light on the development of the tense-mood-aspect system in interlanguage, they also contribute to the ongoing discussion of factors that influence second language acquisition more broadly. The influence of instruction, complexity, learner analysis of the input, and the one-to-one principle are relevant to any area of linguistic development. Learners are often faced with multiple forms for what may appear from their perspective to be "the same meaning" and they manage to construct an economical and efficient interlanguage in the early stages. How they construct the initial stages and how the early systems expand toward target-like form–meaning associations is worthy of continued investigation.

REFERENCES

Andersen, R. W. (1984). The one-to-one principle of interlanguage construction. *Language Learning, 34*, 77–95.

Andersen, R. W. (1990). Models, processes, principles and strategies: Second language acquisition inside and outside the classroom. In B. VanPatten & J. F. Lee (Eds.), *Second language acquisition–foreign language learning* (pp. 45–78). Clevedon, England: Multilingual Matters.

Andersen, R. W. (1993). Four operating principles and input distribution as explanations for underdeveloped and mature morphological systems. In K. Hyltenstam & Å. Viberg (Eds.), *Progression & regression in language: Sociocultural, neuropsychological, & linguistic perspectives* (pp. 309–339). Cambridge, UK: Cambridge University Press.

Azar, B. S. (1985). *Fundamentals of English grammar*. Englewood Cliffs, NJ: Prentice Hall.

Bardovi-Harlig, K. (1992a). The relationship of form and meaning: A cross-sectional study of tense and aspect in the interlanguage of learners of English as a second language. *Applied Psycholinguistics, 13*, 253–278.

Bardovi-Harlig, K. (1992b). The use of adverbials and natural order in the development of temporal expression. *IRAL, 30*, 299–320.

Bardovi-Harlig, K. (1994). Reverse-order reports and the acquisition of tense: Beyond the principle of chronological order. *Language Learning, 44*, 243–282.

Bardovi-Harlig, K. (2000). *Tense and aspect in second language acquisition: Form, meaning, and use*. Oxford, England: Blackwell.

Bardovi-Harlig, K. (2002). A new starting point? Investigating formulaic use and input. *Studies in Second Language Acquisition, 24*, 189–198.

Berretta, M. (1990). Il futuro in italiano L2. *Quarderni del Dipartimento di Linguistica e Letterature Comparate (Università di Bergamo), 6*, 147–188.

Biber, D., Johansson, S., Leech, G., Conrad, S., & Finegan, E. (1999). *Longman grammar of spoken and written English.* London: Longman.

Broen, P. A., & Santema, S. A. (1983). Children's comprehension of six verb–tense forms. *Journal of Communication Disorders, 16*, 85–97.

Bybee, J. L. (1985). *Morphology: A study of the relation between meaning and form.* Amsterdam: Benjamins.

Bybee, J., Perkins, R., & Pagliuca, W. (1994). *The evolution of grammar: Tense, aspect, and modality in the languages of the world.* Chicago: University of Chicago Press.

Comrie, B. (1985). *Tense*. New York: Cambridge University Press.

Coates, J. (1983). *The semantics of the modal auxiliaries*. London: Croom Helm.

Coates, J. (1987). *Epistemic modality and spoken discourse. Transactions of the Philological Society* (pp. 111–131). Oxford, England: Blackwell.

Dahl, Ö. (1985). *Tense and aspect systems*. Oxford, England: Blackwell.

Dahl, Ö. (2000). *Tense and aspect in the languages of Europe*. Berlin: de Gruyter.

Dietrich, R., Klein, W., & Noyau, C. (1995). *The acquisition of temporality in a second language.* Amsterdam: Benjamins.

Ellis, N. C. (1996). Sequencing in SLA: Phonological memory, chunking, and points of order. *Studies in Second Language Acquisition, 18*, 91–216.

Ellis, R. (1990). *Instructed second language acquisition.* Oxford, England: Blackwell.

Fleischman, S. (1982). *The future in thought and language*. Cambridge, England: Cambridge University Press.

Fletcher, P. (1979).The development of the verb phrase. In P. Fletcher & M. Garman (Eds.), *Language acquisition* (pp. 261–284). Cambridge, England: Cambridge University Press.

Gee, J., & Savasir, I. (1985). On the use of *will* and *gonna*: Toward a description of Activity–types for child language. *Discourse Processes, 8*, 143–175.

Giacalone Ramat, A. (1992). Grammaticalization processes in the area of temporal and modal relations. *Studies in Second Language Acquisition, 14*, 297–322.

Klein, W. (1995). The acquisition of English. In R. Dietrich, W. Klein, & C. Noyau (Eds.), *The acquisition of temporality in a second language* (pp. 31–70). Amsterdam: Benjamins.

Krashen, S. (1977). Some issues related to the monitor model. In H. Brown, C. Yorio, & R. Crymes (Eds.), *On TESOL '77* (pp. 144–158). Washington, DC: TESOL.

Leech, G. N. (1971). *Meaning and the English verb.* London: Longman.

Lyons, J. (1977). *Semantics*. London: Cambridge University Press.

Meisel, J. (1987). Reference to past events and actions in the development of natural language acquisition. In C. W. Pfaff (Ed.), *First and second language acquisition processes* (pp. 206–224). Cambridge, MA: Newbury House.

Moses, J. (2002). *The expression of futurity by English–speaking learners of French.* Unpublished doctoral dissertation, Indiana University.

O'Neill, R., Anger, L., & Davy, K. (1981). *AKL: Beginning*. London: Longman.

O'Neill, R., Kingsbury, R., Yeadon, T., & Cornelius, E. T., Jr. (1978). *AKL: Intermediate*. London: Longman.

Palmer, F. R. (1986). *Mood and modality*. Cambridge, England: Cambridge University Press.

Pawłowska, M. (1999). A parallel development in the history and acquisition of *be going to* in English. *Studia Anglica Posnaniensia, XXXIV*, 201–210.

Perkins, M. R. (1983). *Modal expressions in English.* Norwood, NJ: Ablex.

Pienemann, M. (1989). Is language teachable? Psycholinguistic experiments and hypotheses. *Applied Linguistics, 10*, 52–79.

Pienemann, M. (1998). *Language processing and second language development: Processability theory*. Amsterdam: Benjamins.

Reichenbach, H. (1947). *Elements of symbolic logic*. Berkeley, CA: University of California Press.

Salsbury, T. (2000). *The grammaticalization of unreal conditionals: A longitudinal study of L2 English*. Unpublished doctoral dissertation, Indiana University, Bloomington.

Schumann, J. (1987). The expression of temporality in basilang speech. *Studies in Second Language Acquisition, 9*, 21–41.

Wiberg, E. (2002). Information structure in dialogic future plans: A study of Italian native speakers and Swedish preadvanced and advanced learners of Italian. In R. Salaberry & Y. Shirai (Eds.), *Tense–aspect morphology in L2 acquisition* (pp. 285-321). Amsterdam: Benjamins.

CHAPTER 7
Cognitive Linguistics and Second Language Acquisition: Motion Events in a Typological Framework

Teresa Cadierno
University of Southern Denmark

Karen Lund
The Danish University of Education

This chapter discusses how cognitive linguistics can constitute a fruitful paradigm for the study of second language acquisition (SLA) and, more specifically, for the investigation of how learners establish form–meaning connections in SLA. It illustrates the possible contribution of cognitive linguistics to SLA by focusing on one particular line of inquiry— that of cognitive typology. Specifically, it examines how Talmy's typological framework of motion events (1985, 1991, 1996) can be useful for investigating how L2 learners come to interpret and express motion in the L2. It shows how this line of inquiry can constitute the basis for theoretically grounded and testable hypotheses on the types of form–meaning mappings that learners from typologically different L1s make when interpreting and expressing motion events in the L2. The formulation of these hypotheses is based on (a) Talmy's typological framework; (b) an empirical investigation of L1 acquisition conducted by Slobin and his collaborators (Berman & Slobin, 1994) and (c) on Slobin's *thinking for speaking hypothesis* (Slobin, 1996a), which constitutes a modified version of the Whorfian relativity hypothesis on the relationship between language and thought.

The chapter is divided as follows: The first part presents the theoretical background to this line of investigation. This includes a general introduction to its central tenets, and a presentation of Talmy's typological framework and of Slobin's empirical work on L1 acquisition and his thinking for speaking hypothesis. The second part discusses the implications of Talmy's and Slobin's work for SLA and, on the basis of these and the typical form–meaning patterns of Danish and Spanish, posits a series of hypotheses concerning the interpretation and production of manner of motion by learners with typologically different L1s and L2s (i.e., Danish learners of Spanish and Spanish learners of Danish). Here possible research methodologies for the investigation of these hypotheses will also be discussed. The terms *form* and *meaning* are understood as follows: Form refers to the linguistic units of language, including both lexical and grammatical units (i.e., morphological and syntactic). All linguistic forms or expressions are considered to be symbolic units, consisting of the association of a phonological and a semantic representation. Meaning thus refers to the semantic structure of a symbolic unit, which is in turn equated with conceptualization. This conception of form and meaning is elaborated on throughout.

COGNITIVE LINGUISTICS: CENTRAL TENETS

Cognitive linguistics is a functional approach to language that emerged in the 1980s[1] as an alternative to the dominant linguistic theory of the generative school, which focuses on the formal properties of the language and views language as an autonomous system independent from human cognition. Cognitive linguistics does not, however, constitute a totally homogeneous framework given its interdisciplinary nature that draws on a variety of disciplines (e.g., cognitive science, cognitive psychology, neuroscience, and anthropology). Even though different approaches and lines of research have been identified within cognitive linguistics (Cuenca & Hilferty, 1999; Ungerer & Schmid, 1996), they all share a particular view of language, which will be briefly discussed.

Language as an Integral Part of Cognition

In the cognitive linguistics paradigm, language is viewed as intrinsically linked to human cognition and general cognitive processes. In this view, "linguistic structures are seen as being related to and motivated by human conceptual knowledge, bodily experience, and the communicative functions of discourse" (Gibbs, 1996, p. 27). The strategy followed by cognitive linguists is thus to look explicitly for possible links between language and cognition. This has been referred to as the "cognitive commitment," that is, the commitment to provide linguistic descriptions and explanations that accord with what is known about human mental processing in general (Lakoff, 1990; Langacker, 1987). In Langacker's own words (1968, p.1), linguistic structure is, as far as possible, "analyzed in terms of more basic systems and abilities (e.g., perception, attention, categorization) from which it cannot be dissociated."

Language as Symbolic in Nature

The field of cognitive linguistics views language as essentially symbolic, that is, as "an open-ended set of linguistic signs or expressions, each of which associates a semantic representation of some kind with a phonological representation" (Langacker, 1987, p. 11). In other words, all linguistic expressions (i.e., lexical, morphological and syntactic) are viewed as symbolic units consisting of conventionalized form–meaning mappings used for communicative purposes. It is precisely this conception of language as symbolic

[1] As indicated by authors such as Geeraerts (1988) and Langacker (1987), even though cognitive linguistics emerged in the 1980s, some of the underlying assumptions are not new (e.g., work on prototypes and categories carried out by Berlin & Kay, 1969; and Rosch, 1978).

that makes cognitive linguistics a well-motivated paradigm for the examination of form–meaning connections in SLA.

An important consequence of this conception of language is the central role that meaning plays in linguistic description. In cognitive linguistics, meaning is equated with conceptualization (i.e., mental experience), which is viewed as a dynamic activity of embodied minds interacting with their environment. Conceptualization is to be interpreted broadly, subsuming both novel and established concepts, all facets of sensorimotor and emotive experience, and apprehension of the social, linguistic, and cultural context (Langacker, 1996). Linguistic meaning is thus viewed as encyclopedic in scope; everything known about an entity can be regarded as contributing to the meaning of an expression that designates it. This means that a sharp distinction between semantics and pragmatics, and between linguistic and extralinguistic knowledge, is not attainable (Langacker, 1987).

In sum, linguistic meaning is viewed as a cognitive embodied phenomenon, grounded in the human experience of bodily existence (Johnson, 1987; Lakoff, 1987). Linguistic meaning is considered to be subjective and to reflect the ways in which speakers conceive their experiences of the world and the ways in which they choose to construe them and to talk about them.[2]

Cognitive linguistics differs from formalistic approaches to language, such as the generative approach, in four basic aspects: (a) Whereas generative linguistics sees linguistic competence as the proper subject matter of linguistic investigation, cognitive linguistics stresses the importance of examining linguistic performance, and thus taking into account the functions that language serves; (b) whereas generative linguistics adopts a modular view of language (i.e., it views language as largely independent of other mental and cognitive abilities), cognitive linguistics views language as an integrated part of general cognition, and consequently, as reflecting conceptual structure; (c) whereas generative linguistics views grammar (and syntax in particular) as an autonomous system (i.e., independent of semantics), cognitive linguistics views grammar as intrinsically symbolic, and hence meaningful (consequently, semantics is seen as inseparable from grammar); and (d) whereas generative linguistics adopts an objectivist view of meaning based on truth conditions and described by some type of formal logic, cognitive linguistics adopts a conceptualist view of linguistic meaning by considering it a mental phenomenon, which is encyclopedic in nature.

Cognitive linguistics is thus seen as a promising linguistic paradigm for the study of SLA because it offers some insights that other linguistic approaches of formalistic nature cannot due to their underlying assumptions—namely, a

[2] Langacker (1987, 1996) identified several aspects of construal: specificity, which is the capacity to conceive an entity or situation at varying levels of specificity and detail; background, which is the ability to conceive of one structure against the background provided by another; perspective, which subsumes factors such as vantage point and orientation; and the relative prominence given to the different substructures of a conception, which encompasses the concepts of saliency, profiling, and figure-ground alignment.

detailed analysis of the semantic structure of the learners' L2 in comparison to their L1, and an explanation of how semantic structure is related to general cognitive abilities (e.g., the ability to categorize, to impose figure/ground organization, and to conceive of a situation at different levels of specificity). This is discussed in more detail in the rest of the chapter, which deals with how different languages of the world encode motion.

MOTION EVENTS: TALMY'S TYPOLOGICAL FRAMEWORK

A conceptual domain that has received a great deal of attention in cognitive linguistics-based research is the spatial domain. Researchers, such as Lakoff (1987) and Johnson (1987), proposed that our understanding of spatial relations is based on universal image schema that have a kinesthetic basis and can be traced back to bodily experiences of the world (i.e., to the fact that from birth onward people develop an ability to perceive and interpret spatial relationships first visually and then through action). These image schema have been defined by Johnson (1987) as "a recurring, dynamic pattern of our perceptual interactions and motor programs that gives coherence and structure to our experience" (p. xiv). Of special relevance here is the Source-Path-Goal schema, which is at the base of our understanding of motion (Johnson, 1987; Lakoff, 1987), and consists of three components: source (starting point), path (the route from the source to the goal), and goal (intended destination).

It is interesting, however, that even though our understanding of motion is based on a universal image-schema, languages manifest a systematic variation as to how its different semantic components are lexicalized. Talmy (1985, 1991, 1996) addressed the systematic relationship in language between form and meaning in the motion domain from a cross-linguistic perspective. A motion event, which is defined by Talmy (1985) as a situation containing movement or the maintenance of a stationary location, is composed of the following six semantic components: (a) motion: the presence per se of motion; (b) figure: the moving, or conceptually movable, entity; (c) ground: the object with respect to which the figure moves, which can potentially include the source, the medium and the goal of movement; (d) path: the course followed by the figure with respect to the ground; (e) manner: the manner in which the motion takes place; and (f) cause: the cause of its occurrence.

Talmy (1985) offered the following two examples to illustrate the components: *The pencil rolled off the table* and *The pencil blew off the table*. In both sentences, *the pencil* functions as the figure and *the table* as the ground, which in these examples expresses source of movement, whereas the particle *off* expresses the path. Both verbs *rolled* and *blew* express motion, and in addition the former expresses manner of motion and the latter expresses cause of motion.

Languages differ as to how the semantic components of a motion event are packaged into linguistic forms. Depending on the types of lexicalization patterns that take place, Talmy proposed a typological framework that characterizes the typical form–meaning mapping patterns found in the depiction of motion events in different languages of the world. He identified two broad types of languages according to how path information is packaged lexically: satellite-framed languages (S-languages) and verb-framed languages (V-languages). In S-languages (e.g., English, Danish, and Chinese), the verb typically conflates motion and manner or motion and cause of motion, while path is encoded outside the verb, in a satellite (verb particle) (e.g., *The bottle floated out of the cave*). In V-languages (e.g., Spanish and Turkish), on the other hand, the verb typically conflates motion and path, while manner and cause are expressed separately in an adverbial or a gerund (e.g., *La botella salió de la cueva flotando* 'The bottle left the cave floating').[3]

Motion Events in First Language Acquisition

Talmy's typological framework has been empirically investigated within L1 language acquisition by Berman and Slobin (1994) and Slobin (1996a, 1996b, 1997, 2000). Their research examined whether these typological differences had an impact on native speakers' conceptualization and expression of motion events. Their studies thus included children and adults from both S-languages (English, German) and V-languages (Hebrew, Spanish, and Turkish). Data were gathered by means of the "the frog story" elicitation task, a wordless picture book (Mayer, 1969).

The results of these investigations have shown that the two typological patterns—satellite- versus verb-framing—have a clear impact on the rhetorical style with which native speakers from the two language types express motion events. Whereas speakers of S-languages tend to devote relatively more narrative attention to the dynamics of movement along a path, speakers of V-languages tend to devote more attention to scene setting (e.g., *The deer threw them off over a cliff into the water* vs. *Lo tiró. Por suerte, abajo, estaba el río. El niño cayó en el agua* '[The deer] threw him. Luckily, below, was the river. The boy fell into the water') (Slobin, 1996b). In English, the speaker elaborates path descriptions in detail by appending several satellites to a single verb of motion, thus leaving the setting to be inferred (i.e., that the cliff is over the water); in Spanish, on the other hand, the speaker provides stage-setting information, thus leaving the details of the trajectory to be inferred (i.e., that he went from some elevated place down into the water). Important differences were also found with respect to how the semantic component of manner of motion was expressed in the two language types, an issue discussed in the second part of the chapter.

[3] These lexicalization patterns reflect general tendencies and not absolute differences. There are some S-languages, such as English (but not Danish), that contain Latinate verbs (e.g., *enter, ascend, descend*), which conflate motion and path. Likewise, V-languages like Spanish possess verbs conflating motion and manner (e.g., *correr* 'to run', *nadar* 'to swim', *saltar* 'to jump'). This last observation is dealt with in more detail in the second part of the chapter.

Thinking for Speaking

The systematic differences found in children learning typologically different languages have been explained by Slobin (1996a) as reflecting different patterns of what he called, thinking for speaking. The Thinking for Speaking Hypothesis claims that there is a kind of thinking that is intimately tied to language—that is, the thinking that is carried out online in the process of speaking, or in the process of signing, writing, or listening. Thinking for Speaking involves picking those characteristics of objects and events that fit some conceptualization of the event and are readily encodable in the language.

Following claims made by cognitive linguists, Slobin's hypothesis assumes that people cannot verbalize experience without taking a perspective. Slobin especially emphasized that language plays an important role, given that particular linguistic structures in a language may favor particular perspectives. In Slobin's own words (2000), "The world does not present 'events' to be encoded in language. Rather, in the process of speaking or writing, experiences are filtered through language into verbalized events" (p. 107).

Slobin's Thinking for Speaking Hypothesis thus constitutes a modified and more cautious version of the Whorfian hypothesis on linguistic relativity and determinism, given its emphasis on the kind of mental processes that occur during the act of formulating an utterance, and not on the possible effects of language on cognition in general.[4] In this respect, Slobin's hypothesis follows a tradition in anthropological linguistics as exemplified in the work of Boas (1911), who suggested that "any utterance is a selective schematization of a concept—a schematization that is, in some way, dependent on the grammaticized meanings of the speaker's particular language, recruited for the purposes of verbal expression" (as cited in Slobin, 1996b, pp. 75–76).

According to Slobin (1996a), when acquiring a native language, the child learns particular ways of thinking for speaking. Each language thus trains its native speakers to pay different kinds of attention to particular details of events when talking about them. As Slobin (1996a) suggested, this training carried out during childhood could be exceptionally resistant to restructuring in adult SLA.

MOTION EVENTS IN SECOND LANGUAGE ACQUISITION

The aim of the second part of this chapter is twofold: (a) to discuss the implications for SLA research of Talmy's typological framework and of Slobin's thinking for speaking hypothesis and his work on L1 acquisition; this discussion is set in the context of the role of crosslinguistic influence in SLA; and (b) to show how these two lines of research can constitute a useful

[4] Other researchers such as Lucy (1992, 1996) have made stronger claims as to the influence of language on nonlinguistic human cognition.

theoretical basis for the study of form–meaning connections in SLA and, more specifically, how they can be the basis for theoretically motivated hypotheses, which can then be put to empirical test. This second aim is illustrated by focusing on a specific semantic component of a motion event (i.e., Manner of motion). The discussion proceeds by first describing the form–meaning mappings of two typologically different languages (i.e., Danish and Spanish), and then posits a series of hypotheses concerning the interpretation and production of manner of motion by Danish learners of Spanish and Spanish learners of Danish.

Implications of Talmy's and Slobin's Work for SLA

Consider two relevant questions in the light of Talmy's and Slobin's work: How do L2 learners come to express motion events in an L2 that is typologically different from their L1? And how does the performance of these types of learners compare to learners whose L1 and L2 share the same typological patterns? Following Slobin's thinking for speaking hypothesis, a plausible working hypothesis would be that learning an L2 will involve learning another way of thinking for speaking, that is, learning how the semantic components of a motion event are mapped onto L2 surface forms, and learning which particular details of a motion event must be attended to in the input and expressed in the L2. A general hypothesis consistent with the thinking for speaking hypothesis would thus assume that the learners' L1 typological patterns will, at least initially, constitute the point of departure for the form–meaning mappings established in the L2. This hypothesis entails that, independently of the typological patterns of the L1 and the L2, the learner will tend to transfer the L1 form–meaning patterns into the L2. This process, however, would result in different transfer patterns from a descriptive point of view; in cases of typological similarities between the L1 and the L2, positive transfer between the two languages would be expected, whereas in cases of typological differences between the L1 and the L2, negative transfer would be expected.

Manner of Motion

As indicated by Talmy's (1985, 1991, 1996) typological framework, the semantic component of manner shows different lexicalization patterns in satellite-framed and verb-framed languages. According to Talmy's framework, manner in S-languages is typically conflated with motion in the verb whereas, in V-languages, it is typically expressed in a separate expression (e.g., *The bottle floated out of the cave* vs. *La botella salió de la cueva flotando* 'The bottle went out of the cave floating'). However, in order to fully account for the different lexicalization patterns of the two language types, it is necessary to take into account another semantic component, namely, boundary-crossing (Slobin, 1996b, 1997). Boundary-crossing refers to whether or not a path involves the crossing of a boundary (e.g., the difference between *inside,* which expresses no boundary-crossing, and *into,* which expresses boundary-crossing).

Table 7.1. Form–meaning mappings in Danish L1

Figure	Motion	Path	Ground
	Manner	+/- BC	
	Verb	Satellite	PP
Han	*løb*	***ind***	*i huset*
'He	ran	into	the house'
Han	*løb*	***inde***	*i huset*
'He	ran	inside	the house'

Note. BC = Boundary-crossing, PP = Prepositional Phrase

Table 7.2. Form–meaning mappings in Spanish L1.

Figure	Motion		Ground
	Manner (only when –BC)		
	Verb		PP
Él	*corrió*		*hasta la casa*
'He	ran		up to the house'
Él	*corrió*		*en la casa*
'He	ran		inside the house'
Figure	Motion	Ground	Manner
	Path		
	+BC		
	Verb	PP	Separate/omit
Él	*entró*	*en la casa*	*(corriendo)*
'He	entered	the house	(running)'

Note. BC = Boundary-crossing, PP = Prepositional Phrase.

An analysis of the lexicalization patterns of S- and V-languages with respect to manner of motion will be undertaken with Danish, an S-language, and Spanish, a V-language. In line with the theme of this volume, the analysis will be based on the form–meaning mappings of the two languages. As shown in Table 7.1, manner in Danish is typically conflated with motion in the verb, thus resulting in a wide variety of manner of motion verbs. Path and +/- boundary-crossing are mapped onto satellites by means of an elaborate satellite system, which indicates an opposition between translocative and locative function (e.g., *ud/ude* 'out (translocative)/outside', *ind/inde* 'into (translocative)/inside', *op/oppe* 'up (translocative)/upstairs', *ned/ nede* 'down (translocative)/downstairs', and *hjem/ hjemme* 'home/at home'). An example is *Han løb ind i huset* 'He ran into the house' indicating boundary-crossing versus *Han løb inde i huset* 'He ran inside the house'. In Danish, then, one would normally not express path without expressing whether the motion involves boundary-crossing.

On the other hand, as shown in Table 7.2, manner in Spanish can be conflated with motion in the verb only in cases of non-boundary-crossing (e.g, *Corrió hasta la casa* 'He ran to the house (without entering)', *Corrió en la casa* 'He ran inside the house'. When boundary-crossing is involved, this conflation is not possible. If manner and boundary-crossing are to be expressed within the same utterance, manner must be mapped onto a separate phrase, either a gerund or a prepositional phrase (e.g., *Entró en la casa corriendo* 'He entered the house running'). This often results in the omission of manner unless it is in focus. The possibility of conflating manner and motion in Spanish verbs in cases of non-boundary-crossing indicates that Talmy's typological classification must not be understood in absolute terms; and that boundary-crossing is a necessary semantic component in crosslinguistic descriptions of motion events.

The characteristic form–meaning mappings of S- and V-languages have an impact on the types of manner of motion verbs contained in the lexicon, as well as on the frequency with which these verbs are used. Thus, S-languages, such as English and Danish, have a larger lexicon of manner of motion verbs in comparison with V-languages, such as Spanish (e.g., *deslizarse = creep, glide, slip, slither; saltar = bound, jump, dive, hop, spring*). As Slobin (2000) indicated, languages have a two-tiered lexicon of manner verbs: neutral, everyday verbs, such as walk, fly, climb, run, and more expressive or exceptional verbs, such as dash, swoop and scramble. As S-languages have a more extensive and elaborated second tier than V-languages, their speakers are trained to make more manner distinctions than speakers of V-languages. In addition, speakers of S-languages have been found to use manner of motion verbs with a higher frequency than speakers of V-languages (Slobin, 2000).

The different status of the semantic component of manner of motion in the two language types is also reflected in translations from one language type into the other (Slobin, 2000). Spanish translators tend to omit manner of motion, whereas English translators add manner to the Spanish original. So for instance, *They plunged across the road into the long grass on the other side* (taken from *A proper marriage* by Doris Lessing) was translated as *Cruzaron el camino hacia la hierba alta del otro lado* 'They crossed the road towards the long grass on the other side'. In contrast, the following sentence from Cervantes, *Cuando don Quijote salió de la venta* 'when don Quijote left the inn', was translated into German as *Als Don Quijote aus der Schenke ritt* 'when Don Quijote rode out of the inn'.

Hypotheses on the Interpretation and Production of Manner of Motion

The typological mapping patterns of Danish and Spanish and Slobin's research on L1 acquisition and translations are used to discuss discuss several predictions about how Spanish learners of L2 Danish and Danish learners of L2 Spanish both interpret and express manner of motion in the L2. The predictions are divided into motion-manner mapping and boundary-crossing mapping. Following Slobin's Thinking for Speaking hypothesis, the predictions assume that the learners' L1-thinking for speaking patterns will be the point of departure for the interpretation and production of L2 patterns. The hypotheses thus focus on the initial stages of SLA. It is an open question whether more advanced learners will still be influenced by the L1 thinking for speaking patterns or whether they will learn the new form–meaning patterns as they get increasing exposure to the L2. Research with advanced learners will thus shed light on the strength of Slobin's thinking for speaking hypothesis in SLA.

Spanish L1 - Danish L2: Motion-Manner Mapping. Given that Spanish lacks a fine-grained lexicon of manner of motion verbs (especially second-tier verbs), and consequently, its speakers have not been trained to distinguish between different manners of motion in a categorical way, several hypotheses can be postulated.

First, with respect to interpretation, it is predicted that the semantically fine-grained manner distinctions present in L2 second-tier manner verbs will not be initially processed by the learner. The verb will tend to be decoded only for motion. For example, a learner who hears the sentence *Tyven sniger sig rundt inde i stuen* 'The thief creeps around inside the room' will tend to decode first and foremost for motion (i.e., the thief moves around inside the room) and ignore manner information. The learner's interpretation of motion in cases like this will be based on the meaning of the construction itself.[5] On the other hand, when confronted with first-tier manner verbs (i.e., verbs that are also commonly used in the learner's L1), the learner will initially tend to process the manner information in the verb (e.g., *Hun løber i parken* 'She runs in the park'). In general, however, the same predictions can be made for beginning learners irrespective of the typology of their L1, as all beginner learners tend to make use of high-coverage lexical items (e.g., Harley, 1993; Harley & King, 1989).[6] This indicates that for learners in the initial stages of language acquisition, it is not possible to sort out the extent to which the lack of attention to L2 second-tier manner verbs in the input is due to a universal learning principle or to the influence of the L1 typological pattern. This issue, however, can be sorted out in the case of more advanced learners. Following Slobin's thinking for speaking hypothesis, a difference is predicted with respect to the way in which advanced learners from S- and V-languages process second-tier manner verbs.

Second, with respect to production, it is hypothesized that the learner will initially use few manner verbs in Danish (and not any second-tier manner verbs). The tendency will be to overgeneralize a single manner verb or a small number of such verbs to all communicative contexts, meaning that the rich L2 repertoire of manner verbs available in the lexicon is not exploited. For example, the learner would use only one verb for walking (e.g., *gå* 'to walk' in all walking contexts independent of the manner of walking involved, which in Danish could be expressed as *slentre* 'stroll', *spadsere* 'go for a short stroll', saunter' *stavre* 'totter', *traske* 'trudge', or *vakle* 'stagger'). The types of manner of motion verbs that will be overused will depend on factors such as input frequency, perceptual saliency, and prototypicality.

[5] This explanation is in agreement with the Construction Grammar approach (Goldberg, 1995), which states that grammatical constructions have meanings in their own right.

[6] Thanks to an anonymous reviewer of this chapter for this insight.

As it was the case with interpretation, these predictions described for learners with an L1 V-language will also apply to beginner learners with an L1 S-language (i.e., they would tend to use a limited number of high coverage lexical items). For more advanced learners, however, a difference between these two subject populations would be expected in the light of Slobin's thinking for speaking hypothesis.

Spanish L1 - Danish L2: Boundary-Crossing Mapping. The following hypotheses are postulated, given that Spanish does not allow for mapping of manner and motion onto a verb in boundary-crossing situations, whereas Danish does allow this conflation in both boundary- and nonboundary-crossing situations.

First, with respect to interpretation, it is predicted that the learner will interpret Danish boundary-crossing expressions as nonboundary-crossing at the outset, thus establishing incorrect form–meaning connections. For example, if learners hear the sentence *Han løber ind i huset* 'He runs into the house', which is a boundary-crossing situation, they would wrongly interpret it as *Él corre dentro de la casa* 'He runs inside the house', that is, with no boundary-crossing. So, a Spanish learner of Danish will tend to interpret both boundary- and nonboundary-crossing expressions as nonboundary-crossing. This L1-based interpretation might be reinforced by the fact that Danish utilizes subtle phonetic differences between expressions of boundary- and nonboundary-crossing (e.g., +/- glotal stop, +/- stress and vowel length). Following Slobin's Thinking for Speaking hypothesis, however, differences are expected to be found between beginning learners from V- and S-languages, as the latter are not required to learn new mapping patterns in the L2.

With respect to production, it is hypothesized that the learner will initially not conflate manner and motion in the verb in boundary-crossing situations, and will use instead the L1-pattern where manner is expressed separately. For example, despite the complexity of the construction, learners might prefer expressions like *Han kom løbende ind i huset* 'He came running into the house' to *Han løb ind i huset* 'He ran into the house', given that, in Spanish, they would say *Entró en la casa corriendo* 'He entered the house running'. As in the case of interpretation, differences between beginning learners from V- and S-languages would also be expected.

Danish L1 - Spanish L2: Motion-Manner Mapping. Given that Danish contains a fine-grained lexicon of manner of motion verbs and a large variety of second-tier verbs that do not exist in Spanish, the prediction is that learners will tend to add manner information in Spanish L2.

Thus, with respect to interpretation, the learners would tend to initially add manner information to their interpretation of Spanish motion verbs. For example, if learners hear the sentence *El ladrón entró en la casa* 'The thief entered the house', they might interpret *entró* as encoding both motion and manner, thus following the Danish L1 pattern *Tyven brød ind i huset* 'The thief broke into the house'. Based on Slobin's Thinking for Speaking hypothesis, and given the different degrees to which manner of motion is coded in the lexicons of the two languages, a difference would be predicted between beginning learners of S- and V-languages.

With respect to production, the learner might add in a given context some kind of manner information that is not commonly expressed in the target language. For example, if learners want to express the idea that *Folk strømmede gennem gaderne* 'People streamed through the streets', they might say something like *La gente pasaba por las calles como un río* 'People passed though the streets like a river'.[7] As in the case of interpretation, differences between beginner learners from V-and S-languages would also be expected.

Danish L1 - Spanish L2: Boundary-Crossing Mapping. Given that in Danish manner and motion are conflated in the verb in situations that contain both boundary and nonboundary-crossing, the following hypotheses are postulated.

With respect to interpretation, the learners might interpret Spanish nonboundary-crossing expressions like *Corrió en la casa* '(He) ran inside the house' to refer to both a nonboundary- and a boundary-crossing situation; that is, meaning either 'He ran inside the house' (without boundary-crossing) or 'He ran into the house' (with boundary-crossing). Following Slobin's thinking for speaking hypothesis, differences are expected to be found between learners from S- and V-languages, as the latter are not required to learn new mapping patterns in the L2.

With respect to production, it is hypothesized that the learner will conflate manner and motion in boundary-crossing situations, which is not possible in Spanish. Thus, the learner might produce Spanish sentences such as *Ella corrió en la casa* 'She ran inside the house' to mean 'She ran into the house'. As in the case of interpretation, differences between beginner learners of S- and V-languages would also be expected.

As indicated in the predictions, it is important that, when doing empirical research, the data collection includes control groups. So, for example, Danish L2 learners should have native languages representing both V- and S-languages (e.g., Spanish learners of Danish and English learners of Danish). It is also important to collect data from learners with different L2-proficiencies, but data from more advanced learners is of particular interest in order to investigate the strength of the thinking for speaking hypothesis. If, for instance, very advanced Spanish learners of L2 Danish have a reduced repertoire of second-tier manner verbs in comparison with, for example, English learners, then the thinking for speaking hypothesis would be strongly supported. If, on the other hand, no significant differences were found between the two learner groups, this would mean that the L1 typological patterns are influential only at the initial

[7] This is an example found in a commonly used Danish-Spanish dictionary (Hansen & Gawinski, 1996), which is written by Danish native speakers.

stages of SLA. Therefore, the thinking for speaking hypothesis might require rethinking in the light of increasing language proficiency.

CONCLUSIONS

The overall aim of this chapter has been to show how cognitive linguistics can constitute a promising linguistic paradigm for the study of SLA and particularly for the investigation of how L2 learners establish form–meaning connections in the L2. With respect to the contributions in general, it has been argued that cognitive linguistics is a particularly promising paradigm for the examination of form–meaning connections in SLA given its view of language structure as a symbolic instrument that conveys meaning. The central role of meaning in this theory, as well as its view of semantics as inseparable from linguistic structure, makes it especially suited for L2 researchers interested in examining the types of form–meaning mappings that learners make in the process of acquiring a L2. Furthermore, its view of language as an integral facet of cognition, and its commitment to analyzing language in terms of more general cognitive processes and abilities (e.g., perception, categorization, schematization, metaphor, imagery, and attention, to mention a few), allows for the establishment of links between linguistic and cognitive approaches to language—as argued by Tomasello (1998)—and consequently, between linguistic and cognitive approaches to SLA.

These two views on the nature of language, the one concerning the inseparability of linguistic structure and linguistic meaning, and the other concerning the inseparability of language and cognition, allow for a more integrated view of language. This integrated view has already resulted in a fruitful research agenda within L1 language acquisition, as shown in the work of Slobin, Tomasello, and other L1 acquisition researchers (see Berman & Slobin, 1994; Neimeier & Achard, 2000; Slobin, 1996a, 1996b, 2000). Such a view would also be fruitful for the investigation of SLA. SLA research could likewise benefit from the fine-grained analyses of semantic and conceptual structures provided by cognitive linguistics, and take these as points of departure for analyses of the learners' L1 and IL systems.

The last, but not least, important contribution of cognitive linguistics to the study of SLA is that it would allow for a more integrative analysis of the different linguistic levels of learner language (i.e., lexicon, morphology, and syntax). The cognitive linguistics view of lexicon, morphology, and syntax as an interconnected continuum of symbolic structures influenced by common cognitive principles and processes may help provide a more unified picture of the L2 learners' interlanguage.

With respect to the specific contributions of cognitive typology to SLA research, it has been argued that this line of research constitutes a useful framework for the systematic investigation of how L2 learners come to talk about motion in an L2, an area that has not received much attention in SLA research (but see Inagaki, 2001, and Montrul, 2001, for two recent studies from a different theoretical perspective; and Becker & Carroll, 1997, for a broad investigation on the expression of spatial relationships in the European context). Talmy's typological framework in combination with Slobin's empirical work on L1 acquisition and his thinking for speaking hypothesis can constitute the basis for theoretically motivated hypotheses, which could then be put to empirical test. This line of inquiry is heuristically rich in its predictive power, and as such complies with one of the important functions of any theoretical approach, namely, the ability to stimulate research by providing the solid ground from which hypotheses can arise (McLaughlin, 1987).

In addition, it has been argued that this line of research would allow for the systematic investigation of crosslinguistic influence in SLA, and could shed new light on the intricate relationship between crosslinguistic influence and the degree of similarity and difference between the learners' L1 and L2. Moreover, as indicated by Odlin (1989), research based on linguistic typologies is useful for the investigation of transfer, given that it allows for the study of systemic influences and for a clearer understanding of the complex interplay between transfer, developmental sequences, and natural principles of L2 acquisition.

Finally, it should be stressed that the benefits of a link between SLA research and cognitive typology are not unidirectional, but rather bidirectional. It is not only the field of SLA that can benefit from research on cognitive typology. Results from SLA research can also further understanding of the intricate relationship between language and thought and can thus contribute to the ongoing debate on linguistic relativity and determinism.

REFERENCES

Becker, A., & Carroll, M. (1997). *The acquisition of spatial relations in a second language*. Amsterdam: Benjamins.

Berlin, B., & Kay, P. (1969). *Basic color terms: Their universality and their evolution.* Berkeley: University of California Press.

Berman, R. A. & Slobin, D. I. (1994). Development of linguistic forms: English. In R. A. Berman & D. I. Slobin (Eds.), *Relating events in narrative: A crosslinguistic developmental study*. Hillsdale, NJ: Lawrence Erlbaum Associates.

Cuenca, M. J., & Hilferty, J. (1999). *Introducción a la lingüística cognitiva*. Barcelona: Ariel Lingüística.

Geeraerts, D. (1988). Cognitive grammar and the history of lexical semantics. In B. Rudzka-Ostyn (Ed.), *Topics in cognitive linguistics* (pp. 647–677). Amsterdam: Benjamins.

Gibbs, R. W. (1996). What is cognitive about cognitive linguistics? In E. H. Casad (Ed.), *Linguistics in the redwoods: The expansion of a new paradigm in linguistics* (pp. 27–53). Berlin: Mouton de Gruyter.

Goldberg, A. E. (1995). *Constructions: A construction grammar approach to argument structure*. Chicago: Chicago University Press.

Hansen, J. W., & Gawinski, B. (1996). *Dansk–spansk ordborg*. Norbok: Munksgaard Ordbøger.

Harley, B. (1993). Patterns of second language development in French inmersion. *French Language Studies, 2*, 159–183.

Harley, B., & King, M. L. (1989). Verb lexis in the written compositions of young L2 learners. *Studies in Second Language Acquisition, 11*, 415–439.

Inagaki, S. (2001). Motion verbs with goal PPs in the L2 acquisition of English and Japanese. *Studies in Second Language Acquisition, 23*, 153–170.

Johnson, M. (1987). *The body in the mind: The bodily basis of meaning, imagination and reasoning*. Chicago: University of Chicago Press.

Lakoff, G. (1987). *Women, fire and dangerous things: What categories reveal about the mind.* Chicago: University of Chicago Press.

Lakoff, G. (1990). The invariance hypothesis: Is abstract reason based on image schemas? *Cognitive Linguistics, 1*, 39–74.

Langacker, R. W. (1968). *Language and its structure; some fundamental linguistic concepts*. New York: Harcourt.

Langacker, R. W. (1987). *Foundations of cognitive grammar: Vol 1. Theoretical perspectives*. Palo Alto, CA: Stanford University Press.

Langacker, R. W. (1996). Cognitive grammar. In K. Brown & J. Miller (Eds.), *Concise enclypedia of syntactic theories* (pp. 51–54). Oxford, England: Pergamon.

Lucy, J. (1992). *Grammatical categories and cognition: A case study of the linguistic relativity hypothesis.* Cambridge, England: Cambridge University Press.

Lucy, J. (1996). The scope of linguistic relativity: An analysis and review of empirical research. In J. Gumperz, J. John & S. C. Levinson (Eds.), *Rethinking linguistic relativity* (pp. 37–69). Cambridge, England: Cambridge University Press.

Mayer, M. (1969). *Frog, where are you?* New York: Dial Press.

McLaughlin, B. (1987). *Theories of second language learning*. London: Edward Arnold.

Montrul, S. (2001). Agentive verbs of manner of motion in Spanish and English as second languages. *Studies in Second Language Acquisition, 23*, 171–206.

Niemeier, S., & Achard, M. (Eds.). (2000). Language acquisition [Special Issue]. *Cognitive Linguistics, 11*.

Odlin, T. (1989). *Language transfer: Cross–linguistic influence in language learning*. Cambridge, England: Cambridge University Press.

Rosch, E. (1978). Principles of categorization. In E. Rosch & B. B. Lloyd (Eds.), *Cognition and categorization* (pp. 27–48). Hillsdale, NJ: Lawrence Erlbaum & Associates.

Slobin, D. I. (1996a). From 'thought and language' to 'thinking for speaking'. In J. Gumperz, J. John, & S. C. Levinson (Eds.), *Rethinking linguistic relativity* (pp. 70–96). Cambridge, England: Cambridge University Press.

Slobin, D. I. (1996b). Two ways to travel: Verb of motion in English and Spanish. In M. Shibatani & S. A. Thompson (Eds.), *Grammatical constructions: Their form and meaning* (pp. 195–219). Oxford, England: Clarendon.

Slobin, D. I. (1997). Mind, code, and text. In J. Bybee, J. Haiman, & S. A. Thompson (Eds.), *Essays on language function and language type: Dedicated to T. Givón* (pp. 438–467). Amsterdam: Benjamins.

Slobin, D. I. (2000). Verbalized events: A dynamic approach to linguistic relativity and determinism. In S. Niemeier & R. Dirven (Eds.), *Evidence for linguistic relativity* (pp. 107–138). Amsterdam: Benjamins.

Talmy, L. (1985). Lexicalization patterns: Semantic structure in lexical forms. In T. Shopen (Ed.), *Language typology and syntactic description: Vol. 3. Grammatical categories and the lexicon* (pp. 36–149). Cambridge, England: Cambridge University Press.

Talmy, L (1991). Path to realization: A typology of event conflation. *Proceedings of the 7th annual meeting of the Berkeley Linguistics Society* (pp. 480–519). Berkeley, CA: Berkeley Linguistic Society:

Talmy, L. (1996). The windowing of attention in language. In M. Shibatani & S. A. (Eds.), *Grammatical construction: Their form and meaning* (pp. 235–287). Oxford: Claredon.

Tomasello, M. (1998). *The new psychology of language: Cognitive and functional approaches to language structure.* London, England: Lawrence Erlbaum & Associates..

Ungerer, F., & Schmid, H. J. (1996). *An introduction to cognitive linguistics*. London, England: Longman.

CHAPTER 8
Beyond Syntax: Performance Factors in L2 Behavior

Elaine C. Klein
Queens College and The Graduate Center
City University of New York

Second language (L2) learners of English often exhibit the lexical and morphosyntactic errors illustrated in Examples 1 and 2:

1 a. *Which movie are the girls talking?
b. *That's the movie the girls are talking.

2 a. *She paint the house yesterday.
b. *She painting the house every year.

In addition, researchers have presented L2 learners and very proficient bilinguals with sentences like that in Example 3:

3 Someone shot the maid of the actress who was on the balcony.

When asked to decide *who* was on the balcony—the actress or the maid?—respondents from particular native languages like Spanish tend to choose the maid, in marked contrast to native speakers of English who opt for the actress.

In the cases shown in Example 1, L2 learners appear to be exhibiting gaps in their knowledge of verbs requiring a preposition in questions (Example 1a) and relative clauses (Example 1b). In Example 2 their knowledge of tense and aspect comes into question: Example 2a represents a well-known underproduction problem with omission of the inflectional past tense (*-ed*) ending, whereas Example 2b could be said to represent overproduction (or oversuppliance) of the progressive aspect marker (*-ing*), when the simple present (*-s*) is required. The case of Example 3, on the other hand, suggests an interpretation of the input that deviates from expected target language norms of relative clause "attachment," potentially limiting non-native speakers and fluent bilinguals from reaching a level of attainment in the L2 equal to that of native speakers.

The issue addressed here is whether divergence from native speaker behavior as exhibited in Examples 1 and 2, particularly, is related to gaps in L2 knowledge of form–meaning relationships (i.e., a competence deficit). Alternatively, it is suggested that such behavior, along with that illustrated in Example 3, can be better explained by reference to performance factors, particularly when L2 learners attempt to respond to increasingly difficult target language input. It is argued that what appear to be morphosyntactic errors in an L2 learner's grammar are often related to factors that lie beyond syntax; disentangling syntactic versus "interface" phenomena (i.e., the interaction of syntax with other grammatical domains), along with processing effects on the learner, can help explain the lack of form–meaning connections that result in L2 production errors and misinterpretations of the target language input. Grammar construction is input driven, so such an investigation is important for both theoretical and pedagogical reasons, in order to understand the process by which a learner's input becomes intake for new learning (Corder, 1967). Subtle performance factors that affect this process are, thus, the focus of this chapter.[1]

It is well-known, for example, that performance deficits often come about when the input has been pushed beyond the current processing capacities of the L2 learner, creating an overload in the performance system that results in nontarget behavior. An example comes from Valian, Scarpa, and Prasada's (2001) study of English first language (L1) development, where the distinction between the predicates illustrated in Examples 4 and 5 is noted:

4 a. The cat is eating some food.
  b. The cat is eating a sock.

5 a. The dog chews a bone.
  b. The dog chews a crayon.

The direct objects in Example 4a, *some food*, and Example 5a, *a bone*, are entirely predictable from and compatible with their respective verbs.[2] These contrast with the pragmatically odd direct objects in Examples 4b and 5b, *eat a sock* and *chew a crayon*. Such "plausibility cues" (related to semantic or pragmatic relationships, here between a verb and its object) have been found in sentence processing studies to require different degrees of processing resources for native speakers (see, e.g., Babyonysev, 2001, for related studies of adult processing).

An interesting question is whether developing L1 and L2 verb and sentence constituents are more apt to break down in the wake of input with features such as odd objects, inducing familiar errors in verbal morphology as those shown in Example 6, for example:

6 a. The cat eating/is eat a sock.
  b. The dog chew a crayon.

[1] Part of the research reported here was supported by a grant from the City University of New York (CUNY) Collaborative Incentive Grant Program to the author, Gita Martohardjono, and Virginia Valian. I thank my colleagues and research assistants at the second language acquisition research laboratory of the CUNY Graduate Center for their work on some of the research described here. I particularly thank Virginia Valian and Eva Fernandez whose important research I cite in sections of this chapter. Portions of this chapter were also presented at the annual conferences of the American Association of Applied Linguistics (AAAL) and Teachers of English to Speakers of Other Languages (TESOL), both in March 2000, Vancouver, BC. I thank my coresearchers Eniko Horvath and T. Leo Schmidt, along with audience members who provided helpful comments and suggestions. All errors and omissions remain my responsibility.

[2] Valian et al. noted that this follows from Katz (1987), who argued that the semantics of a verb inherently includes direct objects with particular semantic properties.

This chapter returns to studies that address this and related questions involving the effects of different sorts of input on L2 output. Importantly, an argument is made that the empirical evidence needed to understand input effects must necessarily come from highly controlled studies of the kind that Hultsjin (1997), E. C. Klein and Martohardjono (1999), and others argue is crucial in L2 research. It is only from such studies that the precise nature of elements that affect the processing and interpretation of L2 input can be examined, which in turn affect further grammar construction and reconstruction.

This chapter is organized into the following sections: The first section is an overview of the theoretical framework underlying the arguments presented here, a Universal Grammar (UG) model of acquisition. The second section presents three UG-based hypotheses, which provide alternative explanations for the nontarget behaviors illustrated in Examples 1 through 3. In the third section of the chapter, experimental evidence is presented for each type of nontarget behavior: first, omitted prepositions; then, errors in tense and aspect; and finally, relative clause attachments that deviate from those of native speakers.[3] It is argued that the three types of behavior are each explained by one of the hypotheses posited earlier. The concluding section discusses some important implications for L2 theory, research, and pedagogy.

THE UNIVERSAL GRAMMAR MODEL OF L2 ACQUISITION

An underlying assumption is that language development proceeds from a set of universal principles and parameters known as Universal Grammar (UG), with which native and non-native language learners are innately endowed (see White, 1989, for discussion of UG in L2). Such principles provide the skeletal framework on which the rest of language development is built, providing constraints on the hypotheses that learners develop for the target grammar. Other components build on UG: Language specific input enters a parser, which is governed by processing principles, the universality of which is still in question (this issue is discussed later on). It is at this point that form–meaning connections begin to be made. Similarly, the parser's output is governed by learnability principles that guide the processed input as it contributes to the grammar. Importantly, input must be processible in order for it to serve, in some manner, as a trigger for restructuring the grammar—that is, for pushing the grammar on its path toward the target, sometimes a long and arduous trip. (For explanation and illustration of this process, see E. C. Klein and Martohardjono, 1999.)

Importantly, the UG model makes a crucial distinction. The properties that constitute grammatical knowledge, the learner's underlying competence,

[3] All of the experiments described have recently been conducted (or are currently in progress) at the first and second language acquisition and processing laboratories at Hunter College, CUNY, and the CUNY Graduate Center.

consist of UG and the mental representations of learners at each stage of development. On the other hand, process issues relate to the mechanisms that constitute the course of grammar construction, involving the input, processing, learnability, and triggering—how the learner gets from one knowledge state to the next, or just hangs out in the same state for awhile. Properties, then, are related to competence, whereas process involves the performance system.

The question addressed here is whether specific nontarget-like behavior evidenced by an L2 learner is a property issue, lack of language knowledge, or a process issue, attributed to the performance system. Importantly, it is acknowledged that any learner language observed is always measured through performance; there is no way of doing otherwise. However, it is crucial, for theoretical and other reasons, to attempt to distinguish what the learner knows, but cannot access or use, from what the learner does not know. The next section provides alternative hypotheses for the three products of nontarget-like L2 behavior originally presented as Examples 1 – 3, now shown as Examples 7 – 9:

7 a. Which movie are the girls talking?

b. That's the movies the girls are talking.

8 a. She paint the house yesterday.

b. She painting the house every year.

9 Someone shot the maid of the actress who was on the balcony.

Q: Who was on the balcony? A: The maid.

HYPOTHESES

Figure 8.1 displays potential hypotheses to explain the nontarget-like L2 behavior shown in Examples 7 – 9.

Under a UG model, this behavior could be due either to deficits in competence or deficits in performance. Under competence, there are two types of deficits: The right side refers to lack of knowledge in domains of language outside of syntactic (e.g., phonological, semantic, etc.). This chapter considers only "syntax" deficits, implying that learners are hypothesized to lack (morpho)syntactic knowledge of the relevant form–meaning connections in their grammars. This is illustrated in the instances of omitted prepositions shown in Example 7.

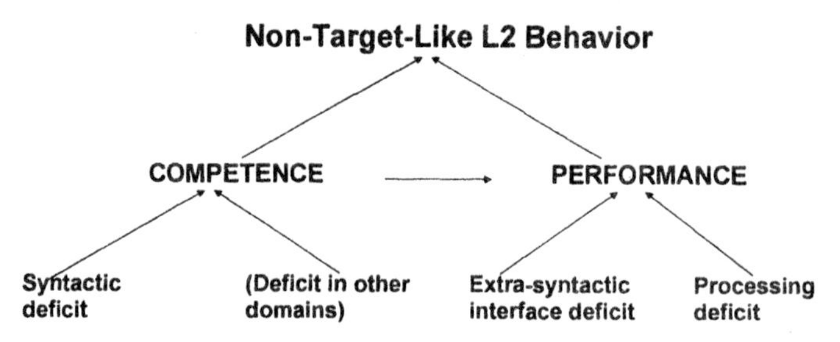

Fig. 8.1. Potential hypotheses to describe non-target-like behavior.

Under performance, there are also two possibilities: One is due to what is being called *interface deficits*. Here L2 learners are hypothesized to have the required structural knowledge, but the interface of the (morpho)syntax with lexical, semantic, phonological, or pragmatic complexities results in an overload to the performance system that causes L2 learners to falter and often err. This explains the tense and aspect deviations under Example 8.

Under performance, as well, are *processing deficits* where learners are also hypothesized to have the required (morpho)syntactic knowledge. However, they exhibit aberrant behavior because of well-known and not so well-known processing effects. For example, a task may strain working memory capacity and thus be too difficult to perform in real time, or a learner's processing resources may be diverted from formal properties of language during a task. Another possibility is that nagging L1 processing strategies are making demands on the learner that she cannot resist. The relative clause attachment deviation in Example 9 will be shown to be a processing deficit of this type.

Recent experimental studies of the behaviors in Examples 7 through 9 suggest how the aforementioned hypotheses help to uniquely explain each behavior.

EXPERIMENTAL EVIDENCE AND EXPLANATIONS

The Null Prep Phenomenon

In a series of studies, E. C. Klein and colleagues (E. C. Klein, 1993a, 1993b, 1995a, 1995b, 2001; E. C. Klein & Casco, 2000) have reported the omission of prepositions among both adult (e.g. E. C. Klein, 1993a, 1995b) and child (E. C. Klein, 1993b) learners of L2 English. In the so-called null prep studies, learners are first tested on their subcategorization knowledge of verbs for their prepositional complements, requiring the acceptance of declarative examples such as Example 10a and the rejection of Example 10b:

10 a. The young girls are talking about the movie.
   b. *The young girls are talking the movie.

If respondents evidence the required subcategorization knowledge and also accept related questions or relatives without the preposition as shown in Examples 11a and 11b, they are considered to exhibit the null prep phenomenon:

11 a. *Which movie are the girls talking?
   b. *That's the movie the girls are talking.

The null prep response pattern has been robustly attested in English L2 as well as French L2 (Jourdain, 1996). Importantly, null prep appears in the grammars of nonprimary language learners from a wide variety of native languages that do not exhibit such structures, eliminating language transfer as an explanation for this mystery.

Now the question is why learners have null prep in their L2 grammars, especially because the evidence appears to show (with some controversy) that null prep questions are not permitted in the world's natural languages. The typical null pattern is illustrated in the Haitian Creole example under Example 12 where a preposition is required by the verb in the declarative sentence in Example 12a, whereas its omission is permitted in the related relative clause shown in Example 12b (from E.C. Klein, 1993a, p. 35):

12 a. *Twa zanmi-yo ap pale de sinema sa a.*
Three friend-pl are talking about movie this-top
'The three friends are talking about this movie.'
b. *Men sinema Ø que twa zanmi-yo ap pale a.*
Here is movie (about) that/which three friend-pl are talking top
'Here's the movie the three friends are talking about.'

By contrast, omission of the preposition is illicit in the question form shown in Example 13a, which requires the fronted (or pied-piped) preposition of Example 13b:

13 a.* Ø Ki sinema twa zanmi-yo ap pale a.
(About) what movie three friend-pl are talking top
'What movie are the three friends talking about?'
b. De ki sinema twa zanmi-yo ap pale a.
About what movie three friend-pl are talking top

This same pattern has been attested in several languages of the world, especially in their vernacular dialects. These include colloquial Brazilian Portuguese, Puerto Rican and Venezuelan Spanish, Catalan, some dialects of Modern Greek, Quechua, Québecois and Montréal French, among others (E. C. Klein, 1993b, p. 126).

In fact, there has been a debate between E. C. Klein (2001) and Dekydtspotter, Sprouse, and Anderson (1998) on whether or not there are languages in the world that permit null prep questions, an important issue if it is assumed that L2 learners should not be exhibiting behavior prohibited in natural languages (E.C. Klein, 1995a). Dekydtspotter et al. and E. C. Klein both proposed an analysis that attempts to explain L2 null prep grammars within UG.

Briefly, Dekydtspotter et al. (1998) proposed a nonmovement analysis to explain null prep in questions, suggesting that learners are not moving the required elements in the formation of these constructions. Under their analysis, Dekydtspotter et al. argued that null prep shows these learners to be evidencing nonmovement grammars when English requires *Wh*-movement to form questions. (See E. C. Klein, 1993b, for detailed discussion of the syntax involved in prepositional pied-piping and stranding constructions, the native speaker equivalents for null prep.[4]) Learners do not use *Wh*-movement, the researchers suggest, because of "computational complexity," which causes them to fall back on less complex (nonmovement) grammars.[5]

However, such an explanation would also suggest that L1 learners should similarly exhibit null prep and they do not (E. C. Klein & Casco, 2000). To better account for these L1/L2 differences, E. C. Klein (2001) alternatively proposed an analysis which posits that many L2 learners optionally choose null operator movement, along with the required *Wh*-movement. (See E. C. Klein, 2001, for details and entailments of null operator movement.) Learners do this because of prior experience with languages where null operator movement is unexceptional, causing them to go through a unique developmental stage in their L2 questions—a stage that does not appear in early L1 development. Importantly in this (usually) temporary stage (i.e., the movement of null operators instead of overt ones), L2 learners are propelled to drop the preposition for UG-related reasons, explaining why null prep occurs in L2 but not in L1 questions.

A Syntactic Deficit Explanation

Whether the null prep phenomenon is explained via a nonmovement or a null-operator hypothesis, L2 learners are clearly exhibiting a gap in their syntactic knowledge. That is, English requires overt and obligatory *Wh*-movement for the formation of questions, and learners with null prep grammars do not have that obligatory rule in their grammars yet, even for simple questions. A syntactic deficit explanation, then, accounts for most cases of the null prep phenomenon.

The remainder of this chapter reports on some new acquisition studies of tense and aspect, along with relative clauses, which draw on explanations that lie beyond syntax, in the realm of performance, to account for the other examples of nontarget-like L2 behavior of concern here.

Tense and Aspect

Horvath, Klein, and Schmidt (2000)

In a study of the development of tense morphology, Horvath, E. C. Klein & Schmidt (2000) examined interface influences on tense in L2 English.

[4] In the following examples, i. represents the so-called pied-piping construction, whereas ii. is the related preposition stranding form, both of which are the accepted (i.e., correct) constructions in standard American English:

i. About which movie are the girls talking?
ii. Which movie are the girls talking about?

[5] This is not unlike Lebeaux's (1988) proposal for first language development (my interpretation).

Research Questions. The researchers posed the following questions regarding the effects of different factors on accuracy of interpretation and production of tensed verbs:

1. What are the effects of contextualization? It was hypothesized that tensed verbs embedded within the context of a story might hinder rather than help accuracy. Following VanPatten (1990), it was postulated that this is because processing resources are often diverted from language form when there is a focus on meaning.

2. What are the effects of lexical adverbs and their locality? Following many other L2 studies in the literature (e.g., Bardovi-Harlig, 1999, 2000; W. Klein, 1993; Lee, Cadierno, Glass, & VanPatten, 1997), Horvath et al. sought to confirm and clarify, with a more controlled experimental design, the finding that lexical adverbs aid comprehension and production of tense. The intent was also to extend the research of Hinkel (1997), who found that the closer an adverb is to a given tensed verb, the more accurately the L2 learner interprets the tense of that verb.

3. What are the effects of phonology? Following Wolfram (1984, 1985), Bayley (1994), and others who found phonological effects in L2 studies of tense, Horvath et al. examined whether L2 learners' responses are affected by allomorphic alternations of English past tense verb endings in the input: [t] as in *watched*, [d] as in *played*, [Id] as in *visited.*

Importantly, participants in the experiment were chosen on the basis of having already evidenced knowledge of present tense (3rd p. sing. [-*s*]) and past tense *[-ed]* in a simple decontextualized cloze task, with vocabulary and sentence length that imposed a minimal processing load on the learner. This was to determine learners' knowledge of the form–meaning connections involved in the English tense system without the confound of difficult material or procedures that might impede the deployment of this knowledge.

Participants. The participants in the experimental group were 54 adults learners of English, at an intermediate proficiency level of English, from varied L1s.[6] Participants were randomly assigned to one of three input conditions, where each condition differed according to the absence or presence of lexical adverbs and their proximity to target verbs:

Condition 1: No lexical adverbs

Condition 2: Lexical adverbs at some distance from target verbs (i.e., not in target sentences)

Condition 3: Lexical adverbs in every target sentence

Materials and Procedures. A perception task and a production task were administered, each containing a story foregrounded in the past tense, but that

[6] Proficiency level was determined by the Michigan Test of English Proficiency (MTEP). There was also a control group of 12 native speakers of English.

included an equal number of sentences in the simple present as background information expressing habitual states or actions. The question was to see the extent to which participants were able to understand and distinguish the forms and meanings of the two tenses throughout each story. For the comprehension task, participants responded via a checklist; for the production task, they were required to produce sentences from prompts (see Horvath et al., 2000, for details).

Importantly, and in contrast to most other studies of tense in discourse, the target sentences were carefully controlled: (a) Past tense verbs were phonologically balanced, (b) All target verbs were followed by an initial vowel to promote salience of the past tense endings, (c) Whenever an adverb appeared under one condition, it was balanced in another condition by the same words, along with a nonadverb having the same number of syllables as the adverb, as shown in Examples 14 and 15:

14 He played at the Green Grass Golf Course yesterday. (Cond. 3)

15 He played at the Green Grass Golf Course by himself. (Cond. 1)

And, finally, (d) Adverbs supporting past tense were also balanced by sentence position (e.g., initial vs. final position).

Results.

Contextualization effects. Learners who had evidenced close to perfect performance on the pretest did not do nearly as well on this discourse task. There was robust overgeneralization of (the *expected*) past tense when present was required, and the differences between native and non-native speakers was significant on analyses of variance (ANOVAs) on both tasks: For the perception task $F(2, 51) = 9.63, p < .001$; for the production task: $F(2, 51) = 4.963, p < .01$.

Lexical and locality effects. As in other studies, lexical adverbs aided in the processing and production of tense: Participants in Condition 3, with lexical adverbs in every target sentence, significantly outperformed those in the other two conditions on both tasks. ANOVAs demonstrated the extent of these effects: In the perception task across the three conditions $F(2, 51) = 9.63$, $p < .001$, a post-hoc Scheffé attributing the effect to Condition 3: $p < .002$; in the production task $F(2, 51) = 4.963$, $p < .01$, a post-hoc Scheffé also attributing the effect to Condition 3: $p < .01$. Because there were no differences between Conditions 1 and 2, only local adverbs (those in Condition 3) were beneficial.

Phonological effects. In Condition 1 on the perception task, where learners relied on inflectional morphology alone, responses to verbs ending in devoiced [t] were significantly less accurate on than those with voiced [d]: (df = 17) $t = 2.5, p < .02$ and those with voiced epenthetic [Id] (df = 17), $t = -2.64, p < .01$. Differences between the two voiced endings, however, did not reach significance.

This study is important because it shows how discourse context, degree and proximity of lexical support, as well as phonology, clearly contribute to L2 variability in comprehension and production of tense. Recall that L2 learners in this experiment had already demonstrated their knowledge of tense forms and meanings in a task with a lighter processing load, namely, one without the added burden imposed by interfaces between the morphosyntax and another domain of the grammar.

Although not in the research design, Horvath et al. also suspected potential semantic influences on the accuracy with which the participants made tense distinctions. This led to the follow-up study described next.

Horvath and Klein (2000)

In this early pilot study, Horvath and E. C. Klein (2000) investigated the extent to which preferences and acceptability of tense in L2 English are affected by subtle semantic differences in a verb's direct object, where slight changes in form result in corresponding meaning differences. These are shown in Examples 16 and 17:

16 a. She visited an art gallery in her hometown.
   b. She visits an art gallery in her hometown.
17 a. She visited art galleries in her hometown.
   b. She visits art galleries in her hometown.

It can be seen that the sentences in Example 16 contrast with those of Example 17 where either form of Example 17, a or b, is completely *natural*. On the other hand, Example 16b is somewhat odd unless a specific context is manufactured (e.g., *She visits art galleries in her hometown whenever she visits her mother*). Following early work in semantics by Dowty (1979) and later by Enç (1991), the contrasts can be explained by distinctions in *specificity* of the relevant NP. Thus, in Example 16 *an* art gallery is indefinite but *specific* (+ spec), and the plural art galleries in Example 17 is also indefinite, although *not specific* (- spec).[7]

According to Dowty (1979, p. 54), such contrasts in specificity appear to motivate *preferences* for past versus present tense in English. An object NP that is -spec, for example, is neutral as to tense; that is, its verb can suggest a completed event or action as is usual in the English past tense. It can also suggest an event or action that has extended from past to now, as the English present tense generally does. This explains why either past or present tense is perfectly natural in Example 17, even without adding a context.

By contrast, objects like those in Example 16 are +spec. As such, according to Dowty, they are biased toward the past tense, which is generally associated with completed events or actions (as in Example 16a) and not ongoing activities (as in Example 16b). Similarly in Example 18 the feature of

[7] It should also be mentioned that other semanticists have made slightly different distinctions, for example, equating +spec as *individuated*, and –spec as *generic*, but the point is essentially the same.

+spec remains, with definiteness increased, showing the expected pattern of preference:

18 a. She visited the art gallery in her hometown. = preferred
 b. She visits the art gallery in her hometown.

Although it appears that the present tense in English is only natural with plural objects (as in Example 17b), because such objects are nonspecific or generic, it is important to note that all the present tense examples in Examples 16 to 18 are *grammatical* sentences of English. That is, the form–meaning distinctions seen earlier result in subtle degrees of preference for naturalness in the language, but not differences in grammaticality.

The Horvath and E. C. Klein (2000) pilot study investigated the extent to which native and non-native speakers of English are aware of these subtle distinctions: Whether speakers differ in their preferences for use as well as acceptance of past versus present tense, when the specificity of the NP object is presented in three conditions as shown in Example 19:

19 a. -spec, where the direct object (DO) appears in its plural form, and is nonspecific:

With her painting class the new girl _____ art galleries in her hometown.
(visit)

b. +spec, where the determiner of the DO is indefinite, and is specific:

With her painting class the new girl _____ an art gallery in her hometown.
(visit)

c. ++spec, where the determiner of the DO is definite, and is very specific:

With her painting class the new girl _____ the art gallery in her hometown.
(visit)

Participants. The participants were similar to those in the previous study, this time with two proficiency groups (total N = 42); proficient bilinguals were also included as a control group, along with native speakers of English (control groups: N = 17). L2 learners again were pretested to ensure present and past tense knowledge in a simple cloze task.

Materials and Procedures. There were two tasks. The first task was a cloze preference task requiring participants to fill in their choice of a verb form to determine their preferences given the varieties shown in Example 19, which were randomized throughout the written test. Specifically, the desire was to find out whether non-native speakers would use simple present tense at times when it was hypothesized that native speakers (and perhaps proficient bilinguals) would not do so, as in the +spec conditions. If present tense were chosen, then it should predictably be in the –spec condition, which suggests ongoing activity.

The second task was an acceptability judgment task where participants were given the present and past forms of a particular verb, and had to judge and rank the degree to which paired sentences were more or less acceptable in English. Because both present and past tense are acceptable, the control groups were expected to respond as such; also it was predicted that they would not rank present tense as being more acceptable than past tense in the +spec conditions, whereas non-native speakers might do so.

Results. Importantly, the two control groups responded similarly in both tasks, with no significant differences between them. In the cloze preference task, however, the L2 learners' choices contrasted significantly with both control groups in all conditions indicated by ANOVAs performed: -spec, $F(3, 38) = 6.24, p < .002$; +spec, $F(3, 38) = 5.43, p < .003$; ++spec, $F(3, 38) = 5.18, p < .004$.

Differences between the proficiency levels were evidenced as well, the lower proficiency level group differing most from the control groups. The degree to which the lower proficiency group selected *nonpreferred* forms (i.e., present tense in +spec conditions (which the higher proficiency group and control groups hardly ever did), might be evident on this task where a slight trend appeared: +spec: $F = 2.76, p = .06$; ++spec: $F = 2.34, p = .09$. This clearly needs to be further supported with more participants and stimuli.

In the acceptability judgment task, the two control groups considered both past and present to be acceptable, again with no differences between them under any condition. However, both L2 learner groups differed significantly from native speakers in all conditions: -spec: $F(3, 38) = 4.21, p < .01$; +spec: $F(3, 38) = 4.97, p < .005$; ++spec: $F(3, 38) = 5.47, p < .003$, again with the lower proficiency level furthest from the control groups. Analysis of the selection of nonpreferred *forms* this time showed both non-native groups differing statistically from the control groups, but inexplicably in the ++spec condition only (i.e., the least preferred variety), $F(3, 38) = 4.97, p < .005$. Again, further research with more data will clarify whether this difference can be taken seriously.

Conclusions. Until further research is done, it is tentatively concluded that proficient bilinguals do not differ from native speakers in perceiving subtle semantic biasing effects that specificity and related aspectual distinctions have on the usage of tense. By contrast, the L2 learners in this experiment had not yet perceived these subtle distinctions. As such, the L2 deficits that have emerged are not due to lack of (morpho)syntactic knowledge of tense but rather to complexities imposed here by the interface of (morpho)syntax with semantics.

Valian (2000); E. C. Klein, Martohardjono, and Valian (2001)

These experiments also examine outcomes of tense and aspect interfaces, but in a different way. Here. the performance of L1 learners is directly compared to that of L2 learners.

The pilot L2 experiment currently in progress (E. C. Klein et al., 2001) derives from a first language acquisition study by Valian (2000) of tense and aspect among 2-year-old native English learners.

Research Questions. 1. Do L1 and L2 learners of English at early stages of proficiency show distinctions between past and present tense?[8] 2. How do L1 and L2 learners compare in their usage of tense?

In addition, the intent was to examine whether it was possible to use the same materials and procedures with L1 and L2 learners to make such comparisons.

Participants. In the L1 study, participants were 21 young L1 English-speaking children (age: 24–35 months; MLU: 1.53–5.11). In the pilot L2 study of English in progress, adult participants include 9 Korean and 10 Russian speakers[9] with the Russian speakers at a higher mean level of proficiency than the Koreans, as measured by the MTEP (see footnote 6).

Materials and Procedures. The variables tested were based on predicted complexity of the distinctions between the pairs in Example 20, representing increasingly complex tense/aspect relationships as extensively described in the L1 study (Valian, 2000):

20 a. Did/will = (predicted to be) easiest (e.g. The daddy did/will bake cookies.)

b. Was/is (copular) = moderately easy (e.g. The swing was/is in the park.)

c. Was/is +ing (progressive) = very hard (e.g. My sister was/is coloring.)

[8] This question follows from the much-debated issue in the UG literature about the learner's initial state and whether the nodes for functional categories are instantiated from the beginning of development. The issue has been framed, for example, as some form of the Strong Continuity Hypothesis where children at the earliest stages of development are argued to have adultlike functional nodes (e.g., Boser, Lust, Santelman, & Whitman, 1992; Hyams, 1994; Pinker, 1984; Poeppel & Wexler, 1993). This contrasts with various forms of the Maturational Hypothesis or Weak Continuity where it is hypothesized that functional nodes develop during the course of acquisition (e.g. Clahsen, Eisenbeiss & Vainikka, 1994; Guilfoyle & Noonan, 1992; Radford, 1990).

[9] These are the only data thus far analyzed. The larger study of which this is a pilot includes more adult L2 participants, and child L2 participants and L2 learners who speak native languages other than Russian and Korean.

In both studies, participants were tested individually in two tasks. In Valian's unique comprehension task, an object or picture is presented to a learner, who points to the one corresponding to a given prompt. Each request elicits either present or past tense, thus testing the learner's knowledge of the form–meaning connections required for the English tense system. (e.g., Props: two small plastic buckets with monkeys. Experimenter: "I have two baskets full of monkeys (empties one). "Show me the one that *is/was* full.")

The second task involved taped elicited imitation, where learners imitated sentences like those in Example 20. For the L2 study, an extra condition was included to compensate for learners' longer memory spans. Thus the task was presented under two conditions, the short condition as shown in Example 20 and a long condition, where a prepositional phrase was added to each sentence as an adjunct (e.g. Short condition: *My sister was/is coloring.* Long condition: *My sister was/is coloring with her crayon.*) Whereas the position of the target remained constant in both conditions, the prepositional phrase was placed sentence initially in half the sentences of the long condition and in sentence-final position in the other half. By manipulating sentence length, it was expected to be testing for performance effects as longer sentences clearly bring with them a heavier processing load.

Valian also conducted a follow-up comprehension task with younger and older 2-year-olds, in which lexical adverbs were added to the stimuli.

Preliminary Results. Results of the comprehension task showed that all learners understood tense distinctions to some degree, although their performance varied depending on which morphemes were presented: The Koreans, at a lower proficiency level overall, patterned like 2-year-old L1 learners, from easiest to most difficult morphemes as predicted: *did/will* → *was/is* (cop) → *was/ing +ing.* By contrast, the more advanced Russian speakers performed almost at ceiling on the task.

Interestingly, like the L1 study, where there were no differences based on MLUs, the measure of proficiency used in L1 experiments, the Korean learners showed no differences based on proficiency. This suggests that general knowledge of tense distinctions develops very early (i.e., learning to *distinguish* the form–meaning mappings of past vs. present), but the complexities involved in the development of the tense and aspect system develop gradually.

The comprehension task with lexical adverbs was performed by participants in the L1 study only. The results showed that the addition of lexical adverbs made no difference among younger 2-year-olds. However, the adverbs aided older 2-year-olds in making tense distinctions. This suggests that lexical support is not integrated into children's performance of tense distinctions in the earlier stages, contrasting with L2 development where such support is helpful from the beginning.

Results on the elicited imitation task for L1 and L2 learners in the short condition were as follows: The predicted pattern held for L1 children and the L2 Koreans, who again patterned more like the children than like the L2 Russians who were equal on all verb types. Interestingly, no L2 (or L1) learners reached ceiling for any verb types, showing that the task (i.e. in the short condition) was not too easy for anyone.

Results for the elicited imitation task in the long condition, performed by the L2 learner groups only, were surprising. For both learner groups, performance was severely depressed for all verb types and both tenses, and no results could be tabulated. Across both groups, the long sentences were repeated at an average of only 19%.

Conclusions. On a general note, these experiments found that L1 and L2 learners of different ages can be effectively tested using the same procedures and materials, an important finding for future language research.

The specific results of the comprehension task clearly indicate that L1 and L2 learners at very early stages of development show distinctions between past versus present tense form–meaning correspondences, suggesting that the functional projections for tense are present in their grammars from the start.

L1 and L2 learners also appear to be remarkably similar in early stages of development, showing gradual knowledge of tense/aspect relationships of increasing complexity (e.g., *did/will* → *was/is*). Valian (2000) suggested that although children know the syntax and meaning of tense early on, they gradually learn to fit together more complex form–meaning correspondences. These correspondences involve relationships between the tense/aspect system with semantics/pragmatics that relate to temporal and aspectual notions. It seems that beginning L2 learners can be said to show a similar pattern, although they appear to differ from very young L1 learners in the extent to which more cognitively mature older learners (both L1 and L2) are aided by lexical support.

These pilot experiments also show that additional processing load in the form of longer sentences can result in breakdowns in L2 performance. This was not expected, particularly because most elicited imitation tasks in L2 research have standardly used sentences with about 15 morphemes (originally following Naiman, 1974). The maximum length of the sentences in this experiment was 13 syllables. The study of such performance effects will clearly benefit from more extensive controlled research.

Performance factors related to different input types have been investigated more thoroughly in L1 research than in that of L2,[10] so this section concludes by briefly noting one such study introduced earlier, along with its follow up.

[10] For example, Bloom (1991) and Valian, Hoeffner, and Aubry (1996) examined this issue in L1 studies of null subjects. A notable exception for L2 is Leow (1998), who investigated the effects of different types of input on L2 responses.

Valian, Scarpa and Prasada (2001)

Recall the earlier contrasts of Examples 4 and 5, now Examples 21 and 22, where the b versions are pragmatically less predictable from the verb's meaning:

21 a. The cat is eating some food.
 b. The cat is eating a sock.

22 a. The dog chews a bone.
 b. The dog chews a crayon.

Two-year-old native learners of English (N = 24) tested on sentences such as these in an elicited imitation task showed that they include the verb (and the subject as well) more often when the direct object is predictable than when it is pragmatically odd, the latter carrying a heavier processing load.

To examine whether such effects hold for older subjects, Valian and colleagues are testing native and near-native speakers of English on similar sentences using a rapid serial visual presentation task (RSVP), following Forster (1970). By adjusting the speed of the input on a computer screen, as participants see and repeat sentences like those in Examples 21 and 22, the researchers are trying to induce the same processing problems in adults that are evident in children learning language.

The results, thus far, show that unlike children learning their native English, native and near native English-speaking adults appear to have no trouble at all producing subjects and verbs, even when the input is presented very quickly. Participants also do not stumble when the verb phrase appears with pragmatically odd objects, although they respond more slowly than when predictable objects are presented. Thus, it appears that adult proficient speakers cannot be turned into children developing language, or L2 learners, because the latter groups are seriously affected by the weight of a heavy processing load. Once the constituents of the verb phrase are very firmly established, however, the only effect of processing load on performance, is to slow it down.

A different type of variability comes from work in sentence processing, which serves as a final instance of experimental evidence showing performance factors in L2 behavior.

Relative Clause Attachments

Fernandez (2000, 2002)

An important debate in bilingual processing research involves the following questions, among many others: First, how can so-called performance deficits be explained among highly proficient bilinguals? Such deficits show up in the literature as slower reading times and more errors, especially in a bilingual's nondominant language (see Cook, 1997, for an outline of the issue). Second, how does the bilingual process two languages? It has been generally assumed that bilinguals appropriately process the input in a language-dependent way, namely, based on the particular language they are receiving. Therefore, the form–meaning mappings in the L2 are developed through the ambient language alone. However, more recently, it has been proposed that a bilingual may be processing her two languages using the same processing strategies required of her first or dominant language. That is, form–meaning connections are influenced by prior linguistic experience. These are the issues Fernandez investigated, but first consider some necessary background.

The Role of the Parser. It is generally understood that once a speaker recognizes a stream of words, form–meaning connections begin. That is, this stream of input gets propelled into the *parser* and it is there that the input is assigned a structure. By standard proposals (for review, see Mitchell, 1994), the parser begins this work very early and very fast, and starts to build a tree—of the syntactic sort—preferring the simplest tree possible. If the structure of the input does not match any preferences the parser might have, then a more complex tree must get built—and this takes time and energy for the parser. That is, more computationally complex tree-building is more work.

For the second language learner, the computations are even more difficult, and processing the input may be impeded for many reasons, as suggested throughout this chapter. Once a string of language is in the parser, the question also arises as to how much interaction there will be between the parser and the learner's current grammar, and whether such operations are similar for monolinguals and these potential bilinguals.

A universalist account argues that tree-building within the parser involves universal principles, among which is the principle of low attachment (Frazier, 1979; Frazier & Fodor, 1978; Mitchell, 1994; for reviews, see Frazier & Clifton, 1996). According to this principle, the parser prefers attachments that are "low on the tree" (or closest to the word or words to which a linguistic item is linked), which goes back to the original example now shown as Example 23:

23 Someone shot the maid of the actress who was on the balcony.
Who was on the balcony? The maid? The actress?

Although the form–meaning relationships of this sentence are potentially ambiguous (i.e., the connection of the relative pronoun *who* with its referent), the parser prefers to attach the pronoun and its relative clause *who was on the balcony* to the lower NP (i.e, the *actress*), rather than the higher NP (i.e., the *maid*). Thus, the principle of low attachment predicts that speakers of all languages should disambiguate the sentence by first choosing *the actress*. On the other hand, attaching the relative clause to the higher NP would be a possible but dispreferred option because it violates late attachment. Being dispreferred, the structure should be much harder for the parser to handle and anything that is hard to handle will cause an overload to the parser. Such an overload can affect performance, including longer reading times and sometimes errors.

Now if the parser operates in a universal way, all language learners, no matter their native language, would be expected to attach low initially; a high attachment might then occur later because of extra- or post-syntactic factors that have little to do with the parser's initial work—factors like semantics, prosody, or pragmatics. On the other hand, if the parser does not operate in a universal way, but rather its strategies vary from language to language, then low versus high attachment differences across languages would be expected from the start. In addition, if L2 learners bring their L1 processing routines along with them, it might be very hard—maybe impossible—to switch to L2 routines needed to interpret the L2 in a native-like way.

The Study. Fernandez (2000, 2002) tested these questions both offline and online. Importantly, processing researchers argue that offline tasks tap late stages of parsing, where extrasyntactic factors are involved. By contrast, online tasks attempt to tap very early parsing stages, as the parser is assigning structure to the input as form–meaning mappings. Both are important for the developmental picture.

Participants. There were equal numbers of monolingual English (N = 40) and Spanish (N = 40) speakers in the study, as well as Spanish-English bilinguals who were English-dominant (N = 28) and Spanish-dominant (N = 28).

Materials and procedures. In the offline experiment, Spanish and English monolinguals and bilinguals were tested in a questionnaire task where all the target sentences were ambiguous, as in Example 23. It was expected that high attachers would choose the *maid*, while low attachers would choose the *actress*.

The online experiment consisted of a self-paced reading task where subjects read disambiguated sentences where some were *forced high* and others *low* by means of grammatical number agreement (e.g., Andrew had dinner yesterday with the *nephew* of the teachers that *was* in the communist party. This is *forced to attach high* because the lower verb, *was*, must agree with the higher NP, *nephew*).[11]

When a respondent is forced to attach to a site that her parser does not prefer, this will take more time than if the forced attachment matches the parser's preference. Measurements were taken of the time it took to read two disambiguated sentence types—those forced low vs. those forced high—with attachment preferences determined by the difference in reading times between the two types of sentences.

Results. Among the monolinguals in the online task, both Spanish and English participants had significantly faster reading times in sentences where they were

[11] This very simplistic explanation does not take into account any details on the syntax of relative clauses, but serves only to make the relevant point concerning required agreement features.

forced to attach low, $F1(1, 72) = 7.77, p < .01$; $F2(1, 20) = 6.15, p < .05$, with no significant difference related to language group. This contrasted with results from the offline task: As in earlier experiments, the behavior of the two language groups differed significantly. English monolinguals preferred to attach low and Spanish monolinguals preferred to attach high, $F1(1, 44) = 5.48, p < .025$; $F2(1, 10) = 56.05, p < .001$. As noted earlier, these differences have been argued to result from postsyntactic factors—mostly pragmatics and prosody—that occur after the parser has done its initial work.

Among the bilinguals, the results were not so clear. In the online task, there were no significant differences in attachment preferences among the Spanish/English bilinguals, but there were also no reliable attachment preferences (e.g., low attachment, as with the monolinguals). Overall, their reading scores were *slower* than those of monolinguals, confirming evidence of a performance deficit. Fernandez believed that these slower reading times help explain the null results for bilinguals in this online task, which she argued is not sensitive enough to tap their very early processing.

In the offline task, the results paralleled those for the monolinguals: The bilinguals whose dominant language was Spanish imposed their Spanish preference on English sentences, exactly as the Spanish monolinguals did. Likewise, English-dominant bilinguals acted like English monolinguals and imposed their English parsing routines on Spanish. This effect was significant, $F1(1, 40) = 9.04, p < .005$; $F2(1, 20) = 59.36, p < .001$.

Conclusions. Initially, these results indicate that the parser's earliest tree-building strategies are universal, as shown for both the Spanish and English monolinguals, who consistently favored low attachment. More refined tests will determine whether this is true of bilinguals as well.

The offline experiment, on the other hand, supports others that show crosslinguistic parsing differences for Spanish-English bilinguals (e.g., Cuetos & Mitchell, 1988; Dussias, 2001). Proficient bilinguals appear to bring their L1 strategies to the task of parsing the non-dominant L2 but only after an initial parse is made. Thus, variability in relative clause attachments is due to processing deficits of (some) bilinguals, related to native language processing routines.

SUMMARY OF EXPERIMENTAL EVIDENCE

The following may be concluded from the experimental studies described in the previous section: Null prepositions in a learner's grammar can arguably be explained by a *syntactic deficit* in the L2 grammar. On the other hand, errors related to form–meaning mappings in the L2 tense system are often caused by factors that lie *beyond syntax*: Specifically, such tense errors may be attributed to the interface between morphosyntax and features of phonology, semantics, pragmatics, or discourse that create an overload to the learner's performance system. Thus, many errors have erroneously been attributed to gaps in L2 knowledge of English tense when, more precisely, they may be due to *interface deficits* related to performance. In addition, the *processing deficit hypothesis* can potentially account for tense errors in interpretation of input with long (or complex) sentences, for example, as well as the nontarget-like behavior found in relative clause attachment differences between native and non-native speakers of English.

IMPLICATIONS

The evidence presented in this chapter suggests implications for L2 theory, research, and pedagogy. Theoretically, L2 grammars may be less variable or deficient than is often assumed. That is, further examination of performance factors in L2 studies may change the view that L2 learners are such gross underachievers, falling far behind L1 learners. In fact, non-native speakers appear to be poorer performers, with access and deployment of their L2 knowledge affected by variables not generally, or specifically, understood very well or yet studied closely. This chapter has shown, for example, performance effects that are generally attributed in the research literature to gaps in L2 knowledge.

Continued research in the study of performance, and more specifically processing, effects will help further understanding of the conditions under which form–meaning connections are made as the input is parsed, and how that processed input affects the current and subsequent grammars of an L2 learner. A theory of L2 acquisition should also postulate how such form–meaning connections are retrieved and used, as well as which grammatical features are readily available (or not) to the incipient language user and why. It may be that differences in L1 and L2 acquisition patterns and attainment lie in such performance factors.

Important methodological considerations must drive research in this area: Researchers must distinguish *process* from *property* issues; rigorously control for input factors that overload the performance system, across tasks of differing types and levels of difficulty, manipulating input from decreased to increased performance demands; test for preferences and optional choices as well as categorical choices; and use proficient bilinguals as controls.

Finally, the results of carefully controlled research will obviously inform pedagogy, as language instruction differs markedly for a learner who needs to fill a knowledge gap versus one who needs practice using L2 knowledge under increasingly complex input and task conditions.

REFERENCES

Babyonysev, M. (2001). *The use of syntactic and semantic cues in parsing*. Paper presented at the Psycholinguistics Supper Club, the CUNY Graduate Center, New York, NY.

Bardovi–Harlig, K. (1999). From morpheme studies to temporal semantics: Tense–aspect research in SLA. *Studies in Second Language Acquisition, 21*, 341–382.

Bardovi–Harlig, K. (2000). Tense and aspect in second language acquisition: Form meaning, and use. *Language Learning 50,* (Suppl. 1).

Bayley, R. J. (1994). Interlanguage variation and the quantitative paradigm: Past tense marking in Chinese-English. In S. Gass, A. Cohen, & E. Tarone (Eds.), *Research methodology in second language acquisition* (pp. 157–181). Hillsdale, NJ: Lawrence Erlbaum & Associates.

Bloom, L. (1991). *Language development from two to three*. New York: Cambridge University Press.

Boser, K., Lust, B., Santelman, L., & Whitman, J. (1992). The syntax of CP and V-2 in early child German—(ECG)—the strong continuity hypothesis. *NELS Proceedings 22, GLSA, University of Massachusetts at Amhurst* (pp. 51–65).

Clahsen, H., Eisenbeiss, S., & Vainikka, A. (1994). Seeds of structure. A syntactic analysis of the acquisition of case marking. In T. Hoekstra & B. D. Schwartz (Eds.), *Language acquisition studies in generative grammar* (pp. 85–118). Amsterdam: Benjamins.

Cook, V. (1997). The consequences of bilingualism for cognitive processing. In M. B. deGroot & J.F. Kroll (Eds.), *Tutorials in bilingualism: Psycholinguistic perspectives* (pp. 279–300). Mahwah, NJ: Lawrence Erlbaum & Associates.

Corder, S. P. (1967). The significance of learners' errors. *IRAL, 5* (4), 161–169.

Cuetos, F., & Mitchell, D. C. (1988). Cross-linguistic differences in parsing: Restrictions on the use of the late closure strategy in Spanish. *Cognition, 30*, 73–105.

Dekydtspotter, L., Sprouse, R. A., & Anderson, A. (1998). Interlanguage A-bar dependencies: Binding construals, null prepositions, and universal grammar. *Second Language Research, 14*, 1–33.

Dowty, D. (1979). The aspectual classes of verbs. In *Word, meaning and montague grammar* (pp. 50–131). Boston: Reidel.

Dussias, P. E. (2001). Sentence parsing in fluent Spanish–English bilinguals. In J. L. Nicol (Ed.), *One mind, two languages: bilingual language processing* (pp. 159–176). Oxford, England: Blackwell.

Enç, M. (1991). The semantics of specificity. *Linguistic Inquiry, 22*, 1–25.

Fernandez, E. (2000). *Bilingual sentence processing: relative clause attachment in English and Spanish.* Unpublished doctoral dissertation, the CUNY Graduate Center, New York, NY.

Fernandez, E. (2002). Relative clause attachment in bilinguals and monolinguals. In Heredia & Altarriba (Eds.), *Bilingual sentence processing. Advances in psychology,* (Vol. 134, pp. 187–215). Amsterdam, NL: North Holland Elsevier.

Forster, K. (1970). Visual perception of rapidly presented word sequence of varying complexity. *Perception and Psychophysics, 8*, 215–221.

Frazier, L. (1979). *On comprehending sentences: Syntactic parsing strategies.* Unpublished doctoral dissertation, University of Connecticut, Storrs, CT.

Frazier, L., & Clifton, C. (1996). *Construal.* Cambridge, MA: MIT Press.

Frazier, L., & Fodor, J. D. (1978). The sausage machine: A new two-stage parsing model. *Cognition, 6*, 291–325.

Guilfoyle, E., & Noonan, M. (1992). Functional categories and language acquisition. *Canadian Journal of Linguistics, 37*, 241–272.

Hinkel, E. (1997). The past tense and temporal verb meanings in a contextual frame. *TESOL Quarterly, 31*, 289–314.

Horvath, E., & Klein, E. C. (2000, March). *Semantic bias in grammatical tense development.* Paper presented at the annual conference of Teachers of English to Speakers of Other Languages (TESOL), Vancouver, BC.

Horvath, E., Klein, E. C. & Schmidt, T. L. (2000, March). *The influence of lexical redundancy on L2 development of tense.* Paper presented at the annual conference of the American Association of Applied Linguistics (AAAL), Vancouver, BC.

Hultsjin, J. (1997). Second language acquisition research in the laboratory: Possibilities and limitations. *Studies in Second Language Acquisition, 19*, 131–144.

Hyams, N. (1994). V2, null arguments and COMP projections. In T. Hoekstra & B. D. Schwartz (Eds.), *Language acquisition studies in generative grammar* (pp. 21–56). Amsterdam: Benjamins.

Jourdain, S. (1996). *The case of null-prep in the interlanguage of adult learners of French.* Unpublished doctoral dissertation, Indiana University, Bloomington, IN.

Katz, J. J. (1987). Common sense in semantics. In E. LePore (Ed.), *New directions in semantics* (pp. 157–234). London: Academic Press.

Klein, E. C. (1993a). A problem for UG in L2 acquisition. *Issues in Applied Linguistics, 2*, 33–56.

Klein, E. C. (1993b). *Toward second language acquisition. a study of null prep.* Dordrecht: Kluwer Academic.

Klein, E. C. (1995a). Evidence for a "wild" L2 grammar. When PPs rear their empty heads. *Applied Linguistics, 16*, 88–117.

Klein, E. C. (1995b). Second versus third language acquisition: Is there a difference? *Language Learning, 45*, 419–465.

Klein, E. C. (2001). (Mis)construing null prepositions in L2 intergrammars. A commentary and proposal. *Second Language Research, 17*, 37–70.

Klein, E. C., & Casco, M. (2000). Optionality in English non–native grammars: Differences between L1 and L2 acquisition. *Proceedings of the 23rd annual Boston University Conference on Language Development* (pp. 349–360). Sommerville, MA: Cascadilla Press.

Klein, E. C., & Martohardjono, G. (1999). Investigating second language grammars. Some conceptual and methodological issues in generative SLA research. In E. C. Klein & G. Martohardjono (Eds.) *The development of second language grammars. A generative approach* (pp. 3–36). Philadelphia: Benjamins.

Klein, E. C., Martohardjono, G., & Valian, V. (2001). *How is second language acquisition like first language acquisition?* Paper presented at the Psycholinguistics Supper Club, the CUNY Graduate Center, New York, NY.

Klein, W. (1993). The acquisition of temporality. In C. Perdue (Ed.), *Adult language acquisition: Cross–linguistic perspectives* (Vol 2, pp. 73–118). Cambridge, England: Cambridge University Press.

Lebeaux, D. (1988). *Language acquisition and the form of the grammar.* Unpublished doctoral dissertation, University of Massachusetts, Amhurst.

Lee, J. F., Cadierno, T. Glass, W. R., & VanPatten, B. (1997). The effects of lexical and grammatical cues on processing past temporal reference in second language input. *Applied Language Learning, 8*, 1–21.

Leow, R. (1998). The effects of amount and type of exposure on adult learners' L2 development in SLA. *Modern Language Journal, 82*, 49–68.

Mitchell, D. C. (1994). Sentence parsing. In M. Gernsbacher (Ed.), *Handbook of psycholinguistics* (pp. 375–335). New York: Academic Press.

Naiman, N. (1974). The use of elicited imitation in second language acquisition research. *Working Papers on Bilingualism, 2*, 1–37.

Pinker, S. (1984). *Language learnability and language learning.* Cambridge, MA: Harvard University Press.

Poeppel, D., & Wexler, K. (1993). A full competence hypothesis of clause structure in early German. *Language, 69*, 1–33.

Radford, A. (1990). *Syntactic theory and the acquisition of english syntax.* Oxford, England: Basil Blackwell.

Valian, V. (2000). *Young children's understanding of tense and time*. Unpublished manuscript, Hunter College and the CUNY Graduate Center, New York, NY.

Valian, V., Hoeffner, J., & Aubry, S. (1996). Young children's imitation of sentence subjects: Evidence of processing limitations. *Developmental Psychology, 32,* 153–164.

Valian, V., Scarpa, J. & Prasada, S. (2001) *Direct object predictability: Effects on young children's imitation of sentences.* Unpublished manuscript, Hunter College, the CUNY Graduate Center, and Dartmouth College.

VanPatten, B. (1990). Attending to content and form in the input: An experiment in consciousness. *Studies in Second Language Acquisition, 12*, 287–301.

White, L. (1989). *Universal grammar and second language acquisition*. Philadelphia: Benjamins.

Wolfram, W. (1984). Unmarked tense in American Indian English. *American Speech, 59*, 229–253.

Wolfram, W. (1985). Variability in tense marking: A case for the obvious. *Language Learning, 35*, 229–253.

III
Research and the Classroom

CHAPTER 9
Effects of Instruction on Learning a Second Language: A Critique of Instructed SLA Research

Catherine J. Doughty
University of Hawaii

SLA theorists are not in agreement concerning the potential value of instructional intervention in SLA: Some argue that instruction can have no effect beyond the provision of an environment conducive to SLA (e.g., comprehensible input or triggering input). Others assume the effectiveness and even the necessity, at times, of relevant and principled instruction, and a case is made accordingly for the benefits of instruction of the right kind. Instructed SLA researchers thus investigate the comparative efficacy of different types of pedagogic intervention, particularly with regard to how instruction can assist learners in making the form–meaning connections that are critical for interlanguage development. A fundamental question in instructed SLA research is whether adult SLA involves, in the main, implicit or explicit language processing, and the related question of whether the most effective instruction is implicit or explicit in its approach to making the information needed for form–meaning connections available to the L2 learner.

THE NONINTERVENTIONIST ARGUMENT

As stated here, one view concerning the efficacy of instruction is that learners can only make form–meaning connections on their own:

> 1. Foreign language learning under classroom conditions seems to partially follow the same set of natural processes that characterize other types of language acquisition...there seems to be a universal and common set of principles which are flexible enough and adaptable to the large number of conditions under which language learning may take place. These observations furthermore suggest that the possibility of manipulating and controlling the students' verbal behavior in the classroom is in fact quite limited (Felix, 1981, p. 109).
>
> 2. The only contribution that classroom instruction can make is to provide comprehensible input that might not otherwise be available outside the classroom (Krashen, 1985, pp. 33-34, and passim).

Two arguments, implicit in these proscriptions, motivate what Long and Robinson (1998) called the strong noninterventionist position: (a) SLA is driven by the same Universal Grammar (UG) that guides first language acquisition, and (b) SLA, like first language acquisition, is entirely incidental. Within the first argument, there are also competing views concerning the potential for instruction to influence SLA (see White, 2003). Schwartz (Schwartz, 1993; Schwartz & Sprouse, 1996) argued that second language acquisition involves the resetting of parameterized universal principles (the "full transfer full access hypothesis"), triggered only by positive evidence (i.e., input), and that there is no role for negative evidence (e.g., instruction concerning what is not possible in the L2).[1] The second UG account of SLA is one that allows for, or even requires, negative evidence, such as that provided by instruction, but the need for instruction is strictly limited to cases where triggering evidence is not sufficiently informative. More specifically, when the L2 is a proper subset of the L1 with respect to a certain aspect of language, L2 learners will have to retreat from the overly general hypothesis that emanates from their L1 (White, 1987, 1991), something that cannot be done on the basis of positive evidence alone. By these UG SLA accounts, then, instruction is either entirely or largely unnecessary in the making of form–meaning connections.

The second noninterventionist argument, more commonly known as the Input Hypothesis within Krashen's (1982, 1985) Monitor Theory of SLA, proscribes traditional pedagogic procedures (grammar teaching, linguistic grading, error correction, etc.), citing a so-called noninterface concerning any potential relationship between "learned" and "acquired" knowledge (Krashen & Scarcella, 1978). Krashen (1982, 1985) claimed that the form–meaning connections of consciously learned language are distinct in memorial representation from those of unconsciously acquired language, that only the latter type of knowledge can be deployed in spontaneous language use, and furthermore, that there can be no interaction between these two independent knowledge systems (i.e., the so-called *learning/acquisition* distinction). The noninterface position explicitly states that *learned* knowledge can never become *acquired* knowledge.

Following the arguments of Doughty and Williams (1998c), for at least three reasons, both the no-negative-evidence and noninterface versions of the noninterventionist position are premature in their nearly complete prohibition on L2 instruction that fosters form–meaning connections. First, even if SLA is constrained by UG, the elements of language that are governed solely by UG are limited. Much more of the L2 is potentially acquired more efficiently, provided instruction appropriately engages learners' cognitive processing ability to connect meaning to forms during L2 comprehension and production (see also Doughty, 2001). Second, although there can be no doubt that both spontaneous and more deliberate L2 performance exist, what type of knowledge underlies each, and whether there is any connection between the two during L2 acquisition and use, are contentious issues that are far from settled in SLA, let alone any other domain of human cognition (Berry, 1997; Berry & Dienes, 1993; Stadler & Frensch, 1998.) Finally, in stark contrast to child language

[1] Of course, it should be kept in mind that UG accounts of SLA are limited in scope to the core grammar of language, and have nothing at all to say about the effects of instruction on other aspects of SLA.

acquisition, adult SLA is guaranteed only to be variable both within and across individuals, most typically relatively unsuccessful, and always incomplete, such that non-native speakers can be invariably identified as such, provided judgments are made on adequate samples of performance (see Hyltenstam & Abrahamsson, 2003; Long, 1993). In sum, it is far too soon to announce a moratorium on L2 instruction. Rather, the position taken by Doughty and Williams (1998c) is the prudent one:

> We do not consider leaving learners to their own devices to be the best plan. Does this mean that practitioners should take up the opposite position that [instruction] is appropriate ... for all learners all the time? We think not, and that, between the two poles, there are many ensuing pedagogic decisions to be made. At the outset, it must be said that it is not the case that adult second language acquisition cannot take place in the absence of instruction...; for many learners, clearly much of it can. However, our interest is not limited to what is merely possible, but extends to a determination of what would comprise the most *effective* and *efficient* instructional plan given the normal constraints of acquiring a second language in the classroom. (p. 197, emphasis added)

EFFECTIVENESS AND EFFICIENCY OF L2 INSTRUCTION

The question of whether second language instruction makes a difference was first posed in earnest by Long (1983), who attempted a preliminary answer to this question by reviewing the handful of empirical studies that directly tested Krashen's then influential claim of a learning/acquisition distinction. In those early studies, only very global comparisons were made, for instance between the L2 proficiency of subjects who either had or had not attended L2 classes, or who had done both in varying combinations. In general, the main findings indicated that, for those for whom the classroom is the only opportunity for exposure to L2 input, "instruction" is beneficial. Furthermore, when differing amounts of instruction were added on to a fixed amount of exposure, positive outcomes were interpreted to mean either that more instruction is beneficial or that more instruction merely serves as more L2 exposure. However, when differing amounts of exposure were added on to a fixed amount of instruction, these findings, taken together with instruction-plus-exposure findings, were interpreted as evidence for the benefits of the L2 instruction per se. Finally, although very few in number, when studies independently varied the amounts of instruction and L2 exposure, positive outcomes, taken together with all of the other findings, lent credence to this interpretation.

Although, on the basis of the available evidence, Long indeed concluded that second language instruction does make a difference, there were at least three fundamental research methodology problems. First, the comparisons between instruction and exposure were too global: It was not known whether instruction and exposure constituted different opportunities for SLA, let alone what specific SLA processes, cognitive or otherwise, may have taken place during the course of the investigations. Second, there were no direct comparisons of either instruction or exposure conditions with true control groups; and third, neither the type of instruction, nor any specific aspect of SLA were operationalized in the study variables. Without any information on the type of L2 instruction per se and the relevant SLA processes, study findings were always open to the interpretation that a null finding was due to poor quality or mismatched instruction. Furthermore, it was impossible to infer anything about the psycholinguistic processes that lead to form–meaning connections during interlanguage development.

Several years later, Long (1988) reconsidered the question of whether instruction makes a difference, but this time within four operationalized domains of SLA and covering the additional research. By now, the four SLA domains are well known, if not entirely understood: SLA processes; SLA sequences; rate of SLA, and level of ultimate L2 attainment.

SLA processes include, for instance, transfer, generalization, elaboration, stabilization, destabilization, omission, and oversuppliance, and perhaps most relevant to the concerns of this volume, noticing and mapping L2 forms to meaning (see DeKeyser, 2003; Doughty, 2001; Hulstijn, 1997, 2003; Odlin, 2003; Romaine, 2003; Segalowitz, 2003). By 1990, and even now, the proportion of empirical studies that investigate SLA processes in instructed settings is unfortunately still very small (Doughty, 2003b). The general findings indicate that, although instructed and untutored populations of learners follow similar paths, the SLA processes that were observed differ. For instance, although morphemes emerge in roughly the same order for both groups, naturalistic learners tend to omit obligatory morphemes at lower proficiency levels, whereas classroom learners tend to oversupply them (Pica, 1983), presumably as a consequence of instruction.

In the second domain, SLA "route," clear developmental sequences (i.e., fixed series of stages) have been identified in, for example, the acquisition of negation, interrogatives, relativization, and word order. Progress through the routes can be affected by the L1 in complex ways (e.g., speed-up or delay) (Zobl, 1982), or by instruction (Doughty, 1991; Pienemann, 1989), but only in terms of substages or rate of passage. In other words, stages are not skipped, and the route itself cannot be altered (Pienemann, 1989), a phenomenon that has come to be known as developmental readiness. Despite this, evidence continues to accumulate that the "rate" of instructed SLA is faster than that of naturalistic SLA. However, it is sometimes the case that what is learned quickly is forgotten equally fast (Lightbown, 1983), perhaps depending on the mode of learning that is evoked by the L2 instruction, an issue discussed further in a later section.

In the domain of level of ultimate attainment in the L2, studies indicate that, perhaps owing to the different types of input to which naturalistic and instructed learners are exposed, or to negative feedback, instructed learners make more progress toward the target language. For example, when learners are provided with input that includes marked examples (i.e., infrequent) of systems that enter into implicational hierarchies (e.g., relativization), they are able to acquire both the marked and unmarked aspects of the system (Doughty, 1988;

Eckman, Bell, & Nelson, 1988; Gass, 1982). Uninstructed learners, who may never gain access to marked input, tend to acquire only the unmarked elements in the system hierarchies (Pavesi, 1986).

Evidence in these four domains of SLA, although scant, is the basis of the assumption that L2 instruction of the right kind is effective. The past decade has witnessed a virtual explosion of interest in instructed SLA research of all types (Chaudron, 2001; Lightbown, 2000), and of experimental or quasi-experimental effects-of-instruction studies, in particular (Doughty & Williams, 1998a, 1998b; Norris & Ortega, 2000), and there is every reason to be optimistic about continued progress, given the increasing number of researchers interested in classroom language learning who are also sufficiently trained in SLA theory and research methodology (see Chaudron, 2003; Doughty, 2003b; Norris & Ortega, 2003, for detailed discussions of L2 research and methodology).

Instructed SLA research has now turned to the question of the type of instruction most facilitative of SLA. Like early investigations of the overall benefits of instruction versus exposure in SLA, initial comparisons of the relative effectiveness of types of instruction were also too global. Typically, in such studies, two "methods" of instruction were pitted against one another, and the findings were always the same: no difference between the two (see, e.g., Smith, 1970). This was because, as has been found to be the case in general education research, the variable of instructional method is actually a composite one (Clark, 1985) and, even if a "method" has an overall description (see, e.g., Richards & Rodgers, 1986), any particular implementation by a teacher is subject to significant variation. Furthermore, many typical teaching practices are components of a range of so-called methods, and it may in fact be those specific L2 pedagogic procedures that are responsible for observed effects (and, hence, which cancel each other out when different methods employing the same critical techniques are compared). Thus, method is not the appropriate level of analysis in type-of-instruction studies (Long, 1980).

The problem of overly general comparisons of input, exposure, and instructional conditions meant that, when interpreting research findings, no direct link between learning outcomes and instructional treatments could be made. To remedy this, Doughty (1988) identified three crucial elements of experimental design that need to be present in effects-of-instruction research: (a) a specific learning target must be identified for investigation (i.e., some aspect of the L2); (b) the instructional treatment must be psycholinguistically appropriate; and (c) specific gains in the L2 must be evaluated with respect to the target of instruction (e.g., by including a control group). Furthermore, because of the difficulty noted earlier regarding interpretation of results obtained after a period of unspecified instruction unknown to, and hence not analyzable by, the researcher, instructed SLA research protocols must specify that treatments be documented in some fashion (e.g., through video or audio-recording, computer delivery of treatments, or detailed classroom observation plus intercoder reliability checking).

If these procedures are followed, at some point later in the investigation, the nature of the treatment can be examined in conjunction with the findings, perhaps shedding more light on elusive SLA processes. For instance, to explain similar gains made by both instructional groups in a study of the development of relative clauses in English as a second language, Doughty pointed to the coding features of both computer-delivered treatments, which might have drawn the subjects' attention to the target of instruction in the same psycholinguistically relevant way (i.e., promoting salience of the elements in the input) (see also Doughty & Long, 2003). In addition to facilitating the interpretation of study findings, the documentation of instructional treatments must be reported in detail if systematic replication is to become a regular practice in research on instructed SLA. Following these guidelines *in vivo* is by no means a simple matter, and by 1997, some SLA researchers were arguing that to conduct SLA research was "almost impossible in 'normal' classrooms with real L2 learners" (Hulstijn, 1997, pp. 131–132) and, hence, they recommended that the investigation of SLA issues primarily be pursued under laboratory conditions. This proposal, however, raises the issue of ecological validity, because L2 instruction most often takes place in classrooms.

RELATIVE EFFECTIVENESS OF DIFFERENT TYPES L2 INSTRUCTION

The most recent review of empirical studies of instructed SLA examines both the overall effectiveness of L2 instruction and the relative effectiveness of different types of instruction (Norris & Ortega, 2000[2]). Employing the technique of statistical meta-analysis,[3] it is also the most rigorous assessment of instructed SLA research to date. Notably, Norris and Ortega identified 250 potentially relevant studies from the published applied SLA literature, an indicator that the state of instructed SLA research is more vigorous now than it was 20 years ago when Long published the first review.

Norris and Ortega's investigation included, for each reported study, a careful analysis of the components of the research methodology that, as already noted, had been identified as utterly lacking in precision (e.g., concerning operationalization of instructional treatments and consideration of appropriate research design), as well as a host of new considerations (e.g., comparison of instructional treatment types, influence of measures, and duration and durability of instructional treatments). Unfortunately, only 77 studies of the original pool of 250 studies survived the initial screening for inclusion in the coding phase of

[2] This excellent piece of research, carried out while the authors were doctoral students in the Ph.D. program in SLA at the University of Hawaii, has won two awards: ACTFL's Pimsleur Award and the TESOL research prize. It is important to make two observations at the outset of the discussion of Norris and Ortega's findings: (a) the meta-analysis is a data-driven procedure, and so any problems with conceptualization of L2 instruction are due, at least in part, to the body of research being examined itself; (b) their report of the meta-analysis includes far more than can be considered in this synopsis, so readers are urged to consult the original publication.

[3] Whereas a discussion of the technique of meta-analysis is beyond the scope of this chapter, it is important to note that such an approach takes into account not only reported group differences, but also assesses effect size, thus enabling a more trustworthy level of scrutiny.

the meta-analysis (i.e., that they be quasi-experimental or experimental in design, the independent variable be reasonably well operationalized in the report, and L2 features were targeted). Furthermore, of those, only 49 studies reported sufficient statistical information to be included in the final round of the meta-analysis. Thus, despite the increase in sheer quantity of work and improvement in operationalizing variables, it must be admitted that the state of the instructed SLA research is still far less robust than is required for the findings reported to be considered truly trustworthy. For this reason, a clear understanding of the findings of the meta-analysis and their interpretations are important for an assessment of the state of instructed SLA.

Rather than at the level of "method," the operationalization of instructional treatments is now considered best analyzed psycholinguistically in terms of language processing that facilitates L2 learners' extracting forms, and connecting, or "mapping," them to meaning and function. The general issues are whether an explicit or implicit approach to instruction is best, and to what extent and in what ways learner attention should be directed (e.g., by the teacher or the materials or activities) to the elements of language involved in mapping. Explicit instruction includes all types in which rules are explained to learners, or when learners are directed to find rules by attending to forms (see also DeKeyser, 2003). Conversely, implicit instruction makes no overt reference to rules or forms, as it is assumed that the learner will abstract this information. During instruction, attention may be directed to language forms in isolation, during the processing of meaning, or not at all. These types of attention can be understood as forming a tripartite contrast among options in language teaching (Long, 1988, 1991, 2000): *focus on forms*, *focus on meaning*, and *focus on form*.

Long offered the following definitions of *focus on form*:

> Focus on form overtly draws students' attention to linguistic elements as they arise incidentally in lessons whose overriding focus is on meaning or communication. (Long, 1991, pp. 45-46)

> Focus on form involves an occasional shift in attention to linguistic code features—by the teacher and/or one or more students—triggered by perceived problems with comprehension or production (Long & Robinson, 1998, p. 23)

Doughty and Williams (1998b) contrasted focus on form and the other two options, *focus on meaning* and *focus on forms*, in the following way:

> Focus on formS and focus on form are *not* polar opposites in the way that "form" and "meaning" have often been considered to be. Rather, a focus on form *entails* a focus on formal elements of language, whereas focus on formS is *limited to* such a focus, and focus on meaning *excludes* it. Most important, it should be kept in mind that the fundamental assumption of focus-on-form instruction is that meaning

> and use must already be evident to the learner at the time that attention is drawn to the linguistic apparatus needed to get the meaning across. (Doughty & Williams, 1998b, p. 4)[4]

Particular pedagogic procedures can be ranged along a continuum describing degree of obtrusiveness of attention to form during instruction (see Doughty & Williams 1998c, p. 258).

Building on DeKeyser's (1995) definition of explicit instruction, Long's tripartite distinction of attentional focus, and Doughty and Williams' continuum of degree of intrusiveness of the pedagogic intervention on the processing of meaning, Norris and Ortega (2000) set out to classify each instructional type in the studies they reviewed as (a) implicit or explicit, and (b) focusing on meaning only, forms only, or form. These classifications are displayed in Table 9.1.

Table 9.1: Distribution of Pedagogic Procedures in the Type-of-Instruction Studies

Implicit (30% of the instructional types)

Focus on Form (18% of the instructional types)	*Focus on Forms* (11% of the instructional types)
• form-experimental (anagram) • input enhancement • input flood • recasts • other implicit	• corrective models • pre-emptive modeling • traditional implicit

Explicit (70% of the instructional types)

Focus on Form (26% of the instructional types)	*Focus on Forms* (45% of the instructional types)
• compound focus on form (enhancement + feedback) • consciousness-raising • input-processing • meta-linguistic task essentialness (cross-word) • rule-oriented focus on form	• rule-oriented forms-focused • garden path • input practice • metalinguistic feedback • output practice • traditional explicit (e.g. rule explanation)

[4] Another term sometimes appears in the effects-of-instruction literature: form-focused. Spada (1997), for instance, used this term to encompass both focus on forms and focus on form. The difficulty with this notion (i.e., that all types of attention to form be grouped) is that the psycholinguistically relevant distinction made clear here by Doughty and Williams is lost.

In practice, deciphering operationalizations of L2 instruction has continued to prove difficult. Although initially guided by these constructs, Norris and Ortega (2000) ultimately had to resort to extrapolating the operational definitions for coding the type-of-instruction variable from the studies themselves (a problem returned to later). Attention is said to be directed to meaning via exposure to L2 targets or experience with L2 tasks, but without explicit attempts to effect shifts of learner attention. Attention to both forms and meaning can occur in any of eight ways listed under the heading of "focus on form" (Norris & Ortega, 2000, p. 464).[5] Finally, when other focus-on-form conditions do not apply, and when the learners' attention nonetheless was focused in some particular way on a specific structure targeted for investigation, this was considered focus on forms.[6]

Of the many important comparisons that were made by Norris and Ortega, the following are of greatest interest here: overall effectiveness of instruction in comparison with exposure; relative effectiveness of implicit and explicit types of instruction; and relative effectiveness of attention to forms, to meaning, or to form–meaning connections. The major findings of the meta-analysis concerning the five instructional type variables (the two describing degree of explicitness of instruction, and the three levels of obtrusiveness of attention to form) are displayed in Table 9.2. The general finding concerning the overall effectiveness of L2 instruction (of any type) is consistent with earlier comparisons of the effectiveness of L2 instruction with simple exposure or with meaning-driven communication (Long, 1983, 1988): Second language instruction does make a difference and, furthermore, the difference is substantial (effect size $d = 0.96$, where 0.80 is considered a large effect). However, as discussed later, this finding is limited by a number of important considerations.

With regard to differences among instructional types, the clearest finding (and, according to Norris and Ortega, the only trustworthy one) is an apparent advantage for explicit over implicit types of L2 instruction. Moreover, combining the nature of the instruction with the degree of obtrusiveness of attention to form in the pedagogic procedures employed, the detailed findings are as follows: Explicit focus on form (large effect) > Explicit focus on forms (large effect) > Implicit focus on form (medium effect) > Implicit focus on forms (small effect).[7] Unfortunately, of the twenty or so different pedagogic procedures utilized in these types of instruction, it was not possible to discern

[5] These are flood, enhancement, recasts, consciousness raising, input processing, compound focus on form, metalinguistic task-essentialness, and rule-oriented focus on form.

[6] Norris and Ortega also mentioned the 20 or so different pedagogic procedures employed, alone or in combination, in the instructional treatments of the studies analyzed, and group them according to the categories of implicit/explicit approach and type of attention to meaning, to form–meaning connections, and to forms in isolation. No analysis of these individual pedagogic procedures was possible, because there has not been a sufficient number of studies of any one procedure.

[7] This order should not be interpreted as involving statistically significant differences between contiguous combinations. The only real difference was between all explicit and all implicit instructional types. Also, see Norris & Ortega for treatments that focused only on meaning rather than form-meaning connections.

Table 9.2. Type of Instruction Effects

Type of Treatment	Findings	Interpretation
Control/comparison groups	18% gain	Any of practice effect, effect of exposure, maturation
ALL Instructional Types (vs. all comparison groups)	49 studies examined (98 treatments) Large effect size, but only 70% include a comparison group (e.g., exposure or control)	"As operationalized thus far in the domain, L2 instruction is effective" (Norris & Ortega, 2000)
All Explicit	Large effect size	EXPLICIT > IMPLICIT
All Implicit	Medium effect size	
All Focus on Form	Large effect size	(FONF > FONFS)
All Focus on Forms	Large effect size	1. FONF EXPLICIT
Implicit Focus on Form	Medium effect size	2. FONFS EXPLICIT
Explicit Focus on Form	Large effect size	3. FONF IMPLICIT
Implicit Focus on Forms	Small effect size	4. FONFS IMPLICIT
Explicit Focus on Forms	Large effect size	

any patterns of effectiveness due mainly to the lack of sufficient replication studies. Therefore, Norris and Ortega (2000) interpreted the results of their meta-analysis to mean that "L2 instruction can be characterized as effective in its own right, at least as operationalized and measured within the domain" (p. 480). The validity of this domain is considered in subsequent sections.

Another clear finding in this phase of the meta-analysis was that, where a comparison could be made between instructed groups and control (true) or comparison groups (defined as nonfocused exposure), the control/comparison groups experienced 18% pretest to posttest gains (see also Doughty, 1991; Hulstijn, 1997). In addition, although instructed subjects experienced greater improvement, the nature of interlanguage change exhibited by instructed subjects was variable, whereas that exhibited by control/comparison subjects was more homogeneous. Nonetheless, at delayed posttesting (in studies where this was carried out), instructed groups both maintained a modest advantage in gains over control/comparison groups, and had become more homogenous.

These findings can be interpreted in a number of ways. The most plausible explanations concerning the progress made by groups not receiving targeted instruction are the already-demonstrated rate advantage for instruction (i.e., uninstructed subjects improve, but instructed subjects improve more, hence they are faster) and test effect. These possibilities have not yet been systematically teased apart. Individual variation in effects of instruction shown by subjects in experimental treatment groups could also have been due to true individual differences factors (e.g., aptitude for language learning), or to mismatches between cognitive learning style and instructional type. Again, such factors have not routinely been included in the design of instructed SLA studies, although they have figured prominently in the very recent SLA literature (see Dörnyei & Skehan, 2003; Robinson, 2003). That the individual variation has disappeared by the time of the delayed posttest is also in need of explanation. Given that the delayed posttest interval is typically quite short (4 weeks, on average), it might be expected that the effects of instruction demonstrated would not remain after a longer period of time, either because control subjects have caught up (a common finding), or because the particular type of instruction favored in this set of studies leads to the type of knowledge that is easily forgotten (as found in earlier research).

Finally, by virtue of somewhat improved reporting in the published literature, Norris and Ortega were able to revisit the question of the differential effects of exposure and instruction originally raised by Long (1983). In the more recent published studies, exposure is operationalized as pure exposure or experience with L2 tasks without any focus on form or forms, or some minimal amount of both. Results are straightforward: The effect of instruction in comparison with exposure is still substantial, but smaller than when instructed subjects are compared with true controls. This finding is consistent with the rate advantage for instruction already discussed.

PROBLEMS OF RESEARCH BIAS

To interpret the relative effectiveness of instructed SLA findings properly requires careful examination of the operationalizations of instructional treatments in the studies now forming the instructed SLA research base, and, crucially, attention to the accumulation of research bias reported by Norris and Ortega. Recall that the operational definitions of types of instruction, derived directly from the studies themselves, unfortunately comprise a rather unsystematic set of features, which as noted earlier simply reflects the state of the current research. In fact, Norris and Ortega reported that coding the types of instruction using these categories involved a high degree of inference in comparison with other variables examined in the meta-analysis.

More importantly, perhaps, a strong bias was identified concerning the number of comparisons made to date of each approach to L2 instruction: Within the 49 studies reported in Tables 9.1 and 9.2, there were 98 distinct instructional treatments, owing to some studies comparing two or more types of treatment with a control or an exposure-only group. Of these, 70% were explicit in approach, and only 30% were implicit. With regard to attention to form, 56% were focus-on-forms type, and 44% were classified as focus on form. The bias is also prominent in the hybrid classifications: Of the focus-on-forms type treatments, 80% were explicit in approach. And, of the focus-on-form type treatments, 58% were explicit in approach. It must be emphasized that, given the completely decontextualized nature of explicit focus on forms, this type of instruction promotes a mode of learning that is arguably unrelated to SLA, instructed or otherwise, in that the outcome is merely the accumulation of metalinguistic knowledge about language. Thus, a bias of this kind in the instructed SLA research domain is a serious problem.

A third bias in the design of effects-of-instruction studies concerns the duration of the instructional treatment. Norris and Ortega reported four lengths of duration: brief (< 1 hour), short (1–2 hours), medium (3–6 hours), and long (> 7 hours). The typical period of instruction was 1–4 hours. One study provided 50 hours of instruction, but this was rare (and also involved instruction on a large number of L2 features). The only real empirical difference found among these durations was that between "short" and "medium" length treatments, with shorter treatments of 2 hours or less being more effective. However, instruction that is intensive, but only of short duration, is well known to be the most vulnerable to rapid forgetting (Lightbown, 1983).

In addition to problems of study design and conceptualization of L2 instructional treatment types, there is an enormous problem concerning validity of outcome measures. This problem has at least three dimensions: (a) a bias in favor of testing only explicit, declarative knowledge (which is not surprising, given the pedagogic procedure bias just outlined); (b) insensitivity to interlanguage change; and (c) a lack of concern with the reliability of the measures used. This discussion elaborates on only the first two here, except to note that just 16% of the studies included in the meta-analysis reported reliability estimates for the dependent measures (see Norris & Ortega, 2000, 2003, for a detailed discussion of reliability and other research methodology issues).

The 49 studies of instructed SLA employed 182 measures (studies typically measuring outcomes in more than one way), which were coded by Norris and Ortega according to the type of L2 knowledge that was tapped by the measure. Most striking is that approximately 90% of the type-of-instruction studies implemented discrete-point or declarative knowledge-based measures, rather than requiring any real deployment of L2 knowledge under anything like spontaneous conditions. Thus, the problem of type of L2 knowledge assessed is even more severe than might be surmised from Norris and Ortega's own interpretation. The essential difficulty is that most of the outcome measures do not appear to be measuring L2 ability in any valid sense (see Doughty, 2003b, especially Appendix A). Fundamentally, recognizing that unconstrained data collection is not likely to result in a sample of L2 ability sufficient for study, the bias in instructed SLA research to date has been toward overly constraining outcome measures, such that their construct validity is severely compromised. On Chaudron's (2003, p. 764) continuum of available data collection measures, ranging from naturalistic to decontextualized, the vast majority used to date in type-of-instruction studies would appear on the far right, and many of them test metalinguistic rather than usable L2 knowledge.

These types of measures, termed "constrained-constructed responses" by Norris and Ortega, typically involve giving subjects much of a linguistic construction, together with some directions as to how to complete it (e.g., fill in blanks, given verb in its infinitive and told to use direct object). Moreover, the tests look very much like the dominant approach to instruction, that is to say, explicit focus on forms. Such decontextualized focus-on-forms instruction and metalinguistic assessment measures draw neither on L2 competence nor L2 performance during either the instruction or assessment phases of the studies. Rather, they merely teach and require knowledge of language as object.

Furthermore, it should be noted that, even when L2 targets were taught by implicit pedagogic procedures, they still tended to be measured in this discrete, decontextualized fashion. Thus, compounding the problem of outcome measures being overwhelmingly explicit in nature and number, measures are often mismatched with instructional type. At the very least, both types of measures, implicit and explicit, should be employed. This constitutes not only an extreme bias in the response type, but a serious threat to the validity of the interpretation of the findings of studies employing such measures.

The validity of instructed SLA outcome measures is compromised not only by decontextualization and the tapping primarily of metalinguistic knowledge, but also in terms of the analytic framework typically used to measure language change. Measures of interlanguage development have tended to be inappropriate, in the sense that they are overly target-language oriented. Child language researchers have long been employing analyses that enable the precise tracking of L1 development unencumbered by comparisons with the adult target. Adult SLA, known likewise to be systematic and nonlinear in its progress, and, furthermore, seldom reaching the accuracy levels of the target language, must be studied in an interlanguage-sensitive fashion. For example, Doughty and Varela (1998) showed that L2 instructional effects can be traced by looking at three types of evidence: (a) decreases in the complete absence of an L2 feature (zero marking or base form); (b) increased attempts at expressing the L2 feature (in whatever form); (c) temporary oversuppliance of the L2 features, and, eventually, (d) increasing accuracy. Measures that set the target language as the only criterion for success of an instructional treatment will often fail to capture relevant evidence of interlanguage development.

The research requirement to target (in order to be able to measure improvement in) a particular aspect of the L2 may, in part, be responsible for the overrepresentation of explicit and target-language oriented instructional and assessment procedures that has resulted in the severe research biases outlined earlier. Whereas the early instructed SLA did not operationalize the instructional treatment in any way, the current state of affairs is that L2 instruction is typically designed and measures in ways that are not psycholinguistically valid. In other words, processing in which learners typically engage in instructed SLA research to date is not of the kind relevant to SLA processes. This dilemma in instructed SLA research protocols must be resolved if future research is to succeed at investigating the more implicit approaches to L2 teaching.

FUTURE DIRECTIONS FOR INSTRUCTED SLA RESEARCH

Although much progress has been made, and great interest has arisen in instructed SLA research, there is still a long way to go. What can be done to advance the research agenda? At least six research methodological problems must be resolved, some of them very difficult:

1. The proportion of instructed SLA studies that investigate the processes involved in making form–meaning connections must be increased.
2. The operationalization of processes must be systematic, drawing upon SLA theoretical constructs.
3. Coding procedures must involve not only an examination of the instructional treatments as implemented, but also an evaluation of pedagogic procedures with regard to underlying SLA theoretical constructs.
4. The proportion of instructed SLA studies that investigate implicit approaches to L2 instruction must be significantly increased.
5. Studies that operationalize instruction in a completely decontextualized fashion and promote only language manipulation or metalinguistic processing and measurement should be labeled as such and be removed from consideration in the assessment of instructed SLA. More specifically, they should not be included in the category of explicit instruction.
6. Whereas features of the L2 must be targeted for instruction so that the processes involved in acquiring them can be tracked, and so that learning outcomes can be measured, research protocols must be discovered that eliminate severe biases toward explicit or metalinguistic instructional and measurement procedures.

Figure 9.1 presents a framework of analysis developed for the purpose of assessing instructed SLA research protocols *before* they are implemented.[8] It has been piloted on the set of instructed SLA studies that were examined by Norris and Ortega, and also applied to those that have appeared since the publication of the last study included in the Norris and Ortega meta-analysis (i.e., 1998–2002), and subsequently revised (Doughty, 2003a).

The central purpose of the framework is to examine the construct validity of the treatments in studies of instructed SLA, with special attention paid to L2 learner processing. An important issue that arose during the development of this instrument is worthy of mention, and needs to be added to the list of problems to be resolved:

7. Features must be built into the protocol that enable the instructed SLA researcher to investigate SLA processes, such as those involving the allocation of learner attention (i.e., orientation, explicit processing, implicit processing, etc.) (Schmidt, 2001), or any other processes implicated in the theoretical constructs.

In Phase I of the detailed coding of studies of form–meaning connections during L2 instruction, the treatment is examined closely with regard

[8] Of course, the framework can also be applied to completed studies.

to the target structure, as to the possibility that the treatment is only of a metalinguistic nature, and whether the treatment involves one or many pedagogic procedures. The researcher's reason for choosing the target feature must be evaluated in terms of psycholinguistic optimality for the learner. This is a difficult dilemma because, ideally, L2 instruction should be provided at the moment when the psycholinguistic need arises. However, considerations of proper measurement require the researcher to predetermine the target feature. Nonetheless, if the L2 learning difficulties have been profiled in advance, and if the instructional materials create the need for the relevant form–meaning connections, then the conditions may be optimal for SLA, with the important caveat that learner readiness must have been established a priori as well. Another key feature of Phase I of the coding is that purely or overly metalinguistic treatments simply are eliminated from further consideration. Metalinguistic treatments are those that involve talking about language forms or systems in isolation, or activities that require the understanding of meaning for the sole purpose of assessing an example of a grammar point. Removing such studies from the coding procedure will contribute to the validity of claims made about instructed SLA, because findings concerning the one type of process that is known not to be relevant to SLA are culled early on.

The main purpose of Phase II of the framework is to establish the validity of the SLA construct that underlies the design of the L2 instructional treatment. There are three possibilities: First, the instruction may have been based on a valid tenet of SLA theory, and this is stated by the researchers. Second, sometimes the motivation for a particular study is a pedagogic one, but nevertheless a valid SLA construct, even if not stated, could be gleaned. Phase II also ascertains whether the construct has been truly operationalized in the L2 instructional treatment. Third, at times, it ultimately had to be concluded that the underlying construct, stated or otherwise, was not valid, and that coding should not be continued.

Determining the nature of the psycholinguistic processing that learners engage in during the instruction is the aim of the third phase of the coding framework shown in Fig. 9.1. In addition to examining whether the instruction promotes implicit or explicit processing overall, a more detailed characterization of processing during instruction was developed, and includes three stages: preinstruction (e.g., alerting, orientation to process in a particular way, and planning opportunities); input or output processing (e.g., comprehension, production, plus a number of microprocesses thought to be relevant to making form–meaning connections—see IIIb2 and IIIb3); and postprocessing or subsequent processes (e.g., feedback on error).

Phase I

- **Describe the L2 Instructional Treatment**

1. Why/how was the target structure chosen? Examples: psycholinguistic optimality (learning problem, communicative need), pedagogy, and requirement for no prior exposure as possibilities. Was readiness considered?
2. Is the L2 instructional treatment purely metalinguistic or overwhelmingly metalinguistic (definition = talking about language system in isolation and/or understanding meaning only for the purpose of assessing an example of a grammar point). If yes, STOP HERE, code as Metalinguistic, and describe the treatment and outcome measure.
3. Is the L2 instructional treatment a pure/composite variable? If pure, describe and then → Q5 If composite → Q4, then Q5
4. Where the instructional treatment involves a sequence of pedagogic procedures, exactly, what was involved (step by step)? (and code each separately) And, → Q5
5. What were the precise directions to the learners (for each step, if steps differ)?

Phase II

- **Assess Validity of Construct(s) as stated**

1. Is the theoretical construct (instructional treatment) valid (definition = based on SLA research/evidence)?
   Y → Describe the theoretical motivation, briefly and → Q3
   N → Q2
   ? → Can't tell
2. Is the construct motivated by pedagogy?
   Y → Can you see an inherent SLA motivation?
      If so → Q4
      If not → Invalid
   N → Invalid
   ? → Can't tell
3. Is the construct operationalized in a fashion that is true to the theoretical construct/motivation?
   Y → Q4
   N Describe and → Q4
4. Is the new (or inherent) construct valid?
   Y Describe
   N → Invalid, describe

Phase III

- **Code the Mode of L2 Processing (Coding/Labels)**

III (a) from the perspective of what the instruction/pedagogic procedures/ materials are designed to do

Regarding learners' attention to target features, choose ONE of explicit/implicit/incidental:

- EXPLICIT: Attempts to DIRECT learners' attention to target features.
- IMPLICIT: (+/- salient) No attempts to direct or divert learners' attention to/from target features.

Fig. 9.1: Coding framework for L2 instructional treatments.

III (b) from the perspective of learners' processing

Code the following as O (opportunities) and E (for evidence). For each E type, provide a brief description of the EVIDENCE on which the coding was based. NOTES: Unlike Set 1, these are not mutually exclusive categories (with the exception of primary learning mode). Awareness refers to awareness of the target feature(s).

1. PRE-PROCESSING Choose one of alerting and orientation (the latter entails the former)
   - ➢ ALERTING: (assume -Awareness) an overall readiness to process incoming stimuli.
   - ➢ ORIENTATION: (+/-Awareness) prepared to process the material containing the target feature(s) in a certain way, i.e., beyond simply reading or listening (when matched with expectation, then code as facilitative; when mismatched, then inhibitory)

   For studies involving output:
   - ➢ PLANNING (+/-Awareness): organizing thought and language toward articulation

2. PROCESSING – INPUT
   - ➢ COMPREHENSION: understanding meaning of material that contains the target input
   - ➢ DETECTION (+/- Awareness): noticing or cognitive registration of the target features

3. PROCESSING – OUTPUT (processes involved in trying to say/write something in the L2)
   - ➢ ARTICULATING (+/-Awareness): the physical act of speaking or writing utterances that contain contexts for the target features
   - ➢ MONITORING (+Awareness): detecting (+/- trying to repair) problems in own plan or articulation

4. POST-PROCESSING
   - ➢ COGNITIVE COMPARISON (+/- Awareness): noticing or registering similarities or differences
   - ➢ OF FEEDBACK (on success of input or output processing of target features) Describe

5. METALINGUISTIC PROCESSING: talking or thinking about system in language.

6. PRIMARY LEARNING MODE: this will normally be inferred from how the materials are set up, and will only be coded when the research methods include think-aloud or some other relevant measure.
   - ➢ INDUCTIVE LEARNING: Working out system from input
   - ➢ DEDUCIVE LEARNING: Applying system to organize processing

Fig. 9.1: Coding framework for L2 instructional treatments, continued.

Because the interpretation of cognitive processing on the basis of learner behavior is quite challenging, the coding of L2 learner processing is approached from two perspectives. First, the materials themselves can be examined with respect to the conditions that they set up for learner processing (see Fig. 9.1, IIIa). In some cases, it will be clear that the conditions force a certain type of processing (e.g., choosing a picture to match the meaning of utterance, the choice depending on making a crucially correct interpretation in the L2). In most cases, however, merely setting up the right conditions for learner processing cannot be taken as a guarantee that such processing has occurred. Thus, evidence must be sought for indications of actual (as opposed to intended) learner processing during the L2 instruction (Fig. 9.1, IIIb). Unfortunately, although considerable progress has been made in reporting on the nature of the instructional treatments used in empirical studies, interpretation of reported learner behaviors as evidence for L2 processing was found to be next to non-existent in most research protocols spanning the time period from 1980 to 2002. A few researchers included think aloud or retrospective protocols, or debriefing sessions from which some processing behaviors can be inferred. However, as online thinking aloud has been demonstrated to alter the normal SLA processing (Jourdenais, 1998, 2001), other ways beyond debriefing, which itself may not be accurate owing to the memory requirement in retrospection, must be developed to detect evidence of L2 learner processing. Perhaps the most important outcome of piloting the coding framework was the revelation that instructed SLA research is still in its infancy regarding the ability to infer anything specific concerning the psycholinguistic processing of instructed L2 learners.

CONCLUSIONS

This overview of the empirical research on instructed SLA has furthered understanding of the nature of instructional effects in the domains of rate, route, and ultimate attainment in SLA. In contrast, still little is known concerning the SLA processes that are vital to making form–meaning connections in instructed settings. In particular, careful attention must be paid to operationalizing the constructs that are proposed in theories of L2 processing (see Doughty, 2003b for detailed discussion), and to establishing what kind of evidence is sufficient for inferring that the processing has taken place as planned by the instructed SLA researcher.

With respect to research on type of instruction, which has been the central focus of the past decade or more of instructed SLA research, only some progress had been made, and numerous research methodology problems continue to surface. Taking together biases in approach to and duration of L2 instruction, and the demonstrated biases in measurement, the reported apparent advantage for explicit instruction has more properly been interpreted as an artifact of cumulative research bias. More specifically, all that can be said at present is that, when the outcome of very short-term, explicitly focused instruction is measured on language manipulation tasks, it has proven effective.

Like any other type of memorized knowledge, L2 knowledge learned in this way would be expected quickly to be forgotten. Furthermore, although not enough studies included delayed posttests, a few studies have shown that explicitly learned knowledge is indeed forgotten, unless the feature is subsequently encountered in the input for a period of time (Lightbown, Spada, & White, 1993; Spada & Lightbown, 1993).

In sum, the case for explicit instruction has been overstated. In addition, given that only 30% of studies have employed implicit pedagogic techniques, and that outcome measures have been severely biased toward constrained construction, language manipulation, and the assessment of declarative knowledge (90% of measures), any advantages for implicit instruction have likely been understated. In other words, under the present biased research conditions, any observed effects of implicit instruction are remarkable indeed!

REFERENCES

Berry, D. (1997). *How implicit is implicit learning?* New York: Oxford University Press.

Berry, D., and Dienes, Z. (Eds.). (1993). *Implicit learning: Theoretical and empirical issues.* Hove, England: Lawrence Erlbaum & Associates.

Chaudron, C. (2001). Progress in language classroom research: Evidence from *The Modern Language Journal*, 1916–2000. *Modern Language Journal, 85*, 57–76.

Chaudron, C. (2003). Data collection in SLA research. In C. Doughty & M. Long (Eds.). *The handbook of second language acquisition* (pp. 762–828). Oxford, England: Blackwell.

Clark, R. (1985). Confounding in educational computing research. *Journal of Educational Computing Research, 1*, 137–148.

DeKeyser, R. (1995). Learning second language grammar rules: An experiment with a miniature linguistic system. *Studies in Second Language Acquisition, 17*, 379–410.

DeKeyser, R. (2003). Implicit and explicit learning. In C. Doughty & M. Long (Eds.). *The handbook of second language acquisition* (pp. 313–348).. Oxford, England: Blackwell.

Dornyei, Z., & Skehan, P. (2003). Individual differences in second language learning. In C. Doughty & M. Long (Eds.). *The handbook of second language acquisition* (pp.589–630). Oxford, England: Blackwell.

Doughty, C. (1988). *Effects of instruction on the acquisition of relativization in English as a Second Language.* Unpublished doctoral dissertation, University of Pennsylvania.

Doughty, C. (1991). Second language acquisition does make a difference: Evidence from an empirical study of SL relativization. *Studies in Second Language Acquisition, 13*, 431–469.

Doughty, C. (2001). Cognitive underpinnings of focus on form. In P. Robinson (Ed.), *Cognition and second language instruction* (pp. 206–257). Cambridge, England: Cambridge University Press.

Doughty, C. (2003a, March). *Designing psycholinguistically valid instructional treatments.* Paper presented at the annual meeting of the American Association of Applied Linguistics, Arlington, VA.

Doughty, C. (2003b). Instructed SLA: Constraints, compensation, and enhancement. In C. Doughty & M. Long (Eds.). *The handbook of second language acquisition* (pp. 256–310). Oxford, England: Blackwell.

Doughty, C. & Long, M. H. (Eds.). (2003). *The handbook of second language acquisition*. Oxford, England: Blackwell.

Doughty, C., & Varela, E. (1998). Communicative focus on form. In C. Doughty & J. Williams, (Eds.), *Focus on form in classroom second language acquisition* (pp. 114–138). Cambridge, England: Cambridge University Press.

Doughty, C., and Williams, J. (Eds.). (1998a). *Focus on form in classroom second language acquisition*. Cambridge, England: Cambridge University Press.

Doughty, C., and Williams, J. (1998b). Issues and terminology. In C. Doughty & J. Williams, (Eds.), *Focus on form in classroom second language acquisition* (pp. 1–11). Cambridge, England: Cambridge University Press.

Doughty, C., and Williams, J. (1998c). Pedagogic choices in focus on form. In C. Doughty & J. Williams, (Eds.), *Focus on form in classroom second language acquisition* (pp. 197–261). Cambridge, England: Cambridge University Press.

Eckman, F., Bell, L., & Nelson, D. (1988). On the generalization of relative clause instruction in the acquisition of English as a Second Language. *Applied Linguistics, 9*, 10–20.

Felix, S. (1981). The effect of formal instruction on second language acquisition. *Language Learning, 311*, 87–112.

Gass, S. (1982). From theory to practice. In M. Hines & W. Rutherford (Eds.), *On TESOL '81* (pp. 120–139). Washington, DC: TESOL.

Hulstijn, J. (1997). Second language acquisition research in the laboratory: Possibilities and limitations. *Studies in Second Language Acquisition, 19*, 131–143.

Hulstijn, J. (2003). Incidental and intentional learning. In C. Doughty & M. Long (Eds.), *The handbook of second language acquisition* (pp. 349–381). Blackwell Handbooks in Linguistics. Oxford, England: Blackwell.

Hyltenstam, K., & Abrahamsson, N. (2003). Maturational constraints in SLA. In C. Doughty & M. Long (Eds.), *The handbook of second language acquisition* (pp. 539–588). Oxford, England: Blackwell.

Jourdenais, R. (1998). *The effects of textual enhancement on the acquisition of Spanish preterit and imperfect*. Unpublished doctoral dissertation, Georgetown University.

Jourdenais, R. (2001). Cognition, instruction, and protocol analysis. In P. Robinson (Ed.), *Cognition and second language instruction* (pp. 354–375). Cambridge, England: Cambridge University Press.

Krashen, S. (1982). *Principles and practice in second language acquisition*. Oxford, England: Pergamon.

Krashen, S. (1985). *The input hypothesis: Issues and implications*. London: Longman.

Krashen, S., & Scarcella, R. (1978). On routines and patterns in language acquisition performance. *Language Learning, 28*, 283–300.

Lightbown, P. (1983). Exploring relationships between developmental and instructional sequences in L2 acquisition. In H. Seliger & M. Long (Eds.), *Classroom–oriented research in second language acquisition* (pp. 217–243). Rowley, MA: Newbury House.

Lightbown, P. (2000). Classroom SLA research and second language teaching. *Applied Linguistics, 21*, 431–462.

Lightbown, P., Spada, N., & White, L. (Eds.). (1993). The role of instruction in second language acquisition. *Studies in Second Language Acquisition, 15* (Thematic Issue).

Long, M. H. (1980). Inside the "black box": Methodological issues in classroom research on language learning. *Language Learning* , *1*, 1–42.

Long, M. H. (1983). Does instruction make a difference? *TESOL Quarterly, 17*, 359–382.

Long, M. H. (1988). Instructed interlanguage development. In L. Beebe (Ed.), *Issues in second language acquisition: Multiple perspectives* (pp. 115–141). Rowley, MA: Newbury House.

Long, M. H. (1991). The design and psycholinguistic motivation of research on foreign language learning. In B. Freed (Ed.), *Foreign language acquisition research and the classroom* (pp. 309–320). Lexington, MA: Heath.

Long, M. H. (1993). Second language acquisition as a function of age: Research findings and methodological issues. In K. Hyltenstam & Å. Viberg (Eds.), *Progression and regression in language* (pp. 195–221). Cambridge, England: Cambridge University Press.

Long, M. H. (2000). Focus on form in Task–Based Language Teaching. In R. Lambert & E. Shohamy (Eds.), *Language policy and pedagogy* (pp. 179–189). Amsterdam/Philadelphia: John Benjamins.

Long, M. H., & Robinson, P. (1998). Focus on form: Theory, research, and practice. In C. Doughty & J. Williams (Eds.), *Focus on form in classroom second language acquisition* (pp. 15–41). Cambridge, England: Cambridge University Press.

Norris, J., & Ortega, L. (2000). Effectiveness of L2 instruction: A research synthesis and quantitative meta-analysis. *Language Learning, 50*, 417–528.

Norris, J., & Ortega, L. (2003). Defining and measuring SLA. In C. Doughty & M. Long (Eds.). *The handbook of second language acquisition* (pp. 717–761). Oxford, England: Blackwell.

Odlin, T. (2003). Crosslinguistic influence. In C. Doughty & M. Long (Eds.). *The handbook of second language acquisition* (pp. 436–486). Oxford, England: Blackwell.

Pavesi, M. (1986). Markedness, discoursal modes, and relative clause formation in a formal and an informal context. *Studies in Second Language Acquisition, 81*, 38–55.

Pica, T. (1983). Adult acquisition of English as a second language under different conditions of exposure. *Language Learning, 33*, 465–97.

Pienemann, M. (1989). Is language teachable? Psycholinguistic experiments and hypotheses. *Applied Linguistics, 10*, 52–79.

Richards, J., & Rodgers, T. (1986). *Approaches and methods in language teaching.* Cambridge, England: Cambridge University Press.

Robinson, P. (Ed.). (2003). *Individual differences and instructed language learning.* Amsterdam: Benjamins.

Romaine, S. (2003). Variation. In C. Doughty & M. Long (Eds.). *The handbook of second language acquisition* (pp. 409–435). Oxford, England: Blackwell..

Schwartz, B. (1993). On explicit and negative data effecting and affecting competence and linguistic behavior. *Studies in Second Language Acquisition, 15*, 147–164.

Schwartz, B. & Sprouse, R. (1996). L2 cognitives states and the full transfer/full access model. *Second Language Research, 12*, 40–72.

Schmidt, R. W. (2001). Attention. In P. Robinson (Ed.), *Cognition and second language instruction* (pp. 3–32). Cambridge, England: Cambridge University Press.

Segalowitz, N. (2003). Automaticity and second languages. In C. Doughty & M. Long (Eds.). *The Handbook of Second Language Acquisition* (pp. 382–408). Oxford, England: Blackwell.

Smith, P. (1970). *A comparison of the audio–lingual and cognitive approaches to foreign language instruction.* The Pennsylvania Foreign Language Project. Philadelphia: Center for Curriculum Development.

Spada, N. (1997). Form–focussed instruction and second language acquisition: A review of classroom and laboratory research [State of the Art Article]. *Language Teaching, 30*, 73–87.

Spada, N., & Lightbown, P.M. (1993): Instruction and the development of questions in L2 classrooms. *Studies in Second Language Acquisition, 15*, 205–224.

Stadler, M., & Frensch, P. (Eds.). (1998). *Handbook of implicit learning*. Thousand Oaks, CA: Sage.

White, L. (1987). Against comprehensible input: The input hypothesis and the development of second–language competence. *Applied Linguistics, 8*, 95–110.

White, L. (1991). Adverb placement in second language acquisition: Some effects of positive and negative evidence. *Second Language Research, 7*, 133–161.

White, L. (2003). On the nature of interlanguage representation: Universal Grammar in the second language. In C. Doughty & M. Long (Eds.). *The handbook of second language acquisition* (pp. 19–42). Oxford, England: Blackwell.

Zobl, H. (1982). A direction for contrastive analysis: The comparative study of developmental sequences. *TESOL Quarterly, 16*, 169–183.

CHAPTER 10
Implicit Learning of Form–Meaning Connections

John N. Williams
University of Cambridge

There is a widespread conviction among cognitive psychologists that humans, and indeed all animals, are equipped with powerful learning mechanisms for extracting regularities from the environment. Many believe that regularities are learned as an inevitable consequence of encoding individual events in memory, through learning processes that can be broadly classed as "superpositional." Events are represented as sets of features, and as the representations of successive events are "superimposed" on each other, common features and underlying generalizations are extracted. Exemplar-based memory models (Hintzman, 1986) and connectionist networks (McClelland & Rumelhart, 1985) are computational instantiations of this principle. Typically, such models take no account of conscious states because learning is assumed to operate unconsciously, and as an inevitable by-product of the way in which events are encoded in memory. Learning mechanisms of this type do not in any way depend on conscious states; they operate implicitly.

Winter and Reber (1994) defined implicit learning as the "human ability to derive information from the world in an unconscious, non-reflective way" (p. 117). Implicit learning does not require an intention to learn; that is, it occurs incidentally while performing some other task. Nor does it require conscious hypothesis testing, or comparisons between consciously recalled events. Such processes fall under the province of explicit learning. However, whereas the implicit learning *mechanism* may not depend on conscious states, it is generally assumed that learners do at least need to be conscious of stimuli for them to contribute to the learning process. This is because focal attention appears to be necessary for encoding novel events in memory (Cowan, 1993; P. Robinson, 1995). Familiar stimuli outside of focal attention may activate preexisting memory representations, but in order to learn novel stimuli, or novel conjunctions of familiar stimuli, focal attention is assumed to be necessary. This assumption forms the basis of Schmidt's (1994) "noticing" hypothesis, according to which learning requires attention to the relevant stimuli, but not as he has recently clarified (Schmidt, 2001), to the underlying regularities: "My intention is to separate 'noticing' from 'metalinguistic awareness' as clearly as possible, by assuming that the objects of attention and noticing are elements of the surface structure of utterances in the input, instances of language, rather than any abstract rules or principles of which such instances may be exemplars" (p. 5).

Consider what this means in relation to learning form–meaning mappings. In the present context *form* will be used to refer to grammatical morphemes (e.g. articles, noun inflections) and *meaning* to refer to those conceptual features that determine their distribution (e.g., definiteness, plurality). Suppose there is a systematic relationship between form A and meaning B in the grammar (e.g., between the *-s* noun ending and the notion of plurality). According to Schmidt's argument, so long as a person attends to A and B, it is possible for the relationship between them to be learned implicitly. But, in a natural language utterance, the person's conscious understanding of the situation being referred to will comprise many conceptual features. Even if it is assumed that there is just one "noticed" element of surface form (perhaps because it is the only element that cannot be interpreted according to the learner's current grammar), there will still be a large number of potentially relevant conceptual features with which it could be associated. Thus, one utterance could be characterized as a pairing of form A and conceptual features C, R, B, X, and another event as a pairing of A and D, W, B, Z, and so on. The question concerns whether learners can unconsciously extract the regularity relating A and B across these utterance-meaning pairs. According to the kind of superpositional memory system that is assumed to underlie implicit learning, provided that the relevant elements are attended and encoded in memory, the A–B association should be extracted. For learning to be truly implicit, however, it would be necessary for the learner to be unaware that there is a systematic relationship between A and B at the time of encoding the events, because this would constitute awareness of the regularity to be learned.

There is evidence that, at least when A and B are both visual stimuli, it is possible to learn their association without being aware that they are related. Jiménez and Méndez (1999) reported a sequence learning experiment in which characters appeared at either of four different positions on a screen and subjects simply had to indicate the position of each character by pressing one of four response buttons. The sequence of positions was in fact generated by a complex finite state grammar similar to those used by Reber (1976) but with the addition that another, simpler, regularity was built into the sequence. The identity of each character predicted the position of the next stimulus, such that, for example, if the character was a '?', the next stimulus appeared at one position, but if it was '*', it appeared at another.

Subjects' response times were compared for sequences that were generated by the grammar or correctly predicted by the preceding character and those that were not. Faster responses in the former case would suggest that subjects had learned the relevant regularities. In the first experiment, the subjects were simply told to respond according to the position of the stimulus. In this single-task condition there was evidence that they learned the complex sequencing rules as defined by the finite state grammar, but they were not using the predictability of position from character, even though this rule is much simpler. In a second experiment, the subjects were told to count how many times the characters 'x' and '*' appeared over a block of trials. They had to do this at the same time as responding to the position of the character by pressing the keys. This is a dual-task condition. Now it seemed that they were sensitive both to the predictability of a position in terms of the grammar, and in terms of the identity of the preceding character. Crucially, however, the participants did not appear to be aware of the relationship between character and position. Thus, it appears that associations between stimuli (in this case, character and position) can be learned without awareness of their relationship, but the subjects have to be attending to the relevant aspects of the stimuli. Similar results were obtained by Logan and Etherton (1994), although in that case it was not clear whether the subjects were aware of the associations during training.

The Jiménez and Méndez (1999) experiment demonstrates implicit learning of an association between visual stimuli under conditions where they are both attended but their relationship is not. But is this also possible in the case of form and meaning?

Undoubtedly, the most relevant previous investigation of implicit learning of form–meaning associations is DeKeyser's (1995) experiment on learning a miniature artificial language. This language contained rich inflectional morphology for marking (sexual) gender, number, and case. A typical sentence in that language was *hadeks-on walas-in-it meleks-is-on* (queen-plural build-feminine-plural castle-accusative-plural). The participants simply observed combinations of sentences and pictures. Periodically, there were trials on which they had to verify whether the sentence was a correct description of the event in the picture. Crucially, the only errors on negative trials concerned vocabulary, not grammar. After 2,480 training trials spread over 20 learning sessions, participants were tested on a production task in which they had to type the correct sentence to describe a picture. Although the sentences were all novel, some involved combinations of stems and suffixes that had been received in training. They were 87% correct for these items showing that they had good memory for trained stem–suffix combinations. However, when the response required a stem–suffix combination that had never been presented during training, they were only 33% correct (which DeKeyser estimates to be at chance). The participants had not learned the associations between individual components of meaning and specific suffixes. Although the good performance on trained stem–suffix combinations suggests that form–form associations between stems and suffixes had been learned implicitly, associations between individual morphemes and specific aspects of meaning had not been learned.

It should be noted, however, that in DeKeyser's (1995) experiment the training task did not require the participants to pay attention to those aspects of meaning that were potentially relevant to the suffixes; the task could be performed simply by matching stems to pictures. Of course, this was intentional because if the sentences had included inappropriate suffixes, the participants would have begun to search for rules. This training condition is, therefore, more like Jiménez and Méndez's (1999) single-task condition where the relevant information was presumably processed, but not attended. Perhaps, it is not surprising that the relevant form–meaning mappings were not learned. What is not yet known is whether form–meaning mappings can be learned implicitly when both form and meaning are attended, but the participants are not aware of their relevance to each other. The purpose of the present experiments was to investigate such a situation.

Some methodological issues need to be considered before the experiments are reported. First, in order to satisfy the requirement that the relevant elements of the input are attended but the relationships between them are not, it is necessary to contrive rather artificial laboratory tasks that do not resemble real-life language learning activities. Whether this limits the relevance of the research ultimately depends on whether language learning is viewed as a process of acquiring knowledge or as one of acquiring task-specific skills. The present approach is based on the assumption that, regardless of the specific tasks being performed by the individual, an underlying superpositional learning mechanism operates in the background. The purpose of this mechanism is to learn correlations between environmental events. Cleeremans and Jiménez (2002) referred to this as "model learning," and distinguished it from "task learning," which is the process of learning associations between inputs and outputs in order to perform a specific task: "Regardless of how these two classes of learning mechanisms can be combined, the important point to remember in the context of this framework is that model learning operates whenever information processing takes place, whereas task learning operates only in specific contexts defined by particular goals" (Cleeremans & Jiménez, 2002, p. 18).

The present experiments of necessity required the critical elements of the input to be perceived as relevant to different tasks (as in the Jiménez & Méndez, 1999, experiment). What is at issue, then, is whether there is some mechanism for learning the correlation between input elements just by virtue of their being co-present in the environment, regardless of the tasks that are being performed on them. The present experiments investigated this issue in the context of learning form–meaning connections.

Second, a central concern in research on implicit learning is how the investigator can be sure that implicit, rather than explicit, learning processes took place during training. It is always possible that participants will enter an explicit, intentional, learning mode even if the task does not appear to demand it. The present approach was to exclude from the data analysis participants who became aware of all, or just some, of the relevant form–meaning connections during training; that is, to apply a criterion based on the explicitness of knowledge rather than of the learning processes. This is, perhaps, a rather conservative criterion because it is likely that conscious awareness can result from implicit learning. After all, implicit knowledge shapes conscious perception (Perruchet & Vinter, 1998). On the other hand, because there are likely to be interactions between implicit and explicit learning processes (Mathews & Roussel, 1997), it is unlikely that a person who becomes aware of the target rules during training does so purely as a result of implicit learning. It is therefore prudent to exclude participants on the basis of rule awareness.

A third methodological issue is the potential influence of participants' knowledge of other languages. Most psychological research on implicit learning has employed target systems that bear little relation to natural languages. The issue of how, or whether, prior knowledge facilitates implicit learning has not been addressed. In contrast, in SLA research, the issue of transfer has been of central concern. Experiment 1 employed a target system based on naturally occurring noun class systems and so it was relevant to consider the extent to which participants' knowledge of structurally similar systems impacted on learning outcomes.

EXPERIMENT 1

Method

Subjects. There was a total of 37 participants. They were predominantly Cambridge University students and researchers with various language backgrounds.

Materials. This experiment employed the artificial microlanguage shown in Table 10.1. There were 8 determiners and 8 nouns. Nouns that refer to living things took the determiners *ig, i, ul,* and *tei*, and nouns that refer to nonliving things took the determiners *ga, ge, ula,* and *tegge.*[1] Participants in the experiment were only exposed to the nonitalicized items in Table 10.1. The items in italics were withheld for the generalization tests.

Table 10.1. The Items Used in Experiment 1

	Definite Singular (the)	Definite Plural (the)	Indefinite Singular (a)	Indefinite Plural (some)
Living things				
monkey	*ig johombe*	i johombi	ul johombe	tei johombi
bee	ig zabide	*i zabidi*	ul zabide	tei zabidi
lion	ig wakime	i wakimi	*ul wakime*	tei wakimi
bird	ig migene	i migeni	ul migene	*tei migeni*
Non-living things				
shoe	*ga shosane*	ge shosani	ula shosane	tegge shosani
clock	ga tisseke	*ge tisseki*	ula tisseke	tegge tisseki
chair	ga chakume	ge chakumi	*ula chakume*	tegge chakumi
vase	ga nawase	ge nawasi	ula nawase	*tegge nawasi*

Note. Items in italics were not presented during training.

[1] This system is actually based on Italian. By substitution of consonants the masculine determiners *il, i, un, dei* became *ig, i, ul* and *tei*, and the feminine determiners *la, le, una, delle* became *ga, ge, ula, tegge*. The *-e/-i* noun endings were based on irregular Italian nouns such as *tegame* ('saucepan,' masculine) and *stazione* ('station,' feminine). The noun stems themselves were devised so as not to be similar to English or Romance words. Given the similarities to Italian, no native Italian speakers were tested. In the main experiment, only 2 participants had any knowledge of Italian at an intermediate level or better, whereas in the control experiment none did.

Two types of knowledge could underlie the ability to respond correctly to generalization items. The first, and the simplest, would be knowledge of the association between determiners and noun animacy. It was the acquisition of this kind of form–meaning association that was of primary concern in the experiment. However, it would also be possible, in principle, for participants to perform a distributional analysis of the input (Maratsos, 1982). Participants could learn that the determiners in each class are associated with each other via their occurrences with common nouns, and they could infer the correct determiner for a generalization item from their memory for which determiners the noun occurred with during training. In this case, responses to generalization test items would be made without any reference to the semantic properties of the nouns at all. In the event of above-chance performance on the generalization test, it would be necessary to perform a control experiment in order to establish whether semantic information was in fact used in the learning process.

Procedure. The participants first learned the English meanings of the nouns and determiners as isolated vocabulary items (determiners with the same meaning were distinguished by using English translations printed in different colors). In the training task, determiner-noun combinations from the training set were auditorily presented and for each item participants had to (a) repeat it aloud, (b) indicate whether it referred to a living or a nonliving thing by pressing either the z (nonliving) or / (living) keys on the keyboard, and (c) translate it into English. For example, the participants would hear "i johombi," say "i johombi," hit the 'Living' key, and say "the monkeys." Feedback was provided. Incorrect responses for living–nonliving produced an immediate beep, and translation errors were followed by the correct response in written form. The participants were instructed to perform the tasks as quickly and as accurately as they could. Each cycle of the training task consisted of the 24 training items from Table 10.1. Each participant performed the training task for 15 cycles.

The procedure was intended to ensure that the relevant forms (the determiner and noun) and the relevant aspects of meaning (the animacy feature) were attended whilst not alerting participants to the possibility that they were related. The phrases had to be retained in short-term memory long enough to support the repetition, decision, and translation tasks, encouraging the kind of maintenance rehearsal that would help establish long term memory representations of form. The decision task required explicit computation of animacy information. In order to discourage participants from adopting an intentional learning strategy, they were told that the purpose of the experiment was to see how their decision and translation performance improved with practice.

The test phase consisted of both generalization and trained items. The English translation of a phrase was presented, and the participants had to choose between two alternative expressions in the target language. For example, for the phrase 'the monkey,' they had to decide between *ig johombe* and *ga johombe*. The incorrect choice always contained a determiner of the correct definiteness and number but the wrong animacy. They first performed this task on the 8 generalization items from Table 10.1, followed by 16 items from the training set. The participants were instructed to respond on the basis of which alternative sounded more familiar or "better" and they were not alerted to the possibility that there might be rules. It was assumed that in this forced-choice situation it is possible for responses to be biased even by unconscious knowledge of the relevant rule, just as it is in the kind of grammaticality judgment tasks used by Reber (1976) in artificial grammar research.

Results and Discussion

Only 7 of the 37 participants became aware of the relevance of animacy during the training phase, and their test performance was perfect or near perfect on both generalization and trained items. It was difficult to ascertain whether these participants learned as a result of implicit or explicit processes, however. Three of them clearly reported first "noticing" the relevance of animacy in relation to one pair of determiners (specifically *tei/tegge* or *ul/ula*) and then "working out" the rest of the system either during the rest of the training task or in the testing phase. This might suggest an interaction between implicit and explicit processes. Others simply reported that they "worked out" the system during the training task, but it is unclear whether the intention to do so derived from an intuition that was the result of implicit learning, or from an intention simply to understand why there were alternating forms for the same meanings (e.g, why *tei* and *tegge* both translated to 'some'). In any case, according to the criterion set out earlier, the data from these 7 participants were not included in subsequent analyses because the aim was to see whether there was any evidence of learning in the absence of awareness of the relevance of animacy during the training phase.

The remaining 30 participants said they did not try to work out the system during training, and they were still unaware of the relevance of animacy at the end of the test phase. Two of them seemed to have tried to work out a system during the test phase, but even then only in the latter part (trained items), and they made no reference to animacy. For all 30 participants, responses to the generalization items appear to have been based on intuition. Nevertheless, performance on generalization items was 61%, which was significantly above the chance level of 50%, $t = 3.25$, $p < 0.01$. They scored 71% correct on trained items, which was also significantly above chance, $t = 6.09$, $p < 0.001$.

There were large individual differences among participants in the level of generalization test performance. The strongest predictor was whether the participant spoke an L1 in which noun classes were distinguished by grammatical gender. For the 13 participants who spoke a gender L1, the mean generalization test score was 71%, which was significantly greater than chance, $t = 4.08$, $p < 0.01$. In contrast for the 17 participants who did not speak a gender L1, the mean generalization test score was 54%, which was not significantly different from chance, $t = 0.96$. The difference between the groups' scores was also significant, $t = 2.78$, $p < 0.01$. Of course, researchers must always be cautious about generalizations of this type because the group differences may in fact be due to some other factor. However, the effect of the L1 did not appear to be due to general second language learning experience. The two groups did not differ significantly in terms of the number of L2s spoken to an intermediate level or better (3.54 and 3.12, respectively, $t = 0.92$), or in terms of the number of gender languages spoken as an L2 (1.46 and 1.23, respectively, $t = 0.47$). Nor did differences in memory ability appear to be a factor. A phonological short-term memory test was administered immediately prior to the experiment requiring participants to recall lists of three nonsense words (the singular forms of the nouns in the target language) in the order of presentation. The scores on this test were not significantly different for the gender L1 and nongender L1 groups, being 77% and 68%, respectively, $t = 1.8$.

Before considering these results further, it is important to establish whether participants who were above chance on the generalization test were sensitive to the relationship between determiners and animacy. A control experiment was therefore conducted in which this relationship was removed. The meanings of the nouns were changed so that half in each class referred to living things. The procedure was identical to that used before. There were 18 participants. All participants spoke at least two gender languages to an intermediate level or better, and 12 spoke a gender L1. None was aware of the noun class distinction during training or testing. They scored 56% on the generalization test (not significantly different from chance, $t = 1.3$) and 68% on the trained items (significantly different from chance, $t = 6.4$, $p < 0.001$). Thus, although their memory for determiner-noun combinations received during training was good, they showed no evidence of having learned the underlying noun class distinction. The mean generalization test scores for those participants who spoke a gender L1 was exactly the same as those who did not.

The results of the control experiment suggest that the participants in the main experiment were indeed exploiting animacy information. This does not necessarily mean that they were learning direct associations between determiners and animacy, however, because as discussed earlier, above-chance generalization test performance could also be a result of learning the associations between the determiners. But even if this were the case, it would still have to be concluded that animacy information facilitated the acquisition of the inter-determiner associations.

In the main experiment learning was related to knowledge of gender languages. Williams and Lovatt (2003) used the same system as in the present control experiment (i.e., with no animacy information), and found that learning was positively related both to a measure of the participants' familiarity with other gender languages and their phonological short-term memory ability. However, because of the nature of the training task and the participants (none of whom spoke a gender language as an L1), it could only be concluded that L2 knowledge of gender systems influenced explicit inductive learning. In the present (main) experiment, implicit learning was in fact related to the number of gender languages known, $r = 0.572$, $p < 0.001$, but there was also a large effect of whether participants spoke a gender L1. There is, therefore, good evidence that knowledge of other gender languages has an impact on learning the kind of systems used in these experiments, although whether L1 and L2 knowledge impact differently on implicit and explicit learning remains unclear.

A relevant consideration may be that the determiners had an internal similarity structure that is a vestige of their Italian origins. In one class, *ga* and *ula* share endings, as do *ge* and *tegge*; in the other class, *i* and *tei* share endings, and *ig* and *ul* are the only determiners to end in consonants. The *-a* ending on two of the determiners in one of the classes might have also been a factor, because this is characteristic of feminine words in many languages (Romance languages and Russian). And of course, it is not the case that natural noun class systems are completely devoid of semantic correlates. It is possible that participants with experience of noun class systems in a variety of languages were more sensitive to these cues as indicators of an underlying noun class organization.

Although the role of prior knowledge in implicit learning clearly warrants further investigation, for the moment consider those participants with relatively little knowledge of other gender languages, who failed to achieve above chance generalization performance in the main experiment. This result could hint at potential limitations of the implicit learning mechanism. Alternatively, it could be argued that the training task used in Experiment 1 was so superficial and mechanical that it did not encourage the kind of depth of processing that is necessary to learn form–meaning associations. It is also possible that the target system was too complex. So a second experiment was conducted to test for implicit learning of form–meaning associations using a simpler system and a deeper, more engaging, training task. In an attempt to minimize the influence of prior knowledge, this experiment also used a target system that was superficially less similar to languages that the participants knew.

EXPERIMENT 2

Method

Subjects. A total of 17 university students with varying language backgrounds participated.

Materials. The target language for this experiment is shown in Table 10.2. There were just four determiners: *gi, ul, ro,* and *ne.* There were 12 different nouns, 6 referring to living things, and 6 referring to nonliving things. Living things took *gi* and *ul*, while non-living things took *ro* and *ne.* The items in italics in Table 10.2 were not presented during training, but were reserved for testing generalization ability. Two of the items in each category occurred with both possible articles. None of the articles carried the characteristic *-a* ending for feminine words in many gender languages. Also there was a lack of the kind of surface similarities between the articles that might otherwise suggest that they could form classes. The articles themselves were presented as translations of the

Table 10.2. The Items Used in Experiment 2

Living		Nonliving	
Near	Far	Near	Far
gi dog(s)	ul dog(s)	ro cushion(s)	ne cushion(s)
B gi mouse(s)	ul mouse(s)	ro phone(s)	ne phone(s)
gi lion(s)	*ul lion(s)*	ro table(s)	*ne table(s)*
gi bird(s)	*ul bird(s)*	ro vase(s)	*ne vase(s)*
gi monkey(s)	ul monkey(s)	*ro stool(s)*	ne stool(s)
gi bee(s)	ul bee(s)	*ro clock(s)*	ne clock(s)

Note. Items in italics were not presented during training.

English words *near* and *far*, as opposed to *the* and *a*. Although the participants were instructed to use these words as article-like elements (see later), the conflation with the near–far distinction clearly reduces similarity to article systems in natural languages.

Procedure. In a preliminary vocabulary learning phase, the participants first learned that *gi* and *ro* were associated with the English word "near," and *ul* and *ne* with the English word "far." The English words were printed in different colors to distinguish the alternative translations. It was then explained that the experiment was about a language in which speakers always talked about objects in terms of their distance from the speaker; they use a word that functions like the English word "the," but that also encodes the distance between the speaker and the object. For example, *ul dog* would mean "the-far dog." During the training task, they were presented with phrases such as *ul dog* and had to construct sentences in which they used the phrase in an appropriate context (e.g., *I threw a ball to ul dog at the bottom of the garden*, or for *gi dog, I was happy when gi dog ate from my hand*), taking care to use *gi, ul, ro,* and *ne* in place of the English article "the."

In order to force attention to the animacy feature, the participants were told to construct different contexts for living and non-living things—living things were to be described in outdoor contexts, whereas nonliving things were to be described in indoor contexts. Thus, the two sets of articles were associated with different contextual information, as well as different noun properties, thereby increasing their distinctiveness.

In order to make the constraints on sentence production explicit, for each phrase presented during training, the participants had to select a number of icons from an array on the screen. There was a picture of each object in singular (one object) and plural (three objects) form, geometric representations of the concepts of near and far, and pictures of a tree and a house to symbolize the outdoor and indoor contexts. The symbol for "far" was an oval with an "x" placed outside it to mark the position of the observer. The symbol for "near" was an oval with an "x" inside it. A selected object appeared inside the oval and the tree or house symbol appeared above it.

On each trial of the training task, a phrase from the training set was visually presented for 1 second. The participant said the phrase aloud, and then selected the appropriate icons from the array by clicking on them. These then appeared in a separate window to form a graphic representation of the content they had to express. They then formulated a sentence containing the target phrase. When they had done this, they clicked a "done" button, and the correct graphical representation was presented, along with the written form of the phrase, which they then repeated once again. For example, "gi lion" was visually presented, the participant said "gi lion," then selected the lion, the near symbol, and the tree, constructed a sentence such as "I was scared when gi lion came up to me in the game park," and pressed done. The participant was then presented with the correct graphic and phrase, and said "gi lion" once again. Participants performed this training task for between 4 and 5 cycles through the training set of 32 training items (including equal numbers of singular and plural forms), that is, for between 128 and 160 trials depending on time constraints.

In the testing phase, graphic representations of generalization and trained phrases were presented. The participants had to choose between two alternative expressions for the graphic, where both expressed the appropriate near–far relation. For example, for the graphic representation of "far lion, outside" (the "far" symbol, a lion, and a tree) the choice was between *ul lion* and *ne lion.* They were told that for this specific item they had used one of the forms more often during the sentence production task, and they should select the one that seemed more familiar, or that they thought seemed "better." The testing phase had the following composition: (a) two trained items, (b) eight generalization items, (c) eight more trained items, (d) a further eight generalization items (these had the opposite value of ±singular from the first set of generalization items). The participants were asked what criteria they had been using to make their choices, and in case they reported rules involving animacy, at what point in the experiment they became aware of its relevance.

Results and Discussion

None of the participants became aware of the relationship between the articles and animacy during the training phase. The mean score for the first set of generalization items was 52%, which was not significantly different from the chance value of 50%, $t = 0.45$. In contrast, performance on trained items was 84%, and significantly different from chance, $t = 9.79$, $p < 0.001$. On the second set of generalization items, performance was somewhat better than for the first set, being 60%, and significantly different from chance, $t = 2.52$, $p < 0.05$. This improvement in scores suggests that some learning had occurred during the test phase itself. In fact, two participants were able to describe the system correctly at the end of the test phase, and a third could state the relationship between animacy and the words for "near," but not for "far." All three claimed that this awareness developed in the course of the test phase. Interestingly, however, two were the only participants who scored 100% on the first set of generalization items (whereas the third only scored 37.5%). It is not possible to tell whether some awareness had in fact developed during training, or whether knowledge that was acquired implicitly became explicit in the course of the test phase. The remaining 14 participants scored 46%, 81%, and 57% on the first set of generalization test, trained items, and second set of generalization items, respectively. Only the score for the trained items was significantly different from chance, $t = 8.05, p < 0.001$.

Of the 17 participants, 11 spoke a gender L1 and 6 spoke a nongender L1 (English in all cases). There were no significant differences between these groups on any of the tests. In fact, the nongender L1 group did slightly better than the gender L1 group on all three tests (70% vs. 62%, respectively, averaged over the three tests), but the difference was not significant, $t = 1.30$. Therefore, there was no evidence that the nature of the participants' L1 had any effect in this experiment.

Experiment 2, therefore, provides very little evidence of implicit learning. Only two participants scored highly on the first generalization test, but the fact that they subsequently showed at least partial awareness of the system raises doubts about whether they really had no awareness of the relevance of animacy during the training phase. They may just not have explicitly formulated the system prior to testing. The majority of participants remained oblivious to the relevance of animacy throughout the entire experiment and were at chance on the generalization tests. The lack of an effect of the L1 suggests that in Experiment 1 the similarity structure of the determiners and the characteristic *-a* endings may well have been critical in allowing participants to draw on knowledge of similar systems, and that learning was the result of an interaction between these cues, prior linguistic knowledge, and animacy information.

In contrast to Experiment 1, none of the participants became aware of the relevance of animacy during the training phase. This may well be because the processing demands of the training task were higher in Experiment 2. In Experiment 1, the decision and translation tasks involved repetition of the same simple responses to the same stimuli over blocks. In Experiment 2, the participants were required to formulate a sentence on each trial and, even granted the tendency to recycle contexts, this was presumably a more demanding task than translation. Therefore, participants in Experiment 2 may have had less spare capacity for noticing the relevance of animacy, or for intentionally trying to work out why alternating forms were used. But this only makes Experiment 2 a more valid test of implicit learning because whereas the probability of noticing the relevance of animacy might have been reduced with respect to Experiment 1, there seems no reason to suppose that any less attention was paid to animacy information as such.

DISCUSSION

The failure to obtain implicit learning of form–meaning associations, at least in those participants who were unable to draw on relevant prior knowledge, is consistent with DeKeyser's (1995) results. In both sets of studies, participants learned form–form associations present in trained items, but they showed no ability to generalize on the basis of the underlying form–meaning associations. In the present case, although the relevant aspects of form and meaning had clearly been attended, associations between specific morphemes and specific aspects of meaning were not learned. Despite the repeated pairings of certain forms and certain meanings, and the apparent simplicity of the system employed in Experiment 2, very few of the participants became aware of the relevant relationships during the training task, and those that did not showed no evidence of learning on tests that could, in principle, have been sensitive to implicit knowledge.

These results are consistent with Ellis' (1994) claim that although implicit learning of word forms is possible, implicit learning of form–meaning associations is not. Central to his argument is the fact that amnesics show normal levels of implicit learning of novel word forms as measured by repetition priming (Haist, Musen, & Squire, 1991), yet they are almost completely unable to learn vocabulary, whether it is taught as translation equivalents or it is encountered repeatedly in naturalistic contexts such as watching television (Gabrieli, Cohen, & Corkin, 1988).

Why then are form–meaning connections so resistant to implicit learning? Some clues may be provided by evidence from research on learning form-form associations, for example, learning previously unrelated word pairs like *bell-cradle*. In his review of the literature at that time, Squire (1992) concluded that there was no evidence for implicit learning of novel associations in amnesics. Likewise, Dagenbach, Horst, and Carr (1990) showed that in normal subjects there was no priming between novel associations even after study exercises that extended over five weeks. More recently, however, positive evidence for implicit learning of novel associations has emerged from studies on normals (Goshen-Gottstein & Moscovitch, 1995) and amnesics (Gabrieli, Keane, Zarella, & Poldrack, 1997). What is unique about these studies is that, during study, the word pairs were presented simultaneously, rather than sequentially. Goshen-Gottstein and Moscovitch (1995) argued that for novel associations to be learned the stimuli need to be "unitized" at encoding. Whether unitization is simply a consequence of temporal contiguity is not clear. They suggested that it may also be important that the person elaborate some kind of a perceptually-based relationship between the stimuli, such as comparing the number of vowels.

In a similar vein, but working in the context of artificial grammar research, Perruchet and colleagues (Perruchet & Gallego, 1997; Perruchet & Vinter, 1998) have argued that implicit learning reflects the chunking, or parsing, operations that occur at the moment of encoding, and participants' performance in grammaticality judgment tests can be accounted for in terms of the chunks they formed while encoding the training stimuli. Because chunking is a perceptual process, the implication is that people are in fact conscious of the relevant information structures, although they do not need to be aware of them as targets for learning (learning can occur incidentally), and they do not need to be aware that they are accessing these structures at the time of testing (knowledge can be used implicitly). According to this, and the unitization hypothesis, for learning to have occurred in the present experiments, it would have been necessary for participants to be aware of the relevance of animacy during training, or for them at least to have formed perceptual chunks in which animacy was related to article forms. If the input were parsed in this way, the systems employed in Experiments 1 and 2 would presumably become trivially simple to learn. For example, in Experiment 2, *gi* occurred with the notions living thing, tree, and outside as many as 40 times during training. This should have been more than sufficient to establish the relevant associations in memory. But without an appropriate parsing of the input, there was no evidence of learning in the majority of participants.

However, there are two reasons why caution should be observed in accepting the present results as evidence against implicit form–meaning connections. The first relates to the size of the training sets used in both experiments, and the second to the influence of prior knowledge. Implicit learning may be subject to the influence of both of these factors. With regard to the size of the training set, the present experiments were conducted using very small-scale language systems containing either 8 or 10 nouns, with only 4 or 5 example nouns for living and nonliving things, respectively. Researchers working on first language acquisition have claimed that the child's vocabulary needs to reach a certain size before certain linguistic generalizations emerge. This critical mass hypothesis has been investigated in the context of word order (Tomasello, 2000), past tense morphology (Marchman & Bates, 1994), and number marking (B. F. Robinson & Mervis, 1998). Critical mass effects are also a property of learning in connectionist models (Plunkett & Marchman, 1993). If only a few examples are presented early in training, then these can be stored as individual items, but as more examples are introduced, pressure increases to discover underlying regularities. Thus, while the small training sets used in the present experiments clearly allowed participants to achieve accurate rote memory for individual examples, this might have been at the expense of learning the underlying rules.

With regard to prior knowledge, it was found that in Experiment 1 the more gender languages a person knew, the more likely they were to show evidence of implicit learning. Therefore, problems of unitization, or vocabulary size, may not necessarily set a rigid limit on implicit learning. In this light, it is relevant to recall Hirst, Phelps, Johnson, and Volpe's (1988) study of teaching an English-speaking amnesic French as a second language. Rather surprisingly, this patient's level of learning both vocabulary and grammar was no different from that of the age-matched control subject. But both subjects were ex professors of Spanish, had lived in Spain for some time, and had a strong interest in linguistics. Hirst et al. concluded that it was the availability of these relevant knowledge structures that facilitated learning of French: "The ease with which amnesics can acquire new information…may depend on the relation between the new information and preexisting knowledge" (p. 116).

It is clear, therefore, that it is going to be difficult to make definitive statements about the possibility or impossibility of implicit form–meaning connections. Much is likely to depend on the nature of the participant (i.e., their prior knowledge) and upon the nature of the system (i.e., its intrinsic learnability through implicit processes). Much remains to be done to explore how these factors influence implicit learning.

REFERENCES

Cleeremans, A., & Jiménez, L. (2002). Implicit learning and consciousness: A graded, dynamic perspective. In R. M. French & A. Cleeremans (Eds.), *Implicit learning and consciousness* (pp. 1–40). Hove, Enland: Psychology Press.

Cowan, N. (1993). Activation, attention, and short-term memory. *Memory and Cognition, 21*, 162–167.

Dagenbach, D., Horst, S., & Carr, T. H. (1990). Adding new information to semantic memory: How much learning is enough to produce automatic priming? *Journal of Experimental Psychology: Learning, Memory, and Cognition, 16*, 581–591.

DeKeyser, R. M. (1995). Learning second language grammar rules: An experiment with a miniature linguistic system. *Studies in Second Language Acquisition, 17*, 379–410.

Ellis, N. (1994). Vocabulary acquisition: The explicit ins and outs of explicit cognitive mediation. In N. C. Ellis (Ed.), *Implicit and explicit learning of languages* (pp. 211–282). London: Academic Press.

Gabrieli, J. D. E., Cohen, N. J., & Corkin, S. (1988). The impaired learning of semantic knowledge following medial temporal lobe resection. *Brain & Cognition, 7*, 157–177.

Gabrieli, J. D. E., Keane, M., Zarella, M. M., & Poldrack, R. A. (1997). Preservation of implicit memory for new associations in global amnesia. *Psychological Science, 8*, 326–329.

Goshen-Gottstein, Y., & Moscovitch, M. (1995). Repetition priming effects for newly formed associations are perceptually based: Evidence from shallow encoding and format specificity. *Journal of Experimental Psychology: Learning, Memory, and Cognition, 21*, 1249–1262.

Haist, F., Musen, G., & Squire, L. (1991). Intact priming of words and nonwords in amnesia. *Psychobiology, 19*, 275–285.

Hintzman, D. L. (1986). "Schema abstraction" in a multiple-trace memory model. *Psychological Review, 93*, 411–428.

Hirst, W., Phelps, E. A., Johnson, M. K., & Volpe, B. T. (1988). Amnesia and second language learning. *Brain and Cognition, 8*, 105–116.

Jiménez, L., & Méndez, C. (1999). Which attention is needed for implicit sequence learning? *Journal of Experimental Psychology: Learning, Memory, and Cognition, 25*, 236–259.

Logan, G. D., & Etherton, J. L. (1994). What is learned during automatization? The role of attention in constructing an instance. *Journal of Experimental Psychology: Learning, Memory and Cognition, 20*, 1022–1050.

Maratsos, M. (1982). The child's construction of grammatical categories. In E. Wanner & L. R. Gleitman (Eds.), *Language acquisition: the state of the art* (pp. 240–266). Cambridge, England: Cambridge University Press.

Marchman, V. A., & Bates, E. (1994). Continuity in lexical and morphological development: a test of the critical mass hypothesis. *Journal of Child Language, 21*, 339–366.

Mathews, R. C., & Roussel, L. G. (1997). Abstractness of implicit knowledge: A cognitive evolutionary perspective. In D. C. Berry (Ed.), *How implicit is implicit learning?* (pp. 13–47). Oxford, England: Oxford University Press.

McClelland, J., & Rumelhart, D. (1985). Distributed memory and the representation of general and specific information. *Journal of Experimental Psychology: General, 114*, 159–188.

Perruchet, P., & Gallego, J. (1997). A subjective unit formation account of implicit learning. In D. C. Berry (Ed.), *How implicit is implicit learning?* (pp. 124 – 161). Oxford, England: Oxford University Press.

Perruchet, P., & Vinter, A. (1998). PARSER: A model for word segmentation. *Journal of Memory and Language, 39*, 246–263.

Plunkett, K., & Marchman, V. A. (1993). From rote learning to system building: The acquisition of morphology in children and connectionist nets. *Cognition, 48*, 21–69.

Reber, A. S. (1976). Implicit learning of synthetic languages: The role of instructional set. *Journal of Experimental Psychology: Human Learning and Memory, 2*, 88–94.

Robinson, B. F., & Mervis, C. B. (1998). Disentangling early language development: Modeling lexical and grammatical acquisition using an extension of a case–study methodology. *Developmental Psychology, 34*, 363–375.

Robinson, P. (1995). Attention, memory, and the "noticing" hypothesis. *Language Learning, 45*, 283–331.

Schmidt, R. (1994). Implicit learning and the cognitive unconscious: Of artificial grammars and SLA. In N. C. Ellis (Ed.), *Implicit and explicit learning of languages* (pp. 165–209). London: Academic Press.

Schmidt, R. (2001). Attention. In P. Robinson (Ed.), *Cognition and second language instruction* (pp. 3–32). Cambridge, England: Cambridge University Press.

Squire, L. (1992). Memory and the hippocampus: A synthesis from findings with rats, monkeys, and humans. *Psychological Review, 99*, 195–231.

Tomasello, M. (2000). The item–based nature of children's early syntactic development. *Trends in Cognitive Sciences, 4*, 156–163.

Williams, J. N., & Lovatt, P. (2003). Phonological memory and rule learning. *Language Learning, 53*, 67–121.

Winter, B., & Reber, A. S. (1994). Implicit learning and the acquisition of natural languages. In N. C. Ellis (Ed.), *Implicit and explicit learning of languages* (pp. 115–146). London: Academic Press.

CHAPTER 11
Theoretical and Methodological Issues in Research on Semantic and Structural Elaboration in Lexical Acquisition

Joe Barcroft
Washington University

To learn a new word in a second language (L2) a learner must do at least three things: encode the (phonemic, graphemic, signed) form of the new L2 word, activate an appropriate meaning (semantic representation) for the word within the learner's semantic system (e.g., referential meaning, collocations, syntactic properties), and map the new word form onto the appropriate meaning. Each of these three subprocesses needs to be completed to learn a new word successfully, regardless of whether the word is learned incidentally from context or intentionally in a more direct manner. Therefore, the issue of how learners allocate their limited processing resources toward the completion of each of these three subprocesses is both critical to our understanding of L2 lexical acquisition from a cognitive perspective and pertinent to different types of vocabulary learning across the incidental-to-direct learning continuum (see, Coady, 1997, for a synthesis of research with reference to this continuum).

This chapter reviews research on how learners allocate processing resources to the semantic and formal components of learning new words. Much of this research focuses on the effects of semantic versus structural elaboration and, respectively, increased semantic processing versus increased structurally oriented processing during lexical learning tasks. The review examines the predictions of levels of processing (LOP) theory (Craik & Lockhart, 1972), transfer appropriate processing (TAP) theory (Morris, Bransford, & Franks, 1977), and the type of processing–resource allocation (TOPRA) model (Barcroft, 2000, 2002) for the relationship between semantic versus structural elaboration and lexical learning. It then reports a new study involving two experiments on semantic versus structural elaboration and L2 lexical learning. It discusses the results of this study in terms of both theory and research methodology. In terms of theory, a comparison is made between the results to the predictions of LOP and TAP theories and the TOPRA model. In terms of methodology, the focus is on issues that need to be addressed in future studies in this area.

SEMANTIC AND STRUCTURAL ELABORATION

With regard to individual words, the term *semantic elaboration* refers to a situation in which the focus is on the semantic properties or the meaning of a word. An example of word-level semantic elaboration would be if a learner were considering the extent to which the word *snail* represents an example of an animal, of an insect, of a food, or of another category. Structural elaboration, on the other hand, refers to a situation in which the focus is on the structural or formal properties of a word. An example of word-level structural elaboration would be if a learner counted how many letters or syllables there are in the word snail or thinks of other words that rhyme with it. Accordingly, activities that require semantic elaboration are associated with increased semantic processing at the cognitive level, whereas activities that require structural elaboration are associated with increased structurally oriented processing at the cognitive level.

With regard to memory for known words, such as previously acquired words in a first language (L1), studies on memory have found that semantic elaboration can produce better recall and recognition performance than does structural elaboration (Bower & Reitman, 1972; Craik & Tulving, 1975; Epstein, Phillips, & Johnson, 1975; Hyde & Jenkins, 1969; Johnson-Laird, Gibbs, & de Mowbray, 1978; Tresselt & Mayzner, 1960). Craik and Lockhart (1972) explained this finding in terms of levels of processing (LOP) by equating semantic evaluation of target items with "deeper" processing and structural evaluation of target items with "shallower" processing. According to LOP theory, semantic elaboration yields better memory performance than structural elaboration because semantic processing is deeper in nature. For example, requiring learners to make pleasantness ratings about words yields better memory performance than requiring them to count instances of the letter "E" in words (Hyde & Jenkins, 1969) because the semantic processing associated with the former task is a deeper type of processing.

Given that memory for previously acquired words is fundamentally different than memory for previously unacquired words, the positive effects observed for semantic elaboration in LOP studies on previously acquired L1 words may not obtain for new L2 words as target items. Evidence to support this assertion was provided by Morris et al. (1977), who compared the predictions of LOP theory with TAP theory. According to TAP theory, memory performance depends on the degree of compatibility between processing types at encoding and retrieval such that semantic orientation should facilitate performance on semantic tasks and structural orientation should facilitate performance on structural tasks. The researchers supported this position by demonstrating higher recognition of L1 words encoded via a rhyming task (as compared to a semantic task) on a rhyme-oriented test and higher recognition of words encoded via a semantic task (as compared to the rhyming task) on a semantically oriented test.

The TOPRA model (Barcroft, 2000, 2002), which is consistent with TAP theory, emphasizes the distinction between different types of target stimuli. In this model, different amounts of specific types of processing predict similar corresponding amounts of the same types of learning within a limited capacity view of cognition (see Broadbent, 1958; Wickens, 1984, 1989, on limited processing capacity). In Fig. 11.1, the two bolded outer lines in the model do not move because they represent limits on overall processing capacity, whereas the inner lines separating processing types do move as different types of processing and their corresponding learning outcomes increase or decrease. Therefore, if two processing types a and b increase, so do learning types a and b, but another

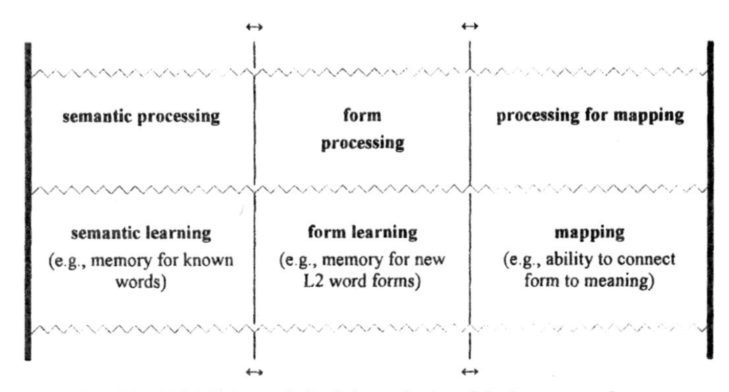

Fig. 11.1. The TOPRA model of the relationship between the semantic, formal, and mapping components of processing and learning.

processing type c and learning type c will have to decrease as a consequence (see Barcroft, 2002, p. 326). Figure 11.1 also depicts a version of the TOPRA model that highlights subprocesses in lexical acquisition. Because each subprocess requires processing resources, as processing for one subprocess increases, overall processing for the other two must decrease in order to accommodate. The resultant amount and type of lexically oriented learning will reflect this kind of trade-off.

The TOPRA model also can be utilized to focus on two subprocesses only, such as semantic processing and form processing (see Barcroft, 2002, p. 325). For this case, the TOPRA model predicts the following (when processing demands are sufficiently high): As semantic processing increases, semantically-oriented learning also increases, but form processing and form learning decrease because fewer processing resources remain available. These predictions for word-level input processing, are consistent with previous research on L2 sentence-level input processing demonstrating tension that can arise between a learner's ability to process for the semantic versus formal components of sentence-level input (VanPatten, 1990, 1996). Lexical learning studies on semantic and structural elaboration have begun to examine the potentially inverse relationship between semantic- and form-oriented processing predicted by the TOPRA model as well.

Many studies have found that semantic elaboration can positively affect memory for known L1 words (LOP studies cited earlier) and for new words when they are recoded as known words as part of a mnemonic device such as Keyword (L1 words: Levin, McCormick, Miller, Berry, & Pressley, 1982; Pressley, Levin, Kuiper, Bryant, & Michener, 1982; L2 words: Atkinson & Raugh, 1975; Ellis & Beaton, 1995). Other studies have found, however, that semantic elaboration (apart from mnemonic devices) had no effect on lexical acquisition rates (L1 studies: Levin et al., 1982; Pressley, Levin, & Miller, 1982; Pressley, Levin, Kuiper et al., 1982, most experiments) or had negative effects on lexical acquisition rates (L1 studies: McDaniel & Kearney, 1984; Pressley, Levin, Kuiper et al., 1982, Experiment 4; L2 studies: Barcroft, 2000, 2003). Pressley, Levin, Kuiper et al. (1982) found that a semantically oriented synonym task in their fourth experiment produced significantly lower scores on an L1 word definition matching test when compared to no-strategy control condition. McDaniel and Kearney (1984) produced a similar finding on using a different type of posttest. Barcroft (2003) found that a condition in which learners had to answer semantically oriented questions about the target words resulted in significantly lower scores on L2 cued productive posttests (view picture, produce target L2 word) when compared to a self-selected strategy condition after controlling for degree of task performance.

Finally, Barcroft (2002) found that semantic elaboration inhibited free recall of new words in an L2 (Spanish) but facilitated free recall of words in a known language (English) when compared to structural elaboration. The results constituted a double dissociation between type of elaboration during learning (semantic, structural) and language of recall (L1, L2) for free recall after an immediate L2 lexical learning task. In that study, English-speaking low-intermediate L2 Spanish learners attempting to learn new Spanish words were required to make pleasantness ratings (+semantic) about some of the words and to count the number of letters that appeared (+structural) in other words. Dependent variables were free recall in Spanish and English and cued recall in Spanish (generate Spanish words when presented with pictures). The results revealed higher Spanish free recall for +structural over +semantic, higher English free recall for +semantic over +structural, higher overall recall for no elaboration over +semantic and +structural, and higher cued recall for control over +semantic and +structural.

To summarize, the combined results of lexical studies in this area suggest that semantic elaboration and the increased semantic processing it invokes do not affect new word learning in the same manner that they affect memory for known words. Some of the results also suggest that increased semantic processing can inhibit the ability to encode the formal properties of new words. These findings are therefore more consistent with TAP theory and the TOPRA model than with LOP theory in terms of their applicability to L2 lexical learning. Given the general paucity of research in this area, however, additional research is needed in order to continue to examine the applicability of LOP, TAP, and the TOPRA model to L2 lexical acquisition.

THE PRESENT STUDY

Motivation

The purpose of the present study was to expand on the current database and repertoire of methodological approaches that have been used in research on semantic elaboration, structural elaboration, and L2 lexical learning. The main theoretical objective of the study was to examine the relative applicability of LOP, TAP, and the TOPRA model to L2 lexical acquisition. To do so, the effects of semantic elaboration versus structural elaboration on lexical learning were examined in two experiments. Unlike Barcroft's (2002) study, the present experiments included two types of cued recall as dependent measures: productive (view picture, produce L2 word) and receptive (view L2 word, produce a known word equivalent; that is, "receptive" with respect to the L2 word form). In this way, the present study was able to examine whether type of cued recall would moderate the effect of semantic versus structural elaboration in any way.

Finally, the study also examined the extent to which L2 learners complete different types of semantic and structural tasks assigned to them when they are concurrently instructed to do their best to learn a set of new words. In both experiments, the participants self-assessed how well they performed the structural and semantic tasks to which they had been assigned. The semantic and structural tasks assigned in the first experiment were less constrained in nature than the tasks in the second experiment, which facilitated exploring the potential relationship between the type of task assigned and the degree to which learners tend to complete the task.

The present study also was designed to explore two specific methodological issues. First, the study examined both less constrained (Exp. 1) and more constrained (Exp. 2) versions of semantic and structural tasks in order to provide information about the degree of task performance that can be expected for different types of assigned tasks when learners are concurrently asked to do their best to learn a set of new words. Exploring this issue is important in order to obtain a sufficient degree of task performance in this area of research. Second, the present study included both within-subjects (Exp. 1) and between-subjects (Exp. 2) experimental designs given that previous lexical learning studies on semantic versus structural elaboration have yet to explore whether the different types of designs result in any obvious differences in performance.

Research Questions

The present study addressed the following questions:

1. Does semantic elaboration have an effect on L2 lexical learning rates when compared to structural elaboration based on immediate and delayed measures of productive and receptive cued recall? If so, what is the nature of the effect?
2. If the answer to Question 1 is "yes," then does the effect of semantic elaboration depend on the type of recall (productive, receptive)? If so, what is the nature of the relationship between type of measure and the effect of semantic elaboration?
3. To what extent do learners complete tasks requiring semantic and structural elaboration when instructed to do these tasks and, concurrently, to do their best to learn new words in an immediate L2 lexical learning task?

With regard to Question 1, if semantic elaboration increases lexical learning rates, this finding would be consistent with the direct applicability of LOP theory to L2 lexical learning without the need to distinguish between different types of tasks at study and between known versus new words when predicting the effects of semantically versus structurally oriented processing. However, if semantic elaboration (as compared to structural elaboration) is found to have no effect or a negative effect, this finding would be more consistent with the applicability of TAP theory and the TOPRA model to L2 lexical learning because it would point to the need to specify the nature of tasks at study and at testing as well as the nature of the to-be-remembered stimulus (known word vs. new word) when predicting the effects of increased semantic processing. The answers to Questions 2 and 3, then, speak to the generalizability of the answer to Question 1 across different types of cued recall and with regard to how learners view the effectiveness of +semantic and +structural tasks during lexical learning.

EXPERIMENT 1

Participants

Participants were English-speaking students in first-semester Spanish at a private university in the Midwestern United States. The original pool was 72, but 4 individuals were removed to create equal cell sizes. The 68 remaining participants were 59 native and 9 proficient speakers of English.

Design

Experiment 1 examined the relative effects of two tasks: semantic elaboration (+semantic) and structural elaboration (+structural). Each participant completed both tasks and was exposed to one of two presentation orders. Participants 1-34 attempted to learn Words 1–12 in the +semantic condition and Words 13–24 in the +structural condition. Participants 35–68 attempted to learn Words 1–12 in the +structural condition and Words 13–24 in the +semantic condition. This counterbalancing of conditions and presentation orders across equal cell sizes was included in order to avoid the potential confounding effects of word groups and presentation orders.

Materials

The following materials were used: a consent form and language background questionnaire, a pretest on the experimental words, a laptop computer and projector, a computer presentation program with the experimental words and pictures, and 4 posttests (2 productive, 2 receptive).

Experimental Words

The experimental words were 24 Spanish nouns. Words of different lengths (two-, three-, four-, and five-syllable words) were included in order to reflect a range of authentic target lexical items, and different dialects of Spanish were represented. To minimize differences in the difficulty for the two word groups, the average number of syllables in each word group was equal. Words 1–12 were *serrote* 'saw', *regadera* 'watering can', *borla* 'tassel', *rastrillo* 'rake', *embudo* 'funnel', *destornillador* 'screwdriver', *imán* 'magnet', and *clavo* 'nail', *taladro* 'drill', *cabestrillo* 'sling', *pinza* 'clothespin', *chiringa* 'kite'. Target words 13–24 were *aletas* 'flippers', *resbaladilla* 'slide', *pala* 'shovel', and *balde* 'bucket', *clavija* 'plug', *sacudidor* 'feather duster', *asa* 'handle', *candado* 'lock', *tenazas* 'pliers', *estantería* 'bookcase', *lupa* 'magnifying glass', and *gancho* 'hook'. Each word had been viewed in a bilingual or monolingual dictionary.

Procedure

Data collection was conducted during regular class hours in the following manner:

1. Each participant completed the consent form, the language background questionnaire, and the pretest. The pretest instructed the participants to translate target words that they knew or thought that they might know into English. The order of the words on the pretest was reversed from the exposure phase in order to avoid habituating the participants to one presentation order while maintaining appropriately structured ordering throughout the study for counterbalancing. None of the 68 participants correctly translated any of the words on the pretest.

2. After reading general directions for the experiment, which included information about presentation interval lengths, numbers of exposures, and the fact that they would be tested on how well they had learned the target words after the exposure phase, the exposure phase began.

3. During the exposure phase, each word and its corresponding picture appeared on the screen for 12 seconds each for 2 trials in the same order. Instructions for the +semantic task were as follows: "For the next 12 words, focus as much as you can on the MEANING of each word. For example, you may focus on (a) whether or not you own this item; (b) how much it might cost to purchase the item; (c) contexts in which the item may or may not be used; (d) the last time that you used the item; and so on. Please do your best to learn these words. Good luck!" Instructions for the +structural task were as follows: "For the next 12 words, focus as much as you can on the FORM of each word. For example, you may focus on (a) what the word looks like; (b) how long the word is; (c) how many syllables there are in the word; (d) the first and last letter of the word; and so on. Please do your best to learn these words. Good luck!"

4. After the exposure phase, the first and second posttests were administered. Instructions on the first posttest (immediate, productive) were to write as much of each target word as possible while viewing pictures only for each target word. Instructions on the second posttest (immediate, receptive) were to write English equivalents for the 24 target words listed on a sheet. The overall amount of time allotted to complete both posttests was 4 minutes, 48 seconds (24 words x 12 seconds for the first posttest). Presentation orders for both posttests had been selected at random.

5. After the second posttest, the participants completed a questionnaire instructing them to self-assess their performance based on the following questions: "(1) Were you able to focus on the meaning of each word when instructed to do so? Please explain. (2) Were you able to focus on the form of each word when instructed to do so? Please explain." The researcher then thanked the participants for their participation without informing them of any subsequent posttests.

6. Two days later, the researcher returned to complete the third and fourth posttests (delayed, productive, and receptive). The procedure was similar to Step 4. The participants then were asked to report whether they had any additional contact with or had practiced the words in the experiment outside of class. Third- and fourth-posttest data provided by any participant who reported having had extensive additional contact with the words were excluded.

Assessment

A lexical production scoring protocol (LPSP-written) (Barcroft, 2000, 2002) was used to score productive cued recall. A trained independent evaluator scored the posttests using blind scoring. LPSP-written allots points for partially produced words incrementally (0, .25, .50, .75, 1) to be sensitive to different levels of word knowledge (see Barcroft, 2002). For receptive cued recall, scores of 1 were assigned for each correctly translated word. Scores for Words 1–12 and Words 13–24 were then totaled to determine scores for the +semantic and +structural conditions.

Data Analysis

Scores were submitted to a repeated measures analysis of variance (ANOVA). Time (immediate, 2 days later), measure (productive, receptive), and task (+semantic, +structural) were treated as within-subjects independent variables. Score was the dependent variable. Responses for self-assessment of task performance were grouped as "yes" responses (including "I think I could," "mostly," etc.) and "no" responses (including "not really," "a little/not too much," "about half the time," etc.). A second repeated measures ANOVA was then conducted using the lexical learning data provided only by participants with "yes" responses for both the +semantic and +structural tasks. For all statistical analyses, the alpha level was set at .05.

Results

Overall means (with standard deviations in parentheses) were 7.29 (2.53) for the +semantic task versus 7.32 (2.35) for the +structural task; 6.42 (2.18) on the productive measure versus 8.20 (2.62) on the receptive measure; and 7.83 (2.22) at Time 1 (immediate) versus 6.78 (2.56) at Time 2 (delayed). Means based on time × measure × condition for the complete sample appear in Table 11.1. Results of the ANOVA on the complete sample revealed significant main effects for time, $F(1, 59) = 38.49, p < .001, \eta^2 = .395$, and measure, $F(1, 59) = 102.03, p < .001, \eta^2 = .634$. No other significant main effects or interactions were revealed. Scores were significantly higher on the immediate measure than 2 days later. Scores were significantly higher on the receptive over the productive measure. However, no significant difference between +semantic and +structural conditions was observed.

Results for self-assessed task performance were as follows (with frequencies in parentheses). For the +semantic task, 67.6% (46) of the participants reported being able to perform the task, 25.5% (18) reported not being able to complete the task, and 5.9% (4) did not answer. For the +structural task, 54.4% (37) of the participants reported being able to perform the task, 27.9% (19) reported not being able to complete the task, and 17.6% (12) did not answer. The data provided by participants with any "no" or no answer responses were excluded from the second ANOVA. In order to achieve equal cell sizes for counterbalancing in this reduced sample, participants were eliminated at random until equal cell sizes were obtained.

Overall means (with standard deviations in parentheses) for the reduced sample of participants who responded "yes" to both questions on task performance were 7.09 (2.28) for the +semantic task versus 7.08 (2.52) for the +structural task; 6.40 (2.24) on the productive measure versus 7.78 (2.56) on the receptive measure; and 7.60 (2.18) at Time 1 (immediate) versus 6.58 (2.66) at Time 2 (delayed). Means based on time × measure × condition for this reduced sample also appear in Table 1. Results of the ANOVA on the reduced sample revealed significant main effects for time, $F(1,19) = 10.45$, $p = .004$, eta squared $= .355$, and measure, $F(1,19) = 22.43$, $p < .001$, eta squared $= .541$. No other significant main effects or interactions were observed. Although actual means were higher for +structural (6.54) than for +semantic (6.26) on the productive measure and higher for +semantic (7.93) than for +structural (7.63) on the receptive measure, this task × measure interaction did not reach a level of statistical significance.

Again, immediate scores were significantly higher than scores 2 days later, and scores on the receptive measure were significantly higher than on the productive measure. Again, no significant difference between the +semantic versus +structural conditions was observed.

Table 11.1. Means Based on Time × Measure × Task (Experiment 1).

			Complete Sample		Reduced Sample	
Time	Measure	Task	M	SD	M	SD
Immediate	Productive	+Semantic	7.10	2.44	6.91	2.41
		+Structural	7.22	2.52	7.18	2.30
	Receptive	+Semantic	8.55	2.77	8.25	2.38
		+Structural	8.45	2.71	8.05	2.68
2 days later	Productive	+Semantic	5.58	2.60	5.61	2.33
		+Structural	5.77	2.49	5.91	2.83
	Receptive	+Semantic	7.93	3.27	7.60	3.14
		+Structural	7.85	3.00	7.20	3.33

EXPERIMENT 2

Participants

Participants were English-speaking students in four sections of third-semester Spanish at the same private university as in Experiment 1. The original pool was 67, but 8 individuals were removed because they correctly translated one or more words on the pretest. The 59 remaining participants were 57 native and 2 proficient speakers of English.

Design

Experiment 2 examined the relative effects of three tasks—semantic elaboration (+semantic), structural elaboration (+structural), and self-selected strategy (control)—using a between-subjects design. Each participant was assigned to one of the three tasks. Each task was assigned at random among the course sections. Two sections were assigned to +semantic, one was assigned to +structural, and one was assigned to control.

Materials and Experimental Words

Materials and experimental words used were the same as those used in Experiment 1.

Procedure

Data collection procedures were similar to those in Experiment 1, with the following exceptions:

1. The +semantic and +structural tasks were more constrained. The +semantic group was instructed to consider the extent to which each word represented an instance of the concept "economic" in the first trial and the concept "recreation" in the second trial. The +structural group was instructed to

consider what each entire word looked like in the first trial and what each individual letter in each word looked like in the second trial. The control group was instructed to do their best to learn each word only.

2. In addition to answering "yes or no" questions about task performance, participants self-assessed their task performance by circling an interval range on a scale between 0% and 100% in order to provide a more precise measure of task performance. The +semantic group was asked "How often (approximately) were you able to consider how each word can (or cannot) be related to the other words (economic, recreation)?" The +structural group was asked "How often were you able to think about what the instructions asked you to think about (what each word looked like, what each letter in each word looked like)?"

Assessment

Scoring procedures were the same as those used in Experiment 1.

Analysis of Results

Scores were submitted to an analysis of variance (ANOVA). Time (immediate, 2 days later) and measure (productive, receptive) were treated as within-subjects independent variables. Task (+semantic, +structural, control) was treated as a between-subjects independent variable. Score was the dependent variable. For all statistical analyses, the alpha level was set at .05. Self-assessment of task performance was analyzed by calculating frequencies for the task performance intervals selected by the participants. A second ANOVA was conducted based on the data provided by participants who indicated at least 40% task performance.

Results

Overall means (with standard error values in parentheses) were 13.62 (.813) for +semantic, 13.53 (1.07) for +structural, and 14.37 (1.15) for control. Based on measure, they were 12.21 (.583) for productive and 15.47 (.647) for receptive. Based on time, they were 14.34 (.623) at Time 1 (immediate) versus 13.33 (.572) at Time 2 (2 days later). Means based on time × measure × condition for the complete sample appear in Table 11.2. Results of the ANOVA on the complete sample revealed significant main effects for time, $F(1, 51) = 25.47, p < .001, \eta^2 = .333$; for measure, $F(1, 51) = 85.00, p < .001, \eta^2 = .625$; and for the time × condition interaction, $F(1, 51) = 47.41, p < .001, \eta^2 = .482$. No other significant main effects or interactions were observed. Immediate scores were significantly higher than scores 2 days later. Scores on the receptive measure were significantly higher than on the productive measure. The significant time × measure interaction was due to a substantial drop in productive scores versus a slight increase in receptive scores between the immediate and delayed posttests.

No significant difference was observed based on +semantic versus +structural tasks, however.

Results for self–assessed task performance were as follows. Of the 46 participants, 3 participants reported 0% task performance; 2 reported 1%–10 % task performance; 6 reported 10%–20% task performance; 1 reported 20%–30% task performance; 5 reported 30%–40% task performance; 4 reported 40%–50% task performance; 3 reported 50%–60% task performance; 7 reported 60%–70% task performance; 8 reported 70%–80% task performance; 6 reported 80%–90% task performance; 0 reported 90%–100%; and 1 did not answer.

A separate univariate ANOVA was conducted to compare task performance in the +structural and +semantic conditions. For this analysis, cases in which participants circled 0% were assigned a value of .00, cases in which 1%–10% was circled were assigned a value of .10, cases of 10%–20% were assigned .20, cases of 20%–30% were assigned .30, and so forth. Results of this separate analysis revealed that mean task performance was .486 or 48.6% for +semantic group and .624 or 62.4% for the +structural group. This difference did not reach a level of statistical significance ($p = .12$), however. Only the data provided by participants who indicated less than 40% task performance were included in the subsequent reduced sample ANOVA.

Overall means (with standard error values in parentheses) for the reduced sample of participants who indicated at least 40% task performance were 14.30 (1.15) for +semantic, 14.64 (1.19) for +structural, and 14.37 (1.15) for control. Based on measure, they were 12.73 (.65) for productive and 16.14 (.75) for receptive. Based on time, they were 15.00 (.72) at Time 1 (immediate) and 13.87 (.64) at Time 2 (2 days later). Means based on time × measure × condition for this reduced sample appear in Table 11.2. Results of the ANOVA on the reduced sample revealed significant main effects for time, $F(1, 35) = 18.89, p < .001, \eta^2 = .351$; for measure, $F(1, 35) = 68.29, p < .001, \eta^2 = .661$; and for the time × measure interaction, $F(1, 35) = 39.40, p < .001, \eta^2 = .530$. No

Table 11.2. Means Based on Time × Measure × Task (Experiment 2).

			Complete Sample			Reduced Sample		
Time	Measure	Task	N	M	SD	N	M	SD
Immediate	Productive	+Semantic	26	13.25	4.21	13	13.58	4.77
		+Structural	15	13.27	5.06	12	14.73	4.34
		Control	13	13.69	3.88	13	13.69	3.88
	Receptive	+Semantic	26	14.92	4.64	13	16.15	4.81
		+Structural	15	14.93	4.93	12	15.83	5.04
		Control	13	16.00	5.07	13	16.00	5.07
2 days later	Productive	+Semantic	26	11.30	3.69	13	11.62	3.74
		+Structural	15	10.65	5.02	12	11.67	4.74
		Control	13	11.08	3.15	13	11.08	3.15
	Receptive	+Semantic	26	15.00	4.39	13	15.85	4.34
		+Structural	15	15.27	5.01	12	16.33	5.05
		Control	13	16.69	4.19	13	16.69	4.19

other significant main effects or interactions were observed. Immediate scores were significantly higher than scores 2 days later. Scores on the receptive measure were significantly higher than scores on the productive measure. The significant time × measure interaction was due to a drop in productive scores and a slight increase in receptive scores between the immediate and delayed posttests. No significant difference between +semantic and +structural conditions was observed.

DISCUSSION

With reference to the research questions that guided this study, the combined results of both experiments suggest the following points. First, semantic elaboration had no effect on L2 lexical learning rates when compared to structural elaboration. This finding is supported by the non-effect observed for task in both experiments. Second, although overall scores on the receptive measure were higher than scores on the productive measure, the noneffect for task maintained across both productive and receptive forms of cued recall. Third, a large percentage of learners did not complete the +semantic and +structural tasks when instructed to do so during a direct lexical learning task. This finding is supported by the results of the self-assessments on task performance reported in both experiments. In Experiment 1, only 67.7% of the participants reported completing the +semantic task, and only 54.4% reported completing the +structural task. In Experiment 2, participants approximated their task performance at an average of only 48.6% in the +semantic group and at an average of only 62.4% in the +structural group.

The results of both experiments are inconsistent with the applicability of LOP theory to L2 lexical acquisition without first distinguishing between the formal versus semantic components of learning new words. A direct, unqualified application of LOP theory would predict that the +semantic conditions in both experiments in this study should have produced better performance when compared to the +structural conditions, but in both experiments this did not happen. The present results are more consistent with TAP theory and the TOPRA model for L2 lexical acquisition because the semantically oriented tasks during the study phase and the semantic processing associated with them did not positively affect memory for form-oriented tasks during the testing phase. Other results showing no positive effects for semantic elaboration concur with this finding (e.g., Barcroft, 2002, 2003; Pressley, Levin, Kuiper, et al., 1982, Exp. 4).

The nature of the present study ties this finding most directly to direct L2 vocabulary learning. The present results are not inconsistent, however, with previous findings on inferencing strategies during incidental L2 vocabulary learning (see Lee & Wolf, 1997; Paribakht & Wesche, 1999). Relating the two areas of research requires defining parameters for levels of input processing. Reading a text involves discourse-, sentence-, and word-level input processing, whereas the present study focused on word-level input processing only and was based on the assumption that access to each target word form and appropriate semantic information had already been obtained. For incidental vocabulary learning, this would imply that a new word had already been identified from the larger input set and that appropriate semantic information for the word had already been made available through inferencing.

The present findings also raise questions, however, as to why inhibitory effects for semantic elaboration have emerged when using free recall as a measure (Barcroft, 2002) more readily than when using cued recall as a measure. One possible explanation is that cued recall of recently learned words is not as good of a measure of form learning as is free recall. Successful cued recall of a word requires activation of a meaning-to-form mapping (e.g., to go from picture to word). Free recall, however, does not necessarily require this type of activation (e.g., recalling a recently learned word without remembering to which picture it refers). This explanation is consistent with TAP theory and with the TOPRA model in that it distinguishes between cued versus free recall as types of tasks and specifies differences between the type of processing needed to perform each of these two tasks successfully. Productive cued recall should continue to be viewed, however, as a reasonably sensitive measure of form learning because, unlike receptive forms of cued recall, it does require production of target word forms. Additional research directed toward distinguishing between receptive versus productive and free versus cued recall as measures of different types of knowledge may help to clarify these issues further. The relationship between task (+semantic, +structural) and measure (productive, receptive) warrants more research as well. Measure by condition interactions may emerge in future studies that yield higher rates of task performance for +semantic and +structural conditions.

With regard to the use of between-subjects versus within-subjects designs, the present results also may be informative to future studies. Both within-subjects (Exp. 1) and between-subjects (Exp. 2) designs were used to examine semantic versus structural elaboration without striking differences in results that one might wish to attribute to design type. Although the fact that learning phase tasks were not exactly the same in both experiments limits what can be concluded on this issue, future studies can address this limitation using exactly the same tasks in within-subjects and between-subjects experiments. In general, between-subjects designs for research on immediate lexical learning tasks should be used with caution given the high degree of between-subjects variation typical on these tasks. This should also be kept in mind with regard to the results of Experiment 2 in the present study.

Regarding task performance, the present results are telling. They reveal an incongruity between externally imposed tasks during lexical learning and the types of strategies that learners prefer to use when doing their best to learn a set of target words. A substantial percentage of learners in the present study reported low levels of task performance for the +semantic and +structural tasks, even though they had been specifically instructed to do these tasks. Participants seemed to find performing these tasks to be incongruous with the other goal assigned to them, that is, learning the target words. A substantial percentage of the participants reverted to their own self-selected strategies, which suggests they viewed these strategies as more optimal for learning the target words than the +semantic and +structural tasks assigned to them.

From a theoretical and research standpoint, this finding emphasizes the need to ascertain taxonomies of learner-selected strategies during immediate lexical learning tasks and to examine quantitatively the relationship between strategy type and performance. Future studies on immediate lexical learning tasks can explore which strategies learners select most often, which strategies result in better or worse performance, and why different strategies result in better or worse performance in terms of processing resource allocation across different subprocesses in L2 lexical acquisition (form encoding, activating meaning, form–meaning mapping). From a methodological standpoint, the present results suggest that future studies need to continue to find ways to increase +semantic and +structural task performance rates. One option is the use of more controlled tasks. Given that neither the less constrained tasks nor the more constrained tasks in the present study resulted in a high degree of task performance, the use of tasks with more direct means of assuring task performance (as in Barcroft, 2002) may be necessary.

Finally, in terms of L2 instruction, the findings of the present study question the effectiveness of having learners engage in semantically elaborative activities during direct L2 vocabulary learning. Although semantically oriented activities can increase learners' knowledge about word meanings, including second language specific semantic information for a word (e.g., the Spanish word *manzana* refers to "apple" and "street block" as English equivalents), they also can exhaust processing resources that might otherwise be utilized to learn the formal component of new L2 words. Therefore, it would be appropriate to replace the general notion that semantically-oriented activities are good vocabulary instruction techniques with the notion that these activities can be good for some aspects of vocabulary learning but not for others.

REFERENCES

Atkinson, R. C., & Raugh, M. R. (1975). An application of the mnemonic keyword method to the acquisition of a Russian vocabulary. *Journal of Experimental Psychology: Human Learning and Memory, 104*, 126–133.

Barcroft, J. (2000). *The effects of sentence writing as semantic elaboration on the allocation of processing resources and L2 lexical acquisition.* Unpublished doctoral dissertation, University of Illinois, Urbana-Champaign.

Barcroft, J. (2002). Semantic and structural elaboration in L2 lexical acquisition. *Language Learning, 52*(2), 323–363.

Barcroft, J. (2003). Effects of questions about word meaning during L2 Spanish lexical learning. *Modern Language Journal, 87,* 546-561.

Bower, G. H., & Reitman, J. S. (1972). Mnemonic elaboration in multilist learning. *Journal of Verbal Learning and Verbal Behavior, 11*, 478–485.

Broadbent, D. E. (1958). *Perception and communication.* New York: Pergamon.

Coady, J. (1997). L2 vocabulary acquisition: A synthesis of research. In J. Coady & T. Huckin (Eds.), *Second language vocabulary acquisition* (pp. 273–290). Melbourne: Cambridge.

Craik, F. I. M., & Lockhart, R. S. (1972). Levels of processing: A framework for memory research. *Journal of Verbal Learning and Verbal Behavior, 11*, 671–684.

Craik, F. I. M., & Tulving, E. (1975) Depth of processing and the retention of words in episodic memory research. *Journal of Experimental Psychology: General, 104*, 268–294.

Ellis, N., & Beaton, A. (1995). Psycholinguistic determinants of foreign language vocabulary learning. In B. Harley (Ed.), *Lexical issues in language learning* (pp. 107–165). Ann Arbor, MI: Benjamins.

Epstein, M. L., Phillips, W. D., & Johnson, S. J. (1975). Recall of related and unrelated word pairs as a function of processing level. *Journal of Experimental Psychology: Human Learning and Memory, 104*, 149–152.

Hyde, T. S., & Jenkins, J. J. (1969). The differential effects of incidental tasks on the organization of recall of a list of highly associated words. *Journal of Experimental Psychology, 82*, 472–481.

Johnson–Laird, P. N., Gibbs, G., & de Mowbray, J. (1978). Meaning, amount of processing, and memory for words. *Memory and Cognition, 6*, 372–375.

Lee, J. F., & Wolf, D. F. (1997). A quantitative and qualitative analysis of word–meaning inferencing strategies of L1 and L2 readers. *Spanish Applied Linguistics, 1*, 24–64.

Levin, J. R., McCormick, C. B., Miller, G. E., Berry, J. K., & Pressley, M. (1982). Mnemonic versus nonmnemonic vocabulary–learning strategies for children. *American Educational Research Journal, 19*, 121–136.

McDaniel, M. A., & Kearney, E. M. (1984). Optimal learning strategies and their spontaneous use: The importance of task–appropriate processing. *Memory & Cognition, 12*, 361–373.

Morris, C. D., Bransford, J. D., & Franks, J. J. (1977). Levels of processing versus transfer appropriate processing. *Journal of Verbal Learning and Verbal Behavior, 16*, 519–533.

Paribakht, T. S., & Wesche, M. (1999). Reading and "incidental" L2 vocabulary acquisition: An introspective study of lexical inferencing. *Studies in Second Language Acquisition, 21*(2), 195–224.

Pressley, M., Levin, J. R., Kuiper, N. A., Bryant, S. L., & Michener, S. (1982). Mnemonic versus non–mnemonic vocabulary–learning strategies: Additional comparisons. *Journal of Educational Psychology, 74*, 693–707.

Pressley, M., Levin, J. R., & Miller, G. E. (1982). The keyword method compared to alternative vocabulary–learning strategies. *Contemporary Educational Psychology, 7*, 50–60.

Tresselt, M. E., & Mayzner, M. S. (1960). A study of incidental learning. *Journal of Psychology, 50*, 339–347.

VanPatten, B. (1990). Attending to content and form in the input: An experiment in consciousness. *Studies in Second Language Acquisition, 12*, 287–301.

VanPatten, B. (1996). *Input processing and grammar instruction: Theory and research.* Norwood, NJ: Ablex.

Wickens, C. D. (1984). Processing resources in attention. In R. Parasuraman & D. Davies (Eds.), *Varieties of attention* (pp. 63–102). New York: Academic Press.

Wickens, C. D. (1989). Attention and skilled performance. In D. Holding (Ed.), *Human skills* (pp. 71–105). New York: Wiley

IV
Commentary

CHAPTER 12
Reflections on Form–meaning Connection Research in Second Language Acquisition

Diane Larsen-Freeman
University of Michigan

My discussion of the chapters in this volume is divided into three sections. In the first part, I deal with the scope of form–meaning connection (FMC) research as represented by the chapters in this collection. Following this, I comment broadly upon the contributions of this type of research. And, in the third, and final, section, I raise some issues for researchers of FMCs to consider.

ON THE SCOPE OF RESEARCH INTO FORM–MEANING CONNECTIONS

One of the first thoughts I had as I read this collection was how broadly research on FMCs extends. Indeed, some of the fundamental questions in second language acquisition (SLA) research are addressed in one or more of the chapters in this volume:

- What is the role of competence and performance in a Universal Grammar account of SLA? (Klein)
- How much of SLA takes place implicitly? How much of the target language has to be noticed? (Gass, Ellis, Williams)
- What effect on SLA does second language instruction have in general and do specific pedagogical procedures have in particular? (Doughty, Barcroft)
- How much of SLA is input dependent? (VanPatten, Ellis, Shirai)
- What are the mechanisms underlying SLA? How does interlanguage develop over time? (VanPatten, Williams, & Rott, Ellis, Shirai, Bardovi-Harlig)
- What is the influence of the native language on SLA? (Cadierno & Lund, Williams)
- How do learner factors and/or the context affect the SLA process? (Shirai, Gass)

Other issues are addressed as well, but these seven constitute enduring core questions in SLA. It could be argued, therefore, that this collection represents a microcosm of the SLA field itself.

To make the point about its broad scope in another way, I note that the linguistic theory that informed initial FMC research has been joined in this volume by generative linguistics (Klein), cognitive linguistics (Cadierno & Lund), and construction grammar (Ellis), as well as traditional grammar

(Bardovi-Harlig, Shirai). Thus, the scope of FMC research is broader in this volume than I had anticipated.

Although its breadth is impressive, it is important that FMC research be seen for its limitations well. A brief example should illustrate this point. Take, for instance, the plural inflection in English, mentioned early on in the volume by VanPatten, Williams, & Rott. One could ask what it is that a learner of English needs to know about the plural inflection. If knowing is construed as acquiring linguistic knowledge, then the answer might be that in order to use the English plural correctly, the learner minimally needs to know the following:

- about count and noncount nouns and which nouns are prototypically count and which noncount in English (and perhaps about ways of imposing countability on noncount nouns)
- its position as a bound morpheme
- its allophonic variants
- its regular and irregular forms
- the changing nature of its irregular forms, for example, is *data* singular or plural?
- its spelling rules and exceptions
- its suppression in adjectival phrases of measurement (**a twelve-inches ruler*)
- its meaning ("more than one")
- its use with noncount nouns to change the meaning to convey "types of" (compare *I prefer white wine* and *the white wines of Australia*)
- in some cases that lexical and morphological number can co-occur to give new meaning to words (e.g., *peoples*)
- its connotation (e.g., many speakers of English will freely use the plural form of the slang term "kids" for "children" but not its singular variant to refer to one child (i.e., they find *kid* to be pejorative)
- its use and nonuse in generic statements and the difference between them (cf. *Researchers work hard* to *A researcher works hard*)
- unlike many other languages, plurality is marked on the noun, but not marked in the determiner phrase or adjective phrase

and perhaps more removed, but still germane,

- how the number of the subject noun phrase intersects with the verb in a sentence, most often agreeing in number, but not always doing so (e.g., *Ten miles* ***is*** *a long way to walk*); or with collective nouns, where plurality can be shown without the plural marker (e.g., *The family are all here*).

Now, even though I have not exhausted the list of factors and although I am talking about one simple inflection in English, it is clear that language is complex, and the learning of it is likely complex, too. I am not suggesting that all the factors are learned in piecemeal fashion, and certainly not that they all must be explicitly taught; however, it is very likely that different learning processes account for the learning of different factors (Larsen-Freeman, 1991). For example, although controversial, some researchers believe there are two learning processes responsible for the learning of just one of these factors—that is, that regular inflectional forms are acquired by a different process from irregular ones (e.g., Pinker & Prince, 1994; also, see Shirai, Chap. 5 in this vol., for an example).

I therefore appreciate the fact that VanPatten, Williams, & Rott are appropriately circumspect regarding the scope of FMC research when they point out that connecting form with meaning does not account for all aspects of the language ("it is likely that different aspects of language are processed differentially"), a position I very much agree with and have written much about (e.g., Larsen-Freeman, 1995, 2000, 2003). In fact, I have pointed out that, at the very least, learners have to learn three things about a form: how it is formed (its morphosyntax and phonology), what it means (its semantics), and when or why to use it (its pragmatics, which I take to mean the contextual factors that influence the choice of form when two forms have the same meaning potential), and that this is true for all linguistic units, be they morphemes, words, grammar structures, formulas, functions, and so forth. From my perspective, FMC research deals exclusively with the second of these three—how learners come to bond a form and its meaning.

Furthermore, what constitutes the learning challenge shifts depending on the linguistic unit and developmental time. For example, I am not convinced that it is connecting the forms and meanings of the verb tense-aspect system that presents the most difficult learning challenge in general, at least for English learners. Rather, in my experience, it is learning when or why to use them; that is, learning to choose one verb form over the other when the forms have the same meaning potential in terms of temporality or modality, but differ in terms of the contribution that they make to, for example, discourse coherence (the obvious example here is the notorious problem that ESL/EFL students have in terms of the simple past tense and the present perfect tense-aspect combination). In my opinion, the learning difficulty is not ameliorated if the source of the challenge is construed as a FMC problem. For discussion of time lines and lexical aspect alone do not get at the root of the conceptual problem learners have (see Larsen-Freeman, Kuehn, & Haccius, 2002). Thus, my point is that FMC research addresses an important part—but only one part—of the SLA puzzle.

THE CONTRIBUTION OF FMC RESEARCH

The specialized focus of FMC research does not detract from its contribution, of course. Understanding how FMCs are made is an important and challenging area of investigation. The specialized focus allows for certain matters to be probed more deeply. Illustrative of this, I note that significant inroads were made by the authors of the present volume in more precisely specifying how FMCs are made and how they contribute to SLA. Subprocesses identified by the authors of various chapters include: making the connection, filling in, strengthening, restructuring (VanPatten, Williams & Rott), input processing (which in turn consists of two subprocesses, namely, the formation of initial FMCs and parsing), accommodation, and restructuring (VanPatten), attending, interacting, extracting (Gass), and associative mapping, noticing, figuring, and tuning (Ellis), among others.

This is extremely important work. Knowing which processes contribute to FM linkages will lead to future understanding that will address how learners come to associate meaning with linguistic form. This understanding, in turn, will inform how we might facilitate learners' making the connections, which leads me to point out another contribution of FMC research.

FMC research has given us another set of tools with which to address pedagogical concerns. VanPatten's notion of input processing offers us a different way to focus language learners' attention on the learning challenge. Input-processing tasks seek to alter the way in which learners perceive and process the input to which they are exposed. Because humans are limited in their processing capacity, they benefit from assistance that directs their attention away from their normal ways of thinking. Applying the heuristic of appealing to contrast is a powerful pedagogical principle, which may facilitate the way that learners connect forms with their meanings.

ISSUES FOR RESEARCHERS OF FMCS TO CONSIDER

In the last part of this review, I put forth some issues for FMC researchers to consider as they advance their research agendas. First of all, VanPatten states that FMC research seeks to account for mental competence. It is, he writes, through a process of forging FMCs that mental competence is constructed. It follows, then, that the goal of researchers is to determine which processes create such links. This seems to me to be a straightforward and sensible approach to FMC research, given what it has sought to explain.

However, a major issue that FMC researchers must contend with these days is that the linguistic ground is shifting. Not everyone accepts that SLA research exists to account for the acquisition of mental competence. Certainly, socioculturalists do not. And, if the nature of the enterprise shifts radically, then the theoretical underpinnings of FMC research may also need to shift, or, at least, FMC researchers will need to say why they should not shift. Now is not the time, nor is it my prerogative, to say which should happen. However, I will briefly enumerate what I see as the linguistic challengers to a view of SLA as the acquisition of mental competence.

One alternative to static models of linguistic competence and its learning lies with emergentist theories of language/learning (e.g., Ellis, 1998; Elman et al., 1998; MacWhinney, 1999). Using connectionist modeling, researchers simulate neural networks in the brain. As language data are taken in to connectionist neural network models, certain connections in the networks are strengthened, others weakened. Nothing is static. A connectionist model of language is therefore constantly changing, best depicted by the dynamic relationships among the network connections. In this way, language is seen to be a "statistical ensemble" of interacting elements (Cooper, 1999, p. ix). Emergentists assert that rules or abstractions are "structural regularities of language [that] emerge from learners' lifetime analysis of the distributional characteristics of the language input" (Ellis, 2003, p. 63). As Ellis put it, cognitivists who favor usage-based views of language and its development believe that a rule-based linguistic description is the explanandum, not the explanans, a view very different from the traditional conception of rules as mental representations that underpin performance. How does emergentism represent a challenge to FMC research? Well, perhaps it does not, but there are, at least, two notable differences between them. First, emergentists are not attempting to account for a mental competence endpoint. Emergentists would not be content with the view that FMCs are forged and remain linked as part of a static mental competence.

Second, it seems that almost all the forms of the FMCs discussed in the chapters in this volume are forms from traditional linguistic descriptions. Who is to say if these are psychologically real forms for learners? For example, many of the authors explicitly or implicitly have chosen not to deal with language chunks or formulas, Ellis being the exception. Chunks are difficult to define linguistically—where they begin and where they end and exactly what the constitutive parts are. To make matters worse, any linguistic definition may or may not correspond to the way learners parse formulas. However, researching the establishment of FMCs with chunks may be extremely important in SLA, for formulas may be what is most psychologically real for learners and what *emerge* "bottom up" from interaction with the input, at least during early SLA.

A second challenge may be probabilistic linguistics, which also assumes that linguistic rules are endpoints, not means. Thus, linguistic phenomena are treated less categorically. Probabilistic linguists, such as Bod, Hay, and Jannedy (2001), are intent on providing the means to account for the gradiency of linguistic behavior, for example, that judgments of well-formedness display properties of continua. Among the authors of chapters in this volume, only Ellis explicitly discusses the fact that FMCs are probabilistic—and that language learning is the associative learning of representations that reflect the probabilities of occurrence of form–function mappings.

A third challenge lies with emergent grammar. Hopper (1988), objecting to Chomsky's depiction of grammar as a static object, which is fully present at all times in the mind of the speaker, proposes instead that grammar is a phenomenon "whose status is constantly being renegotiated in speech and which cannot be distinguished in principle from strategies for building discourses" (p. 118). As Hopper puts it: "Its forms are not fixed templates, but arise out of face-to-face interaction in ways that reflect individual speakers' past experience of these forms, and their assessment of the present context, including especially their interlocutors, whose experience and assessments may be quite different" (Hopper, 1998, p. 156).

Thus, from Hopper's *emergent grammar* perspective, "language is a real-time activity, whose regularities are always provisional and are continually subject to negotiation, renovation, and abandonment" (Hopper, 1988, p. 120). We can see from Hopper's words that he finds no incompatibility with the notion of grammar and the contingent, provisional disorderliness of its use in real time.

To restate my position, what I am calling these linguistic challengers should not dissuade anyone from doing FMC research, in my opinion; however, the ontological foundation on which it rests may need to be reconsidered. For example, unlike Klein who attributes learner errors to performance, rather than competence or gaps in L2 knowledge, which leads her to say that L2 grammar may be less variable or deficient than is often assumed, others see that SLA as the acquisition of mental competence is not an unassailable view these days, and that "competence," if it exists at all, is indeed variable, or at least probabilistic, and continually changing. By straddling the performance/competence distinction (Broeder & Plunkett, 1994), the challengers reflect a more dynamic view of language, and I would suggest that they offer a more dynamic view of learning as well.

Because both language and learning might be thought of as complex dynamic systems (Larsen-Freeman, 1997, 2003), in which "the act of playing the game has a way of changing the rules," I appreciate that VanPatten, Williams, & Rott acknowledge that different teaching procedures may need to be implemented at different points of language development, that Shirai notes that the impact of input factors may differ at different phases of form–meaning mapping, and that Gass has indicated that attention has a differential focus depending on proficiency level. I think all these are right. SLA is not only complex at one point in time; the complexity changes over time.

Another issue with which FMC researchers must contend is the relationship between comprehension and production. As I understand it, the FMC research position is that connections are made through a comprehension process. Then, later, they can be accessed in comprehension and production. While again, this is a neat explanation, I do not think that it corresponds to what is known about comprehension and production, (see, e.g., Keenan & MacWhinney, 1987), which is that although there is clear overlap of the "grammars" from which the two processes draw, the grammars are not isomorphic. Shirai makes this point by reminding us that the Aspect Hypothesis predicts semantic development of tense-aspect morphology, which may or may not be directly reflected in spontaneous production. Although the difference may well be explained by an inability to access the FMCs or the fact that the productive skill is not fully developed, I do not think that this is the whole story.

To turn to another matter briefly, VanPatten's chapter reminds us about the importance of input. I have fully appreciated its importance since the early 1970s, when Hatch pointed out that interlanguage forms could not be accounted for without consideration of the input to which learners were exposed. At the time, there was a shift taking place in the explanandum, from the shaping of human behavior to the acquisition of mental grammar. From the perspective of accounting for the acquisition of a mental grammar, output production came to be seen as possibly useful for skill development and for contributing to fluency, but was considered unnecessary in the development of mental competence. Analysis of input was what fueled the development. Nevertheless, today, if a new, more dynamic view of language prevails, it may not be merely skill development and increasing fluency for which output production is responsible.

In addition to what others have proposed (e.g., Gass, chap. 4 in this volume, proposes that input is not enough—attentional focus is directed as a result of interaction), I have recently raised the question as to whether output production provides an important role in the creation of new language forms. It may not be limited to imitation and rehearsal of previously learned material (Larsen-Freeman, 2003). Of course, in no way can a role for input be denied. However, I do not think that input/reception/acquisition/competence and output/production/skill development/performance align quite so neatly.

The final question that I would pose to FMC researchers has to do with the role of learners. Some authors in this volume do discuss learner factors, but the factors seem to be primarily limited to learners' L1 background and their L2 proficiency. However, there are many other learner factors that play a role in connecting form and meaning. One of the most obvious is the matter of learner agency—that learners can choose to respond to the task at hand in light of their own goals and ways of working. For instance, Barcroft reports that a substantial percentage of subjects in his study did not perform on the tasks as they were instructed to do and that when they did, they adopted their own strategies for accomplishing them, rather than the strategies they were assigned to use. The learners apparently viewed their strategies as being more optimal for learning the target words than the +semantic +structural tasks that were assigned to them. This is not the first such report in the research literature, which has led me in the past (Larsen-Freeman, 1985) to question the customary practice of separating learning from learner. Barcroft's research illustrates and renews my concern.

CONCLUSION

In summary, I am impressed with the scope of the work reported on in this volume. I further feel that there is much to be learned from FMC research. I think its contribution would be greater still if some of the questions that I have posed in this chapter re addressed. SLA is a complex process, and as I have said before (and as Gass says chap. 4 in this vol.), it is important to not only study processes separately, but also to look at how they interact and converge to more truly get at the messy complexity of it all.

REFERENCES

Bod, R., Hay, J., and Jannedy, S. (2001, January). *Probability theory in linguistics*. A symposium presented at the Linguistic Society of America Meeting, Washington, DC.

Broeder, P. and Plunkett, K. (1994). Connectionism and second language acquisition. In N. Ellis (Ed.), *Implicit and explicit learning of languages* (pp. 421–453). London: Academic Press.

Cooper, D. (1999). *Linguistic attractors: The cognitive dynamics of language acquisition and change*. Amsterdam: Benjamins.

Ellis, N. (1998). Emergentism, connectionism and language learning. *Language Learning, 48*, 631–664.

Ellis, N. (2003). Constructions, chunking, and connectionism. In C. Doughty & M. Long (Eds.), *The handbook of second language acquisition* (pp. 63–103). Malden, MA: Blackwell.

Elman, J., Bates, E., Johnson, M., Karmiloff-Smith, A., Parisi, D., & Plunkett, K. (1998). *Rethinking innateness: A connectionist perspective on development*. Cambridge, MA: MIT Press.

Hopper, P. (1988). Emergent grammar and the a priori grammar postulate. In D. Tannen (Ed.), *Linguistics in context: Connecting observation and understanding* (pp. 117–134). Norwood, NJ: Ablex.

Hopper, P. (1998). Emergent grammar. In M. Tomasello (Ed.), *The new psychology of language* (pp. 155–175). Mahwah, NJ: Lawrence Erlbaum Associates, Publishers.

Keenan, J., & MacWhinney, B. (1987). Understanding the relationship between comprehension and production. In H. Dechert & M. Raupach (Eds.), *Psycholinguistic models of production* (pp. 149–155). Norwood, NJ: Ablex.

Larsen-Freeman, D. (1985). State of the art on input in second language acquisition. In S. Gass & C. Madden (Eds.), *Input in second language acquisition* (pp. 433–444). Rowley, MA: Newbury House.

Larsen-Freeman, D. (1991). Second language acquisition research: Staking out the territory. *TESOL Quarterly, 25*, 315–350.

Larsen-Freeman, D. (1995). On the teaching and learning of grammar: Challenging the myths. In F. Eckman, D. Highland, P. Lee, J. Mileham, & R. Rutkowski Weber (Eds.), *Second language acquisition theory and pedagogy* (pp. 131–150). Hillsdale, NJ: Lawrence Erlbaum Associates.

Larsen-Freeman, D. (1997). Chaos/complexity science and second language acquisition. *Applied Linguistics 18*, 141–165.

Larsen-Freeman, D. (2000). Teaching grammar. In M. Celce-Murcia (Ed.), *Teaching English as a second or foreign language* (3rd ed., pp. 365–266). Boston: Heinle & Heinle.

Larsen-Freeman, D. (2003). *Teaching language: From grammar to grammaring*. Boston: Heinle & Heinle.

Larsen-Freeman, D., Kuehn, T., & Haccius, M. (2002). Helping students in making appropriate English verb tense–aspect choices. *TESOL Journal 11*, 3–9.

MacWhinney, B. (Ed.). (1999). *The emergence of language*. Mahwah, NJ: Lawrence Erlbaum Associates.

Pinker, S. and Prince, A. (1994). Regular and irregular morphology and the psychological status of rules of grammar. In S. Lima, R. Corrigan, & G. Iverson (Eds.), *The reality of linguistic rules* (pp. 321–351). Amsterdam: Benjamins.

Author Index

A

B

C

D

E

Subject Index

T

U